up
standers

Heritage University
College of Education & Psychology
3240 Fort Road
Toppenish, WA 98948 #8

Harvey "Smokey" Daniels • Sara K. Ahmed

up
standers

How to Engage Middle School Hearts and Minds with Inquiry

HEINEMANN
Portsmouth, NH

Heinemann

361 Hanover Street

Portsmouth, NH 03801–3912

www.heinemann.com

Offices and agents throughout the world

The authors and publisher wish to thank those who have generously given permission to reprint borrowed material:

Excerpt from *Not My Fault* by Leif Kristiansson. Text and illustration copyright © 1973, 1999 by Leif Kristiansson. Published in the United States by Heyrin Books, Inc. Reprinted by permission of Ia Atterholm Agency/ICBS, Malmö, Sweden.

Home Court Advantage lesson adapted from *Reading and Writing Together: Collaborative Literacy in Action* by Nancy Steineke. Copyright © 2002 by Nancy Steineke. Published by Heinemann, Portsmouth, NH. All rights reserved.

Figures 8.5 and 8.6: "Introduction: Triangle Fire" from *American Experience: Triangle Fire* (www.pbs.org/wgbh /americanexperience/features/introduction/triangle-intro/). Copyright © 1996–2014 WGBH Educational Foundation. Reprinted by permission of WGBH Educational Foundation.

Figure 9.5: Membership Grid adapted from *Reading and Writing Together: Collaborative Literacy in Action* by Nancy Steineke. Copyright © 2002 by Nancy Steineke. Published by Heinemann, Portsmouth, NH. All rights reserved.

Library of Congress Cataloging-in-Publication Data

Harvey, Daniels

    Upstanders : how to engage middle school hearts and minds with inquiry / Harvey "Smokey" Daniels and Sara K. Ahmed.

       pages cm

    Includes bibliographical references and index.

    ISBN 978-0-325-05359-2

    1. Middle school education—United States. 2. Middle schools—United States. 3. Middle school teachers—Training of—United States. 4. Inquiry-based learning. I. Ahmed, Sara K. II. Title.

LB1623.5.H37 2015

373.236—dc23   2014027014

Acquisitions editor: Tobey Antao

Production editor: Patty Adams

Cover and interior designs: Suzanne Heiser

Typesetter: Gina Poirier, Gina Poirier Design

Manufacturing: Steve Bernier

Printed in the United States of America on acid-free paper

19 18 17 16 15 EBM 1 2 3 4 5

dedication

*"All grown-ups were once children . . .
but only few of them remember it."*

**–Antoine St. Exupery,
author of *The Little Prince***

To the kids and the grown-ups who can always
find their inner kid.

contents

acknowledgments

FROM SARA

With deep gratitude to my entire family. To my parents for their bravery in traveling across an unknown ocean in search of the American dream—a dream they found by being vehicles of change in their community for over forty years. I know you wanted three Indian doctors, but you got three educators instead! To Samira and Asra, for your guidance and for giving me the floor of the car on our road trips to Florida. It's tough being the favorite. To my Batavia family and the best girlfriends a middle schooler could ask for: nearly twenty-five years later and no matter the distance between us, I am always home when I am with you.

To my Burley School family. A Dream Team of educators with a spirit of open doors and an unmatched drive to do what is right by kids. To Barbara Kent for raising me to always be in search of my humanity in literature and the world around me. To my friends from the ground floor to the third. Eight years of storied laughter, tears, road trips, and social committee events. Special shout-out to anyone who ever fed me or gave me supplies from their closets—you know who you are. Thank you.

To my Bishop's School family. Thank you for embracing the new kid with welcoming and supportive arms. My first step on that campus every morning is always greeted with warmth and ready laughter. Special thanks to A. C. and Carol for your leadership and support, to Cory Ann, and to Team 6.

To my Facing History family. An international team dedicated to supporting teachers and students through inquiry and the human story. Special thanks to Chuck Meyers for literally being on my doorstep on a moment's notice and the offices in Chicago, Los Angeles, New York, London, and Boston.

To all of my students, near and far. Thank you for always reminding me how important curiosity and laughter really are.

Finally, to my life's mentor, Smokey. You are my Don Graves. This work would not be possible without your guidance, aggressive keyboarding, your NERF basketball hoop, and our mutual love for YA music. I am truly indebted to you and Elaine for sharing your whole hearts and your home on this journey. I am standing on very big shoulders.

FROM SMOKEY

To my mentor, Sara. As Al Pacino once said in a movie, "I am a scary judge of talent." When I first walked into your classroom in Chicago, I immediately thought to myself, now THAT'S what middle school should look like. And I wanted to collaborate with you. Mentoring only works if it is mutual, and whatever I've done for you, I've gained double in return. We didn't just write a book together. We became friends and then family. But still, I am an elder in the profession, and there's one more thing. I am asking you, young one, to carry on the long and always threatened struggle for progressive education in America. That is a lot to put on someone's shoulders. But you are so strong.

To my family. Marny, the hardworking, book-devouring Queen of Retail. Nick, California's Mr. Pathology, a human vacuum of nonfiction, and my financial guru. I'm so proud to call these two upstanders my children. Spouse Elaine, teacher and coauthor, partner and co-conspirator, and the most supportive reader of really rough drafts ever. The best is yet to come, and won't it be fine?

To my school families. I have the greatest job in the world, which now entails serving as a guest teacher across the United States. Just in the past year, I worked with kids and teachers in public, independent, Catholic, and reservation schools. Everywhere I go, I am awed by the dedication of this country's teachers, who work in the face of "reforms" that too often disrespect their precious work. And I am moved and encouraged by the intelligence, creativity, and human decency of our students, young people who are definitely not "data."

FROM BOTH OF US

To Team Heinemann. This is Sara's first book with Heinemann; it is Smokey's fifteenth. So we know a few things about our publisher. Have you ever heard that old joke from *The Peter Principle*? As any organization matures, all of its positions gradually become occupied by people who are incapable of performing their duties? Well, Heinemann is the opposite: every single person we work with is at the very top of their profession. From the principled leadership of Lesa Scott, Vicki Boyd, and Lisa Fowler, through every department, people like Eric Chalek, Brett Whitmarsh, Suzanne Heiser, Sarah Fournier, Victoria Merecki, Anthony Marvullo, and a dozen others make us look good. Our editor, Tobey Antao, seamlessly wove our thoughts and our voices together, despite every obstacle. Tobey, we long for the days we will meet you again in tracked changes! Smokey's longtime production editor Patty Adams took on this new writing team with unfailing patience, contagious serenity, and completely unfounded optimism that we could meet a warp-speed production schedule. And now, when we take our new work on the road, Michelle Flynn, Cathy Brophy, Cheryl Savage, and Cherie Bartlett will guide our professional development events every step of the way. It is incredible to have a team like this around us.

Heinemann, thanks for your commitment to middle schoolers around the country, for believing in the power of the middle school amygdala . . . and ours.

To the Band. Some of this book was actually written while we were sitting in the same room. Despite our vast age difference, we found that we were both energized by the same background music. So, thanks to Taylor Swift, the Beastie Boys, Billy Joel, Justin Timberlake, the Dixie Chicks, and Paul Simon.

To the Posse. We are so fortunate to have a network of dear friends who also happen to be teachers, authors, researchers, and fellow travellers (both literally and metaphorically). For all you do, for who you are, we will be forever grateful for the way you have empowered and cheer-led this project.

Big tweets to @KristinZiemke @NSteineke @StephHarvey49 @StevenZemelman @LiteracySpark @Donalynbooks #yourock #edupstanders

To the Shoulders We Stand On. Donald Graves, Stephanie Harvey, Anne Goudvis, Lucy Calkins, Nancy Steineke, Linda Hoyt, Donalyn Miller, Nancie Atwell, Jerome Harste, James Beane, Richard Allington, Steve Zemelman, P. David Pearson, David and Roger Johnson, and Chip Wood.

PART 1

*

WELCOME

A Core Curriculum
of Heart and Mind

This book is about growing a caring classroom community that deeply supports its own members and also monitors, investigates, and cares for the world beyond its walls. This means helping young people learn to think hard, build knowledge, become skilled researchers, and communicate carefully—in the service of humanity, not just themselves. The new Common Core State Standards (2010) set quite different goals. That four-hundred-page document's announced aims are "Career and College Readiness," with much talk of preparing individual students for "global economic competition." Words like *rigor*, *complexity*, and *argument* proliferate in this burgeoning genre of standards literature. There is no mention of citizenship, either local, national, or planetary. Indeed, in Core-World, many subjects of urgent importance are omitted when the purposes of schooling are enumerated. Among the disappeared topics:

identity	equality	choice	critique
empathy	democracy	responsibility	struggle
altruism	curiosity	courage	change
justice	compassion	peacemaking	collaboration

In the "reformed" American schools of today, these values and principles are treated as naive or simply irrelevant. But that's recent. If you look back at the mission statements of virtually any American school district from fifty or even twenty-five years ago, they unabashedly embraced many of these same ideals. In fact, many contemporary schools retain this kind of visionary language, even though their daily operations may be focused on test prep, and not the development of human character and potential.

You probably didn't become a teacher mainly to raise some child's standardized test score .05 percent—or to ensure that America continues to grab a disproportionately large share of the world's goodies. Instead, you wanted to be part of raising smart, ethical people who would work for their own families—and for a better neighborhood, country, and world.

But we can have both. Nurturing compassionate, collaborative citizens of the world can indeed advance our students into colleges and careers as well as toward the neglected third *C*—citizenship. Our kids can learn, pass tests, find a place in the global economy—and make the world a better place for all. Our school system's passive, top-down pedagogy has already raised generations of bystanders, grown-ups who lack the tools to think critically, the discernment to judge, and the courage to act. Today, we need to nurture a new generation of "upstanders"—active and informed human beings who will make thoughtful and brave choices in their own lives, in their communities, and on the ever-shrinking world stage. The voices of young people must be part of our nation's conversation, not after they leave school, but right now. And the better they learn to read, write, think, investigate, and collaborate, the more effective they will be in creatively solving this planet's problems and extending its future.

In 1930, George S. Counts wrote one of the most famous books in the history of American education, which posed the question, "Dare the schools build a new social order?" Looking at the world around us today, we damn well better.

Hard Work, Heart Work

This is work from our hearts.

SMOKEY: *On one of my visits to Sara's room last year, the TV news was full of the brutal civil war in Syria, and her kids were concerned. Sara's students were reading newspaper and web reports of desperate refugees, many of them children, crowding into IDP (internationally displaced person) camps across the Turkish border.*

Sara explained that one student asked, "Ms. Ahmed, all we keep seeing in the news is that kids are dying. Why are they targeting kids?"

Warren, another student, was drawn to the media coverage, as are many people during atrocities, and even posted something to our class web page one night. See Figure 1.1.

warren Z. to ■ Syria (SocialStudies7)

http://abcnews.go.com/International/doctors-v... it talks about the doctors in Jordan.

☺ ∨ · ◯ 2 Replies · ☐ Share   Sep 19, 2013

Matthew M. · Sep 20, 2013

Wow, that was an interesting article...that was so sad that two year old had a huge opening on the side of her stomach... she should be playing outside , anything but this. She is two!

Michael X. · Sep 25, 2013

She does? Oh my gosh, I feel so sorry for the girl. One more reason why Assad should get out of office. Thanks, by the way, for the life-scarring heads-up.

Figure 1.1 Warren Z., Matthew M., and Michael X. discussion posts.

The images on the Internet were heartbreaking. More than 2.5 million people had already been displaced by the civil war, and prospects for peace were dimming by the day. As Sara always does, she started searching for people, organizations, and websites where she could learn more for herself and find potential resources for her kids. Sara, can you pick up the story there?

SARA: *Sure. Syria was all over the news at the beginning of the school year. There were sickening images of piles of child graves and chemical weapons on every form of media you turned to. We use CNN Student News as another class resource and the kids were beginning to ask questions. I had my own questions too, not knowing too much about the complex history of the conflict.*

One of the other teachers invited a parent who is a news reporter to come in and speak about her experience covering the atrocities. I used our **Edmodo** *page to list links for the kids to read*   69 *and get some of their questions answered, and I also had them search for their own articles to share with the group. We had already done critical literacy lessons on choosing credible sites. With the power of literacy and inquiry, the more they read, the more questions they asked, and the more they felt an urgency to do something.*

I couldn't be a good enough source to them alone, so I started searching on Twitter for anything and everything I could on a Saturday morning. I searched Syria, Syrian children, and Syrian refugees, and came across Camp Zeitouna and the hashtag #Play4Syria. I read some tweets and grew interested in this organization's work with children in the camps through school and soccer. (Selfishly, two of my favorite things.) I googled the camp and found an ambiguous contact email. I wrote to the address asking how we could get involved in a way that would be meaningful and valuable for these kids. I didn't want it to be just about money. I received a response from the director right away. We spoke on the phone the next day, and I couldn't wait to tell the kids about it. That Monday, I showed students an email from Kinda Hibrawi, the cofounder of Camp Zeitouna, who assured them the camp needed our help, but it was up to us to decide how. Here in Figure 1.2 were some possibilities we came up with:

Me to   Syria (SocialStudies7)

This is the website for the Karam Foundation. Let's brainstorm a way to be upstanders for them. It does not need to involve money, we can simply send them art we create to show them we haven't forgotten about them or to show them we value their education too. List your ideas here and we will bounce ideas off each other.
http://karamfoundation.com/projects/camp-zeit...

Me to   Syria (SocialStudies7)

Melanie and Warren made a suggestion on the wall of the Syria page. Can you both repost under here? Thanks!

Melanie S. • Sep 23, 2013

We could make art and send it to the kids in Syria/refugee camps. We could also put a loose change drive outside of the snack bar and vending machines

Warren Z. • Sep 23, 2013

Yeah we could send the art to them.

Warren Z. • Sep 23, 2013

Or we could give them supplies to make art.

Shannon B. • Sep 23, 2013

We could also make bracelets, or other things to sell for fundraising purpposes.

Melanie S. • Sep 23, 2013

Shannon had the idea that we could make and sell bracelets

Alexander V. • Sep 23, 2013

I think we should make a website to donate money to Syria, based on the school. In fact, if possible, we could make it on the school website.

Tate M. • Sep 23, 2013

i like the idea of selling things for fundraising especially food, think about how much people spend on the snack bar

Michael X. • Sep 23, 2013

We could send pictures of motivation, which I did at my old school for the Sandy Hook school.

Melanie S. • Sep 23, 2013

There is something called beads of courage. That people wear for different things we could do something like that and give them to the syrian children and sell them here.

Shannon B. • Sep 23, 2013

We should write books and stories for the children, then send them back with Kinda

Matthew M. • Sep 23, 2013

Since I am in the ASBC, I can communicate/persuade other officers of middle school to make a fundraiser for the refugee camps we are planning to. My idea is to have a "shoot-a-thon" where you shoot 5 balls trying to make as many balls in the hoop as possible. It is $5 per entry. Whoever gets 4-5 hoops will get a prize!

Figure 1.2 Discussion on class website regarding the Karam Foundation.

Melanie and Shannon's idea won out—to make bracelets for the Syrian kids, but the vision was to be like the Tom's shoe company, where you buy one and give one. This was decided unanimously. As my students reflected later, this way those kids will always know someone is thinking about them. We talked about overhead costs for making bracelets and they introduced me to the idea of bracelets made out of strips of T-shirts. Everyone brings in an old shirt or two and there is no overhead! The idea gained momentum and support, as our team of seventh-grade teachers and the kids' peers were instrumental in helping make as many bracelets as they could.

SMOKEY: The next time I came to visit, I found Sara's kids scattered around the floor, weaving multicolored strips of cut-up T-shirts into beautiful bracelets that they planned to sell to raise money for Camp Zeitouna. Around midmorning, Kinda Skyped in from the agency and praised the kids for their dedication. Pumped up, a team of Sara's seventh graders marched into a whole-school assembly (grades 6 through 12) and with exquisite eloquence, told all those older kids about the refugee camp, showed the video they had made highlighting their campaign, called #playforSyria, and why all students had better be buying lots of T-shirt bracelets later that week. Sara's students were not just skilled artisans, but pretty effective sellers, too—I brought home enough bracelets to adorn all my family members and neighbors.

SARA: The ideas for fund-raising, the video, and the sale itself would not have happened without the intense research and reading of articles and media we pored over. We all got increasingly concerned and fired up. But we knew we would have to communicate our sense of urgency to others who lacked our growing schema on the issue. So the kids practiced writing "Convince Me" letters, with The Bishop's School community as the audience. Having a go at this persuasive writing included finding statistics and citing sources, directly quoting evidence while considering audience, and pulling at heartstrings. Figure 1.3 shows Lulu and Sophie's version.

The kids worked at braiding bracelets during every spare moment (and a few minutes in class, too). Everyone who bought a bracelet for $2 could also handpick another one that we'd send to a Syrian child. The sale raised over $700, which was eventually used to buy computer equipment for a makeshift school for the refugee children. That same week, Kinda came to Bishop's to personally pick up the bracelets to take with her to Turkey and the Al-Salaam school. The kids were beyond psyched, and many skipped lunch to come meet her.

SMOKEY: It was amazing to see the kids' commitment and dedication to this project. It also reminded me that teachers like you are sometimes accused of imposing their own politics on kids, making them into little apprentice crusaders working on the teacher's hobbyhorse issues. Some crabby person could probably see your Syria project that way—after all, you did initiate it.

SARA: *It's important to remember where this work began: the issue was prominent in the non-fiction magazines we were reading and the media we were engaged with at the time. The kids became more and more aware, and began to ask more and more questions. I initiated it in the sense that I didn't let it slide, and instead made even more visual and print resources available to students on a topic for which none of us had much background knowledge, me included. They analyzed a variety of complex nonfiction texts to develop answers to their questions, they wrote with specific claims and evidence of the atrocities, and they were able to analyze and validate the credibility of sources they used. The skills and awareness kids gained from this inquiry were invaluable because it was student-driven, they had an authentic audience, and they witnessed the power of their own voices.*

Dear Bishop's Middle School and Upper School Students,

Every Child deserves to **play**, to learn, and to **grow**. But for the 100,000 plus displaced kids in Syrian refugee camps, things like soccer fields and schools are a long way away. Sometimes, being the privileged community we are, we forget about those who aren't as fortunate as ourselves. The kids in Syria have almost nothing; they have lost their houses, their possessions, and in many cases, their families.

Our 7th grade social studies class along with other members in the middle school community, is putting together a fundraising project to help these unfortunate children. We have connected with a Syrian-American woman, **Kinda Hibrawi**, who lives in Irvine. She will be making a trip to a refugee camp in December. Kinda has been working with these kids for a while, providing food, education, and fun! Our class, in an effort to help alongside of her, is creating bracelets that we will sell at middle and upper school lunch. We are using the TOMS idea of a buy one give one program. **If you buy a bracelet, one will also be sent to a child in Syria.** We will give the money we raise and the bracelets to Kinda who will deliver them when she visits the children.

Please help us in an effort to **assist** these poor kids, who are struggling to even **survive**. We have so much, and them so little, it's the least you can do to buy a bracelet and donate a little money!

For info please contact Ms. Ahmed.

Thanks!

Sophie and Ms. Ahmed's SS7 class

Figure 1.3 Lulu and Sophie's letter to the school community.

My job is to have my students unpack challenging nonfiction texts on a variety of topics, so I was teaching directly into the Common Core standards in this project. But also, my time with them is too short—our lives are too short—to study content that doesn't matter. I do teach what I value, which is usually what the kids value. There is no reason that advocacy and action on an urgent issue like Syria should be overlooked in favor of reading Chapter 9 in our textbook. That can wait; refugee children can't.

Months after our fund-raiser, we received a message from Kinda that our idea had spread across the country. Carmel Catholic High School in Chicago saw our video campaign, *Ask Me About My Bracelet*, on the Karam Foundation's Facebook and Twitter accounts. They adopted the idea, generated their own bracelet campaign and fund-raiser, and raised another $3,000 for Camp Zeitouna. Amazing!

We watched the Carmel video as a class and responded to what we saw on a Padlet (see Figure 1.4), an online collaborative "corkboard" (padlet.com).

> Kids are making choices, doing investigative research, sharing their concerns, using their voice for other kids, and watching the seeds of their advocacy and action spread.

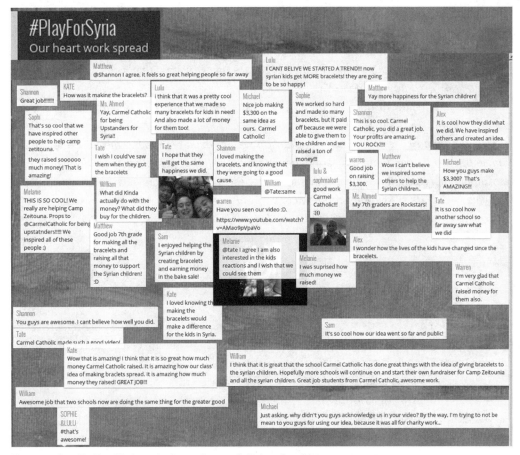

Figure 1.4 Our Padlet filled out before, after, and during the video.

I forwarded the Padlet to my colleague at Carmel Catholic; Figure 1.5 shows her very heartfelt response.

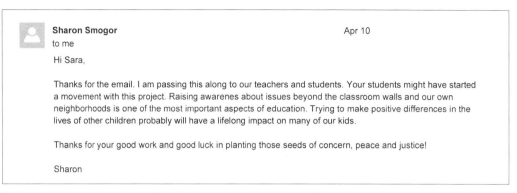

Sharon Smogor   Apr 10
to me

Hi Sara,

Thanks for the email. I am passing this along to our teachers and students. Your students might have started a movement with this project. Raising awarenes about issues beyond the classroom walls and our own neighborhods is one of the most important aspects of education. Trying to make positive differences in the lives of other children probably will have a lifelong impact on many of our kids.

Thanks for your good work and good luck in planting those seeds of concern, peace and justice!

Sharon

Figure 1.5 Email response from Sharon Smogor at Carmel Catholic.

When I first posted the Padlet with its title, Warren blurted out, "Ms. Ahmed! Ha, I get it! Heart work, hard work, ha-ha, get it, you guys?" Warren was thinking this was a play on words.

"Oh, I didn't even intentionally do that, Warren. I was genuinely calling it heart work, and I never realized how 'hard' and 'heart' could be a pun until you said that."

"Wait, then what do you mean?"

Melanie interjected to help her buddy. "No, she means that this is hard work from our hearts, Warren."

Spreading the seeds of advocacy and action was a result of creating the space for inquiry work in the classroom. From the very beginning the catalyst was the kids' wonders, their concern, and compassion. It was their activism, awareness, and aid. It was their readiness to project their voices outside of our classroom walls in order to speak for those who cannot speak for themselves. And they were heard, loud and clear.

🔼 Introducing Ourselves

We are two teachers, a generation apart in our careers, who have been engaging with adolescents, striving to embody progressive values, and using student-centered, inquiry-based classroom practices for a total of 56 school years. Smokey started teaching in 1969; Sara in 2002. You can do the math to determine which of us accounts for most of those decades.

We didn't meet until 2009, when Smokey and comprehension researcher Stephanie Harvey came to visit Burley School in Chicago. He started hanging out in Sara's classroom, getting to know her kids, admiring her skills and her values, and later hosting an annual literacy institute where teachers would come to spend a week with Sara and other great Burley educators. Sara was featured in several of Smokey's subsequent books and videos. Along the way, we became good friends, and when Sara took a new teaching job in California, Smokey began visiting her classroom there, and we started talking more seriously about writing this book. We also talked about why in the world Sara would rent a ground-floor apartment in downtown San Diego, where different homeless people would camp out on her porch every night. Smokey is learning to downplay the fatherly advice. Slowly.

We'll say more about who we are in Chapter 3, when we talk in detail about teacher identity in middle school classrooms. For now, here are some demographics:

SARA: *I was born and raised in the suburbs of Chicago, where my class was the first to attend an early middle school model, and where I made all of my best friends to this day. My teaching journey began in a two-room schoolhouse in the suburbs of Dublin, Ireland, thanks to a great student teaching opportunity offered by the University of Iowa's School of Education. Next, I made a nine-year stop at Burley School in Chicago. There, a team of mentors took me under their wings and said, "Read this professional text," "You have to read this novel," "Try this," and "Let's do this together." Sometimes all at once. And my whole heart fell in love with city kids, coaching them on and off the field. I am a better person and educator for all of it. It was at Burley that Smokey and Steph Harvey walked into my room and lit up my middle school teaching life. It's not every day the books you read in college come to life.*

I couldn't take the polar vortex in Chicago anymore, so I headed west to America's Finest City (San Diego) to explore education in an independent school. I'm feeling like a first-year teacher all over again, but The Bishop's School is the most welcoming and supportive community I could ever have asked for. Here, I have joined a team of colleagues that works together to do what is right by kids. And I am enjoying the weather, ocean, and mountains as well.

FACING HISTORY AND OURSELVES

There's one other important influence on my work that I, Sara, should mention here: Facing History and Ourselves (www.facinghistory.org, @facinghistory). Facing History "combats racism with history," helping secondary teachers and students see history through the eyes of the victims, perpetrators, bystanders, and upstanders. My mentor in this organization, Chuck Meyers, showed me how to view history as the human story. This lens rocked my world, and I've seen it give my students the gift of perspective.

The term "Upstander" and the Facing History and Ourselves resources described in this book were developed as part of the Facing History and Ourselves sequence of study. This powerful sequence begins with identity—first individual identity and then group identities with their definitions of membership—and then moves to a case study of the failure of democracy in Germany and the steps leading to the Holocaust as well

SMOKEY: *Like Sara, I taught in Chicago and fell in love with city kids, so alien to my white-bread Minnesota upbringing. Except that my first year of teaching was 1969. With my kids at Westinghouse and later Lake Forest High Schools, we did inquiries using primary source documents, set up dramatic simulations of mass production lines and lobbyists working members of Congress, and investigated the Soviet Union as a culmination of geographic as well as political features. I've written about twenty books for teachers over the years, and every good idea found in their pages invariably traces back to some great teacher like Sara who let me study and write about her practice. When I moved to New Mexico in 2007, I got back into the classroom with an amazing cohort of sixth graders on Santa Fe's south side. When we did inquiry projects together, my kids investigated questions around climate change, the prospects for our common future, animal extinction, and the use of nuclear weapons in World War II.*

These days, I serve mostly as a guest teacher in other people's schools. Sometimes I do demonstration lessons with kids, sometimes I lead professional development for teachers or coaches, and other times I support whole districts and their leaders. As you might be suspecting, I have the best job in the world.

Sometimes in this book, we will speak in a unified, "we" voice. Like now. Other times, we'll break out under our own names and tell a story or describe a lesson. We'll also be talking to each other along the way. We hope our conversations will give you the flavor of our friendship and the nature of our thinking—and also to show that, for kids or for grown-up teachers, working with a partner is not just sociable and energizing; it can lift up our thinking, too.

With the Syria story above, we wanted to give you a window into Sara's classroom right away, so you can watch how the kids are thinking, the collaborative spirit of the room, and the way our commentary works. It's a quick snapshot of the inquiry classroom: using authentic sources to build curiosity, leading to personal questions, building momentum, and activating emphatic responses. Kids are making choices, doing investigative research, sharing their concerns, using their voice for other kids, and watching the seeds of their advocacy and action spread.

Teaching Middle School Today

There's an old joke among teachers that we gradually assume the characteristics of whatever age group we teach. According to this adage, primary grade teachers tend to be sweet, child-like, gentle, and huggy. (You see where this is going, right?) There are classic stereotypes about middle school teachers, too. But before other people can categorize us, we often label *ourselves* as ADD, impulsive, volatile, and sometimes even hormonal, just like our students.

Of course the stereotypes aren't true about the kids—or us. Mostly. We are simply grown-ups who think that teaching kids from ages ten to fourteen is a unique, demanding, and tremendously satisfying occupation. We enjoy these guys; they crack us up. We teach a distinctive age group that displays the whole range of human development, from cuddly dependence, to narcissism, to total hilarity, to deep questioning, to world-embracing empathy—sometimes all within the same class period. If you love this job, you probably like roller coasters too.

Yet, for all the emotional rewards it offers, this is an especially hard time to be teaching middle school. We feel the pressure of meeting the complex Common Core (or our own state's) standards. We are striving to prepare our kids for the ever-proliferating standardized tests that enforce the standards, rank our students and our school, affect our own performance ratings, and even set our salaries. The kids themselves come to us with more complexity than ever; we see more diversity in our classrooms, more languages spoken, more family income disparities, more diverse experience backgrounds, more exposure to the Internet (and less to books), and more intense attachments to digital pastimes that we don't even understand. Hey, how are we supposed to keep them engaged in the classroom when they have Black Ops and Minecraft at home?

With all these changes and cross-pressures, with all this static in the air, how do we work with young teenagers today? How do we bring out the best in them—and in ourselves, as mentors, models, coaches, and content experts? How do we meet elevated academic goals? And how do we save time for raising citizens, not just consumers, borrowers, spenders, and order-takers?

Maybe we start softly.

 # Passing Periods

In most middle schools, class periods change with a clanging bell, a mad, jostling rush through the halls, and students hustling to their next desks a millisecond before being marked "tardy."

In Sara's current school, there are no bells. The kids filter into their next classrooms gradually, over a few leisurely minutes. Students set down their backpacks and take off their shoes, leaving them beside the door. If they have work to turn in, they silently slide it into a box on the teacher's desk. Then, each kid grabs a book or tablet or magazine, finds a comfy spot, and begins a few minutes of independent reading. Though whispered conversation is not outlawed, the room is mostly quiet. On the whiteboard is a note saying what to bring to the gathering area when the whole group convenes. After eight or ten minutes, Sara gently says, "Meet me at the rug," and the kids promptly shift across the room, materials in hand, ready to work together.

SMOKEY: *Sara, I was really knocked out when I first experienced a "soft start" in your class-room. It's something I'd been trying to perfect for years. When I taught sixth grade in Santa Fe, we always started the day by quietly reading the local newspaper (we had class subscriptions; how great was that?). The kids would come in, grab their copy of the New Mexican, and sit somewhere comfortable. We would all read silently at first; all you would hear was the sound of flipping and folding pages. Then we'd gradually shift to casual, out-loud conversations about the hot stories of the day. One kid favorite I remember was a story about a girl in India who had been born with two heads. The baby was being adored as a goddess by the people in her vil-lage, but my student Nadia saw it another way: "Two heads, more kissing," she mused dreamily.*

Anyway, years earlier, when five of us started a new high school in Chicago, the first thing we did was disconnect the bell system so we could have soft starts something like yours. But at first, managing this was hard for the kids (and some of the teachers). How did you establish these routines?

SARA: *On the first day of school, as each group of kids arrives for class, I meet them outside the door. I introduce myself and talk to them about how we enter the room ready to learn. I give them some guidelines: sit anywhere you want, share the space, everyone has to be included, don't split up by genders. When we come in, we have to get in "the Zone" right away. That means our bodies and minds are focused and ready to take on the day. The same way we get ready before a big game or a performance, our actions show we are ready to be our best selves. The kids know what to do: they walk in; make sure their volume is at a level that isn't disruptive to others; check for a note on the board; turn in any work that is due; kick off their shoes (literally and figuratively); grab a novel/magazine/map/nonfiction book; and find a cozy, safe place to curl up in and read for five to ten minutes while our minds settle in.*

On that first day, it's not exactly serene. They do come rushing in, scour the nonfiction shelves, magazine racks, and library, and eventually nestle into their respective spaces. Gradually, they relax into the reading—a few on a couch, others on beanbags, some on the rug. In stocking feet, minds deep into reading, a few moments of solace in a very hurried day.

SMOKEY: *Dumb question, but why the shoes off?*

SARA: *It started out as a rule because I had a brand-new rug and was being militant about not getting mud and grass on it. I just turned into my mom. (Didn't we all have that living room carpet we weren't allowed to step on somewhere in our childhood?) After the kids went for about a week in stocking feet, we started to discuss why they loved it. Then I started hearing* *from parents that the hot dinner table conversation at home was my shoeless classroom. It was a hit. A mood setter. Of course, I realized that details like this make the classroom feel like home. This small victory, and about a million other climate-building decisions, sets me up for successful classroom management, by making kids feel safe and comfy.*

SMOKEY: *I know that your middle school is departmentalized, so how do you get kids from class to class at Bishop's?*

SARA: *If one class ends at 8:30, the next begins at 8:30. The faculty members trust each other to release kids within a reasonable window. As kids arrive, different teachers have their own guidelines for how to begin their class, and also interventions for any kids who are habitually later than they should be. Soft starts create less of a police action for tardies. No one is standing at the front of the room, itching to teach and playing security guard at the door. The expectation is that learning has already begun through a series of routines and mutually understood practices. These routines can be up to ten minutes long and can begin with simple note on the board; a quiet beginning and autonomy. In my own classroom the same sign is posted near the door all year.*

> Come in ready to learn:
>
> Adjust your volume
>
> Turn in your homework
>
> Check for any notes
>
> Relax and read

We talk about this daily routine for the first days of school, so kids know what it takes to create a positive and calm learning environment. It is a peaceful way to begin; no grown-up is shouting directions and no kid is unclear on what to do (which is what so often causes disruption). I can check in with anyone that I need to, and it gives the stragglers time to come in without a big scene.

Most of us have a box designated for each class period, for kids to turn in work. There is a screen that may or may not have a note on it. If it doesn't, they read their independent novels from home or the library, any of our classroom nonfiction, magazines such as Kids Discover *or* New York Times Upfront, *or a particular reading that we will be tackling together as a class later.*

After about ten minutes, I quietly shift their direction to our minilesson for the day, asking them to meet me on the rug. Some of them are already there, nose-deep in their novels.

SMOKEY: *Could you do this kind of soft start even if there was a bell system in your school?*

SARA: *Of course! During my eight years at Burley School in Chicago, we had fixed passing periods. But once the kids were in my room, we started softly, with some type of independent reading. I guess my consistent principle has been that "time on task" doesn't have to mean the* teacher talking from bell to bell. And that a gentle, reflective interval is a good way to get kids centered and ready to learn. They have ownership and agency when they walk through the door and I am not competing to yell over them with directions.

SMOKEY: *A lot of teachers might say, "Wow, that's a lot of your teaching time to devote to independent reading, every day. Hey, don't you have any curriculum to cover?"*

SARA: *Ha! I hear that all the time. People ask, in a fifty- to sixty-minute class period, how could I allow the kids to read for ten minutes and not begin "teaching" (read: lecturing). My answer is generally this: time spent with a book and reading is far more valuable than my lecturing could ever be for my kiddos. Growing a lifelong love of reading (or sustaining it) in middle school is crucial for our students. Without it, they will only be exposed to the mandated print of the day (test prep, textbooks, teacher-chosen text) for almost the next decade of their lives. I love what Nancie Atwell said in* The Reading Zone *(2007): "A child sitting in a quiet room with a good book isn't a flashy or, more significantly, marketable teaching method. It just happens to be the only way anyone ever grew up to become a reader." I want my kids to be selective and eager text connoisseurs. I want the better part of their sometimes anxiety-filled days to be full of enjoyment, choice, and wonder.*

SMOKEY: *Of course, the research supports your decision. The quantity of free voluntary reading is highly correlated to reading achievement; kids who read lots of self-chosen materials become better, more self-sustaining readers (Krashen 2011). In fact, Richard Allington and Rachel Gabriel (2012) have shown that when kids read books of choice and also talk about them with peers, there is a trifecta of benefits: kids are more engaged in reading, their comprehension improves, and standardized test scores rise. Gotta love that. I also notice a bonus when I visit your classroom—when kids are given a genuine choice of what to read, they often pick materials that are related to content they are studying in class.*

SARA: *Thanks for noticing that. Donalyn Miller (2008) makes it her life's work to ensure kids are making their own choices in what they read and that they feel validated for those choices. I try and flood the room with as many nonfiction sources as I can to let the kids know that reading does not have to mean textbooks only, but also the thousands of trade books and periodicals that are fun to read. I actually take a lot of my "assigned" readings from these materials.* New York Times Upfront, Discovery Kids, Time for Kids, *and* National Geographic Explorer *are all fantastic resources that are designed for kids to grab and dig in. Donalyn writes often of what access to books means, and I am mindful to provide a wide range of reading levels in my classroom in all types of print.*

So, yes, soft starts do some great things for me as a teacher: they help the kids academically and they make classroom management easier for me. But the most important benefit of soft starts, for me, is this: they grow upstanders. This afternoon Sophie came in red-faced after tennis practice, sprawled out upside down on the couch and declared:

> Everyone should start class the way we do . . . so we can all just relax. Then when we are relaxed, we can read for fun. Plus then we read the magazines and get curious about what is going on in the world. And then we want to help like we did for Syria. Like there's bigger things out there, ya know, Ms. Ahmed? It's kind of like, you're looking out for our Common Good, so we have time and want to look out for others' Common Good.

How the Book Works

We wanted this book to begin gently, just like Sara's classes. So we are meeting you here at the door, inviting you to step in, slip off your shoes, get comfortable, and settle in. We have a big agenda for you, but we don't have to rush. There are so many elements in creating a collaborative, inquiry-based, social justice–oriented classroom that getting started can feel overwhelming. So we've begun with one story about young people taking action in the world and one seemingly "small" classroom idea, soft starts, which begins to transform the middle school classroom. Now, piece by piece, we are going to share what we know, and try to make the picture as "3-D" as we can; we want you to see, hear, and feel the everyday contour of middle school kids working hard and doing well.

Upstanders fits loosely under the umbrella of Smokey and Stephanie Harvey's book, *Comprehension and Collaboration: Inquiry Circles in Action* (2009, a new edition comes out in 2015). It is a descendant of that work in that it promotes inquiry-based teaching using small-group investigations, and espouses the explicit teaching of both thinking strategies and social interaction. But the family resemblance remains "loose," because this volume is so profoundly Sara, and so distinctively middle school.

The book has four sections. Here in Part 1, we have been introducing ourselves, giving you a welcome, offering some samples of what's to come, and now, giving directions to help you find the best path through the material have assembled.

Coming up in Part 2, we discuss the key ingredients of great middle school classrooms: the kids, the teacher, the space, the teaching tools and structures. Here, as elsewhere in the book, we try to balance being highly practical—offering lots of instant takeaways and lesson ideas—and sharing stories, narratives of young adolescents learning together. We believe that story is the mother of all teaching methods, both for kids in the classroom and for teachers in professional books.

Not to shock you, but most kids are not born knowing how to operate within a collaborative community. That's why Part 3 shows the specific lessons we use to develop those social skills, values, and attitudes. You'll see how to lead kids through a stepwise series of specific (and easily teachable) lessons in identity and empathy. Many of these activities are adapted from Facing History and Ourselves, the international organization which Sara serves as a member of their Teacher Leadership Team.

Part 4 is the longest section. It shows how to gather everything together—a bunch of lively kids, our teaching selves, our purpose-built spaces, the just-right teaching tools, some powerful language, a set of collaborative values, the commitment to community, the kids' growing self-insight, and their outward-reaching empathy. From all these resources, we co-construct ambitious, engaging, and important inquiry units out of whatever curriculum we are called upon to teach. Here we'll show you all the steps, stages, and materials—and we've parked full-size copies of key handouts on the book's web page, www.heinemann.com /products/E05359.aspx (click on the Companion Resources tab).

We'll also try to get behind the "magic" that sometimes seems to produce these units. Great, mind-expanding, world-embracing units do not result from some teacher's "golden gut" and certainly not from "winging it." They originate in and are sustained by careful teacher thinking every step of the way. But that doesn't mean that everything is foreseen and planned out in detail the previous August. For inquiry teachers, there's always a "skydiving moment" when you decide to jump and cope. Sara calls this process "making game-time decisions," those in-the-moment choices that inquiry teachers must make every class, almost every minute.

For our curricular examples, we have chosen some of the most widely taught middle school topics: civil rights, immigration, child labor, and health and disease, as well as subjects chosen and developed by the kids themselves. Our own definition of inquiry teaching is this: turning the required curricular topics into questions so fascinating that kids cannot resist investigating them.

> **In these units you'll see young adolescents empowered by co-ownership of their own learning.**

In these units you'll see young adolescents empowered by co-ownership of their own learning. They are engaged, they are curious, they are funny, they are moved. They are invited to wonder and question the world. Their wonders range on the profoundness spectrum from "How do the world's religions view death?" to "If I sneeze hard enough, will my brains come out of my nose?" They blog about their questions, research, and new knowledge. They create debate and argument about child labor, and they walk among heroes of the civil rights movement. Before they can do any of this, they question their own identity and grapple with the eternal adolescent question: Who am I? We know very well that literature, history, math, science, and the arts can be better understood if you first understand yourself as a learner and a human being. It is from here we begin our journey.

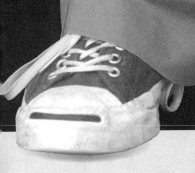
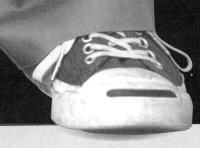

PART 2

*

SCHOOL AS
OUR HOMEPLACE

The Kids

There are many negative stereotypes about kids aged ten to fourteen—and most of them are a crock, in our opinion. The website of one school district lists these characteristics of its own middle school students:

self-preoccupied	easily discouraged	subject to mood swings
callous	critical of others	immature
thoughtless	impatient	intimidated
hyperidealistic	restless	frightened
excitable	awkward	prone to overreact
sleepy	lacking physical fitness	
daydreaming	unpredictable	

Although the list does include some positive traits of young teens, on balance, who'd want to hang with people who have so many personality defects?

Far too often, middle school kids are identified as clusters of symptoms, rather than as people going through a predictable, well-understood life stage. To succeed with kids this age you have to both understand them and like them. If not, you're in for a rough ride. As James Beane says in his preface to *What Every Middle School Teacher Should Know* (Brown and Knowles 2014):

[I]f you see what young adolescents bring to your classroom as a promise rather then a problem, middle school teaching can be one of the most exciting and satisfying things you will ever do. The fact is that young adolescents have tons of questions and concerns about themselves and their world, and their imagination and curiosity work around the clock. They love ideas if those ideas shed light on topics that are personally and socially significant. They love to explore and debate issues of fairness and justice. They love to learn new skills that will help them do something they want to do or think is worth doing. They love to dig deep into projects that are about big ideas or problems. And if you see young adolescents this way and learn how to teach like that, along the way they will learn more and learn better than if you see who they are as a problem you have to solve.

Reframing Stereotypes

Of course, many of the attributes people use to stereotype young teenagers have a kernel of truth. But most of these problematic characteristics aren't just negative; they have a powerful positive side as well. See Figure 2.1.

Stereotype	Brilliant Truth
Are jumpy and squirmy and can't sit still	Are full of energy
Act childish	Love to play and imagine
Are needy	Want meaningful relationships with adults
Are always challenging authority	Are balancing the desire to be independent and the need for guidance
Are rigid and judgmental	Have an acute sense of justice for themselves and for others
Are emotionally volatile	Have a fully developed amygdala (the part of the brain that makes emotional decisions) but a developing frontal cortex (the part of the brain that makes logical decisions)
Are hormone-ravaged	Are going through predictable, common, and positive developmental stages and changes
Are narcissistic	Are actively building their identity and are open to self-reflection and change
Are uncomfortable with intimacy	Are seeking intimacy, but unsure when to act on it

Figure 2.1 Teenagers: The stereotypes and the bright side.

It's Not Easy Being Tween

Some adults are preoccupied with how hard it is to deal with young adolescents. But it isn't always a picnic to be one yourself. Elizabeth, a seventh grader, summarized her student life for researchers Dave Brown and Trudy Knowles: "You wake up early, you work all day at school, and then they expect you to do homework." Rob, an eighth grader, said, "I feel like a cow. They herd us in the building in the morning trying to fit a thousand kids through two doors. Then they make us get into our stalls. Then they make us get in line and serve us all the same food. Then they give us fifteen minutes of pasture time after lunch, then they herd us back into the classroom" (2014, 62–63).

A 2013 study by the American Psychological Association showed that teenagers actually experience higher stress levels than adults: on a ten-point scale, teens rated their stress level during the school year at 5.8, compared to 5.1 for working adults. (Kids' summer stress level went down to 4.1.) The stressors kids named included homework, grades, work, friendships, and family relations. More than a third of the teens said that stress had caused them to feel sad and depressed and to lose sleep.

One might wonder how this squares with the oft-expressed teen lament: "I'm bored." This complaint can often be misunderstood as a marker of laziness. But another study suggests that what young people may label as boredom may actually be stress. Researcher John Eastwood and his colleagues (2012) looked at students who exhibited inattention and who described their schoolwork as "boring." Turns out, *bored* can simply be the word adolescents use to describe feeling stressed, depressed, or overwhelmed. As Eastman put it: "When people are in a negative emotional state, discouraged, or down, we know that causes attention problems. We know when people are stressed it makes it harder to focus and pay attention at a very basic, fundamental level."

Students Explore Middle Level Stereotypes

Young adolescents know that they are stereotyped by adults, but they *really* know how painful it can be to be stereotyped by other kids. Alabama middle school teacher Ambra Johnson shared with us how she and her students directly addressed this issue. The experience culminated with an article written by students Joyce Jung and Justin Locke.

> One day, Ms. Johnson had us all write down ways that we are judged—personal stereotypes—the things that we are NOT—on strips of black and white paper. We moved our desks to a circle, and Ms. Johnson laid out all of the stereotypes (the "I am not . . . " strips) in the center of the room. We had no idea who wrote what

on each piece of paper, but we silently read those words and phrases scattered across the floor:

I AM NOT

always quiet / boring / just a band nerd / rich / a know-it-all / Muslim / helpless / who you think I am / always happy / racist / sure of myself / an American native / often included / indestructible / easy / afraid to live my dreams / always trying my best / a loser / fake / listening to you scream at me / a Christian / perfect

Ms. Johnson asked us to reflect on what was laying on the floor. We could pick any three strips of paper that we could relate to the most, and we had to write about why we connected to those words. We then had to write about how we can shatter these stereotypes or explain some of the ways we can show the world we aren't these things.

This was a little bit awkward because we aren't used to teachers asking us to think this deeply about something that is not really "school related," but after we got comfortable, everyone started writing and didn't stop until she made us.

THE "I AM" STATEMENTS

After the first activity, we focused on the things that we really are. The "I am . . ." statements. We tweeted articles and videos on Twitter using the hashtag #lmsthinksbig about different stereotypes of different people.

For example, one day someone tweeted a news article about how adults (you) consider Generation Z (us) "lazy" and "apathetic." We had conversations in the classroom with each other and with others via Twitter—other students, our assistant principal, a parent, a retired guy in Kentucky we didn't know—about why teens are judged like this. The use of Twitter really enticed us as students to take interest in participating in the activity and motivated us to start taking actions to change the world.

BUILDING THE WALL

Next, we began to make "I AM . . ." statements to create a wall outside of room 114. If you come by and look at our wall, you will see such a wide variety of words and phrases:

I AM . . .

a person / funny / creative / full of anxiety / biracial / an overthinker / trying to find the right path / tired / faithful / reliable / different / bilingual

/ heartbroken / wanting more / real / a person with anger issues / minus two grandparents / Indian / afraid of meeting new people / misunderstood / Christian / someone who makes mistakes / athletic / Egyptian / adopted / ADHD / artistically disabled / pressured / tired of cancer / talented / about to crumble / a brother and a son / forgiving / a person who laughs to keep from crying / a dreamer / here for you / a Mormon / stressed / unsure of where I belong / persistent / constantly worrying / here for a purpose / clumsy / sad / Turkish / younger than you / trying to find the right path / bad with change / unwanted / trying my best to learn English / vulnerable / insightful / more than you think I am . . .

It was fun to see students from other teams coming up to our hallway wanting to add to our wall, asking for paper and Sharpies, reading what was already up there, and really being interested in it. As the wall continued to grow, different students from Team 8 would be in charge of recording using the iPad to document the wall going up. It seemed like the school was taking notice of us and our statements.

More people started coming up to us, asking us what it was and asking about #lmsthinksbig. As awareness grew, our classes bonded closer together, and we think our peers genuinely began to learn what it meant to empathize with others. We can't speak for the teachers, but it is obvious that other students' struggles were not so different from our own.

🔼 Working with (Not Against) Adolescent Development

SARA: Unpaired shoes are strewn about the room. Backpacks are open with folders sprawling out onto the floor. Hoodies are thrown over backs of chairs haphazardly, cascading down to the floor. Magazines and novels are everywhere—in the hands of kids, on their bellies, under their feet, under the desks. Water bottles lie on their sides, condensation soaking homework. The kids are at peace, little angels reading independently in their happy place. I am boiling over with frustration after I trip over my third and final backpack.

Rather than interrupting their Zone, I take some deep breaths. I have already tried to institute the rule that they need to line their shoes up along the wall and their backpacks need to be under their desks. That worked for four days. There has to be a solution to this, I think. I am very open with communicating to them when I am frustrated and invite them to do the same; but when I have reached my limit, it is not the time.

LESSON: CUE THE AMYGDALA AND CORTEX

The next day, after our soft start, I bring the kids to the rug for a chat.

"Guys, I want you to look at the room for a second and talk to me about why I might be frustrated."

They look around and there are some blank stares from kids who accept this kind of mess as normal. A few of the kids who actively try to keep their space clean notice that there is stuff everywhere. They point out the shoes, the bags, and the magazines that are perpetually in the wrong place.

I affirm their keen observations and then explain to them that I am tripping over things, they are tripping over things, and that when guests come to our classroom, I have to warn them of the obstacle course they face.

"I need to let you guys in on a little secret." I pull up a colorful map of the human brain on the doc camera and hand out a paper copy to each kid. "Your brain is part superhero power and part kryptonite." (We read a Superman book at the beginning of the year.) "It is pretty awesome because you have something that I and most adults don't have anymore: you have an amazing capacity for strong emotions because this part of your brain, the amygdala, is more dominant than the amygdala in adults' brains. This enables you to have amazing emotional responses, and it even helps you really understand the characters and people in history that we read about. It may be why you feel extra sensitive to people and events sometimes, but makes for you being a great person too because you are so caring. It's awesome!"

> I suddenly forget why I am explaining any of this to them. It would be much easier to just yell at them.

Crickets . . . I suddenly forget why I am explaining any of this to them. It would be much easier to just yell at them.

"The kryptonite part, though, is your frontal cortex, this part on the diagram, and it is still developing. This is the part of your brain that allows you to slow down and think about your actions, like where you are putting things, and be a little more aware of your space.

"I posted a link to our **Edmodo** page about these parts of the brain. I am going to give you some time back at your desks to research the amygdala and the cortex and figure out what they mean to you. On the brain maps you just labeled, write down two or three characteristics of each part, like a caption right next to it. We will meet back here in a few minutes." 69

A few minutes later, back on the rug, we share our findings and fill out our brains together. They are pretty excited to have more excuses as to why they are tripping over their own two feet, why there is a trail of debris and equipment behind them everywhere they go, and why they lose their things every second.

"So, my initial frustration with you guys has been tamed by this new knowledge we all have, but this just means we all need to work a little harder to keep this a safe space for everyone. We have to work double hard to be aware of our things and how we are actually sharing the classroom with others in our community. We want to be our best selves all the time, so we all need to pitch in with this. Can you try to override your amygdalas a little?"

There's a cheerful chorus of, "Sure, Ms. Ahmed," and on we go. My expectations are realistic—I know progress will be measurable but modest.

SMOKEY: *Love your calm. Your knowledge of adolescent development always seems to override your impulse go all dictatorial on the kids.*

SARA: *Well, usually. But I could never make those moves without my favorite book about the developmental stages and characteristics of my students—*Yardsticks *by Chip Wood (2007). Wood graphically presents the needs and characteristics of kids, one year at a time. So if you look up ten- or fourteen-year-olds, you'll see information on many categories of development: physical, social/emotional, language, cognitive, vision and fine motor, and gross motor. Then Wood takes these developmental characteristics into the classroom and shows what kinds of expectations a teacher should have for that age kid's reading, writing, and math skills and for their engagement in thematic units.*

*   Yardsticks *helped me to understand so many aspects of my students' behavior. It gave me the knowledge and the patience to weather the storm on days when I became frustrated with them for leaving things behind, dropping books, folders, and papers everywhere. It is also a great book recommendation for parents who are trying to understand their kids. I had a mother this year come back to me and declare, "He is totally normal!! Thank you!"*

SMOKEY: *We've already mentioned another favorite book about middle school kids:* What Every Middle School Teacher Should Know, *by Dave Brown and Trudy Knowles (2014). What makes this resource special is that it brings together a wide range of research, not just on kids' physical, social, and cognitive development, but on what works in creating schools well suited to young people at this life stage. Brown and Knowles also document the negative effects of today's corporate reform movement on middle schools. With standardized test scores now promoted as the only accepted measure of students' growth, the developmental aims of middle level education are being systematically discounted—and some middle schools reconverted to junior highs. So this is a great book to put in front of the scoffers who think that middle level education is some kind of feel-good playschool with pimples. Let them grapple with the depth and rigor of the research supporting core middle school practices like personalization and curricular integration.*

WE MAY NOT GET THEM ALL, BUT WE NEVER STOP TRYING

SARA: *Halfway through his eighth-grade year at my school in Chicago, Adam shows up with two new earrings and his pants at a level that makes you cover your eyes. He is walking with the confidence of a cat that just captured a mouse and brought it to your front door. Knowing what is coming in the form of adult response, yet still with head high.*

Later, in humanities class, I get a better look at the new bling he is sporting. We have an exchange, outside the classroom, about who did the piercing (his uncle); if his mother approves (yes); and what he is going to do about basketball games when the ref makes him take them out (Band-Aids will cover them up). I tell him Michael Jordan used to play with jewelry all the time until it was banned from the NBA. Then we discuss where his and Alex's backpacks might be. A simple answer follows; they left them at home. I respond with a smile and slight humor rather than scolding language, because I know that they have already heard too much scolding, and it doesn't work.

Adam and Alex are both at the peak of being fourteen-year-old boys. They are tall, strong, gifted athletically, funny, and cool in the eyes of their peers. Both have been held back, both are in single-parent households with young mothers, and both love the game of basketball. Both also hate school. They are two kids who were dealt a hand of adversity the day they were born. They are up against too many statistics: racial, social/emotional, and academic. They are also up against years of adults and teachers expecting them to make the wrong choices, to not care about school, to be aggressive in language and conduct, to always be on the defensive.

Adam and Alex's statistics precede them and shape them; if you hear something enough, you will begin to believe it yourself. I watched them battle to meet and debunk these expectations in middle school. I watched teachers and administrators wait for them to mess up, and when they did, never listen to their story or understand their perspective, and conclude that the boys were just nasty and apathetic. And sometimes they were.

But I also watched other teachers go above and beyond the call of duty to embrace them and peel back the layers. I watched their math teacher sit with them for count-less hours before and after school. I watched their basketball coach model countless skills, drills, and athletic character in order to grow them into the successful athletes he saw in them.

I'm in another part of the country now, and a few years have passed. I have heard that neither Adam nor Alex is playing basketball anymore, and that both have been either suspended or nearly expelled from school, and have been in and out of gangs. They were given chance after chance by some of the most loving faculty members I have ever worked with, and they could not meet these caring adults halfway con-sistently. Years and years of battling the statistics could not be reversed in just two years, but that does not mean that there is no hope for Adam and Alex. My wish for them is that they continue to cross paths with adults willing to see and expect only the best from them. Adults who will try to empower them so they can rewrite the statistics, rewrite their identity. We never know when we'll have a breakthrough with a kid, which is why we have to keep at it every day, with every kid.

What Middle Schools Should Look Like

Just as with the kids, there are also some pretty negative stereotypes about middle schools themselves. The Urban Dictionary offers this dispiriting definition:

middle school

1. A place where your parents drop you off to be ripped apart by your equals.

2. Where you go from being a sweet, cute, elementary school kid to being a poser goth cutter listening to Avril Lavigne.

3. Where your hopes and dreams are shattered just in time for the next pit of hell: high school.

Mom, don't make me go back to middle school today. I'll be given wedgies and noogies and have my lunch money stolen!

In schools where such sad and destructive rituals are lived out—and they do exist—the adults running that school have not yet taken all the actions that are available to change this cartoonish but genuinely destructive dynamic. In fact, even adults who know better may buy into these stereotypes when they feel things are out of their control.

We think that the idea of middle schools, developed by progressive educators in the 1960s and '70s, was a wise, healthful, and sophisticated design for kids. The original and still best design for middle schools is exquisitely well suited to the developmental tasks and needs of kids at this age. An authentic middle school experience embodies the following characteristics, keeping kids at the center of the school's mission and vision:

- personal relationships between kids and teachers
- small-group advising and individual conferring
- collaboration and teamwork
- democratic living
- authenticity/relevance
- heterogeneous grouping (no leveled tracking)
- curriculum integration across disciplines
- project/inquiry-based/exploratory learning
- social justice/action/problem solving
- choice and exposure to a well-rounded curriculum
- individualized assessment
- community spirit

These design principles attracted teachers who not only loved the kids and learning, but who also wanted to raise upstanding, principled, engaged citizens.

Sadly, today there are more signs marking "middle schools" than there are actual middle schools behind the signs. If you look up the number of official middle schools in America, you will find over fourteen thousand buildings so designated—and only about six hundred still calling themselves junior highs. This might lead you to think that these thousands of schools are carrying out middle level education as we described above. Unfortunately, that is not the case. Many were never actual middle schools to begin with. Others started strong but gradually shed their principles. Most today are middle schools in name only, with few if any of the key design features in evidence. What is somewhat easier to find are individual teachers or teams carrying on within schools that have otherwise given up on the model.

Now, much as we believe in the middle school model, we are not dogmatic about what specific grade levels constitute a "real" middle school: no matter whether you're teaching in a 6–8 school, a 5–8 school, on the top floor of a K–8 school, or in a 6–12 arrangement like Sara's current setting, you can help to build a strong middle level culture for your students. And you do that by living out the principles of personalization, collaboration, choice, exploration, authenticity, democracy, and all the rest.

For anyone wishing to better understand the origins, development, and struggles of the middle school movement, we strongly recommend the resources by James Beane listed in the Works Cited. Jim was one of the leaders of the true middle school movement back in the 1970s. His wife, Barbara Brodhagen, was an ace middle school teacher making it happen in the classroom for kids. Their work is documented in several practical and inspiring books, the best known of which is *Democratic Schools* (2007), which Jim edited with Mike Apple.

Team or Island?

What does all this history and politics mean to you? We have used the term *middle school* advisedly in the title of this book. That's where most of us teach. But we do not assume that you are working in a full-fledged, purely implemented, old-school middle level program, with all those beautiful elements in operation—with every support that teachers need in place (e.g., ample common planning time). Most of us live in a compromise; maybe we still have advisory, but it is weekly instead of daily. Maybe we still have integrative curriculum units, but only a few times a year. Maybe we have tracking by levels, and a concomitant lack of democratic practice in school affairs. Maybe we are islands in a channel of classrooms laid out to form pods and teams. Maybe we are connected to our interdisciplinary partners, our administrators, and our exploratory teachers, and middle school life is harmonious. Whatever the case, we thrive in the name of why we got into this profession to begin with: the kids.

SARA: *I have been an island sometimes, and sometimes part of a super well-supported team. It sure isn't easy to be an island in your early years of teaching, fresh and bright-eyed out of college, knowing you want to change the world, one kid at a time. You can get bogged down with mandates and red tape; next door to you may be teachers who have felt disenfranchised for decades and scoff as you hang polka-dot borders around your room the day before school starts. Being an outlier is always hard. But when I've felt isolated, gently reaching out to colleagues has helped me. Sending out articles, inviting others into your classroom, taking the minutes at a meeting, or volunteering to facilitate professional development are all ways to make your island connect with others. It's up to you to find ways to connect if you truly believe in what you do. Teachers are the smartest, most fortunate souls in the world. We benefit from schools with open door policies that allow us to share and learn together. As an island, you have the power to begin this movement; just start small.*

SMOKEY: *Sara, you went to a middle school yourself, and then taught in middle schools in Illinois and California. I recently taught sixth grade in New Mexico and every year I am on the road working with kids and teachers in fifteen or twenty states, and I can testify, many average Americans think that middle schools are either insane asylums or behavioral sinks. Any ideas why that happens?*

SARA: *Ha! I think it is because we forget that we have all been there ourselves. So many people admit to wanting to erase their middle school years from their memories completely. Like how everyone hates hearing that I teach middle school, as if I just dug up the worst memories of their life for them.*

It's difficult but important work to honor the internal conflict that most middle school students are going through. They are caught somewhere between wanting full independence as adults and still really needing guidance, attention, and love. My classroom is designed with this in mind and my approach in teaching, coaching, or casual conversation informs them that I absolutely know and value this. Remembering that we went through this stage of life as well gives us the empathy that lets us establish mutual ground with them.

I can empathize with the people who have actually raised middle schoolers; my own dad has told me a few times that he didn't like me when I was thirteen. Chip Wood would argue that adolescents actually behave best when they are away from home. Sorry, parents. Middle school kids need as much empathy, compassion, and humor from adults as we give to young children.

This is much easier if you immerse yourself in the research about the adolescent brain and social/emotional development. And then put those books down and do as much "kid watching" as possible. The more you know, the more you will smile rather than rage at kids' behavior. Sometimes the stuff that drives you craziest is just kids hitting their developmental targets right on schedule! Once you grasp this at the DNA level, it becomes natural to laugh with, not disapprove of, their life stage. Your empathy and understanding alone will empower kids to walk out of your room as the movers, thinkers, and creators they are, the growing, engaged citizens they are on track to be.

The Teacher

SMOKEY: *If you mention to everyday civilians that you teach middle school, they usually express some kind of discomfort: they roll their eyes, shake their heads, offer condolences, or say things like, "Wow, that must be a rough job" or "You're lucky you didn't have me in your class, I was such a pain in the ass in middle school." Sometimes they express gratitude, as if you were a first responder to the "hurricane of hormones" that middle schools are supposed to be. Sometimes they say, "Well, I certainly could never handle those kids." And you think, right, you probably couldn't.*

SARA: *The responses I get range from amusing (horrifying) personal stories about the "worst years of my life" to condolences ("God, I hated middle school, I'm sorry"). It's always a wonder to me that people feel so bad about their early adolescence. My first response to these confessions is generally an awkward laugh, but I always try to pacify or sugarcoat their memories. I reassure them that I actually love middle schoolers and they are a really fun group of humans to learn alongside. It's as though I need to convince people that adolescents are also real human beings, with normal feelings, who are trying to find a comfortable zone within their identity, just like everyone else. And really, they are funny—funnier than any adult I've met.*

SMOKEY: *And that's a serious point. I've had some colleagues who were angry at the kids a lot of the time, mostly for stuff that just comes with the territory, y'know? If these kids don't amuse you, if you aren't laughing with them a fair amount of the time, you might be working at the wrong grade level.*

SARA: *If we practice a habit of perspective, we can try to understand why people respond so strongly to this age level. Sixth graders can enter your room at ten. They leave the middle school environment when they are fourteen or nearly there. The social, emotional, physical, and cognitive growth is rapid and ethereal. This can cause turbulence for parents and teachers, but mostly the middle schoolers themselves. Any and all relationships can be challenged during these years: parent vs. child, teacher vs. child, coach vs. child, peer vs. peer. There is no magic wand to fix this, no blog that has the right advice and tools. There is only compassion and empathy, and definitely, a good sense of humor. We love these kids the way the youngest part of them needs us to.*

⬆ Starting with Ourselves: A Teaching Identity

Our selves are our main teaching tool. Hopefully, we also have some content knowledge and a few instructional skills, but before everything, trumping everything, is our *self*, our *person*. This is especially true when we work with kids whose overriding developmental task is forming an adult identity. Our students are learning from how we are, how we act, and what we say, all day, every day.

Successful middle school teachers know themselves well and mange themselves mindfully around the kids. The students want to know us as people, not as teaching machines. Our appropriate and measured self-disclosure is the leading edge of our relationship with young people. How much to share, what to share, how close to get: these are questions we grapple with actively.

> Our students are learning from how we are, how we act, and what we say, all day, every day.

SMOKEY: *Sara, the very first thing that struck me when I visited your room in Chicago was how close you were to the kids. Physically, at a literal level. But mostly how open, available, personal, and casual you were. You openly talked about your wide array of out-of-school interests, your own questions and curiosities, your deeply felt responses to the Bulls and the Bears and the Hawkeyes. (Sorry, couldn't resist that.) You also brought kids news of the world's problems and struggles in a way that made them concerned partners.*

Your basic stance seemed almost like an older sibling or a favorite aunt. You were an example of what a grown-up could be—a learner, a coach, a seeker of justice, a cheerleader, an empathic ear, an adult that kids had good reason to trust. The students could play with you, but still very much respect you. As they say in social psychology, you were highly congruent*; no teacher mask, pretty much straight-up Sara. As I told you then, this was the middle school of my dreams—but I have strange tastes. But this level of intimacy with students some teachers find uncomfortable—they don't want it or seek it. How much of this closeness is necessary and how much of it is a style or personality choice?*

SARA: *One of the first pieces of advice typically emphasized in a teacher ed program, or offered by a veteran colleague to a new, young teacher, is about your relationship with the students: "You are not their friend; you are their teacher. Walk in with a professional outfit on the first few days so they understand this. Don't smile for the first few days."*

SMOKEY: *In my day, the advice was "Don't smile until Christmas." No lie!*

SARA: *Whew! And people told me stuff like, "Don't get their attention by saying 'guys.'" You could imagine my surprise when I walked into Burley and my buddy, Kristin Ziemke, was greeting her students with a "Hi, friends!" She has been a model for me in regard to student relationships ever since. In middle school, I may not use* friends, *but I definitely smile on the first day, and every day after that. How could you not? They are hilarious! (And I do call them "guys.")*

While there is merit to establishing a positive and respectful rapport with your students from the get-go, I always lean toward mutual *respect and letting them know you are also a human being who doesn't sleep under her desk at night. In his infinite wisdom, Donald Graves reminds us to always know our students in facts and actions; to really know who they are before we can teach them (1983). There should be an expectation that we are sharing our lives with the students the same way we are asking them to share their lives with us. We do this by sharing our reading lives and our writing lives in workshop lessons and book talks, and in those first weeks when we ask them to create "Me" projects that share pieces of their identity.*

I introduce identity webs and create my own in front of the kids the first day or two of school. I talk about why I have National Geographic, Time for Kids, *and* Sports Illustrated for Kids *bursting out of the baskets in the classroom. I am a reader, I love to travel, and I love sports. I notice what the kids are wearing and find ways to connect with them via jerseys or shoes, or by offering validation for a fashion risk they decided to take. There are some personality and style liberties that I take as well. I am a sports fanatic, I love fashion, and I would rather read YA and watch YA television and movies than anything else. My family and friends will tell you that I also have YA eating habits. I share these things in snippets and I ask questions to empower kids to reciprocate. I share how important my relationships with my family and friends in Chicago are to me. I have already lived middle school and I don't plan on living vicariously through them, but I often talk about my middle school experience when it is appropriate. My favorite thing to tell is that my best girlfriends today became my best girlfriends when I was eleven, in middle school.*

I reveal personal information when it makes sense to strengthen a rapport or extend an olive branch, or if the kids simply ask. There is a balance between overexposure and opening a window into who you are. I work to find that place each day, a place where I gain a piece of them, and they have a takeaway of me. I am approachable, open, and friendly, but not their friend. Walking this fine line appropriately makes me available to them as a teacher, but also as an adult they can connect with on any given day. Being able to recommend great books or magazine and newspaper articles on the things we love in common is a plus.

Things I don't share include any love stories, from middle school to present day, and in turn, I don't ask about their budding romances either. And if they ask me for love advice, I let them know I have a little schema about this, but I don't go any further than asking, "Well, would you rather continue talking to them and be friends, or say you are 'going out' and then pretend to ignore each other and act super weird when you are in the same room?" The kids laugh, but I have seen more teddy bears thrown in the garbage on Valentine's Day than Gund would care to know about.

Yourself as a Learner

Just as we need to know and manage our self-sharing around kids, we also need a deep understanding of how we think and learn; how our brains, as well as our hearts, work. We need to know our own minds. Our main academic job, after all, is to model and teach *thinking*.

SARA: *When I was fifteen, I sat through driver's ed class and listened as my teacher, Coach D, gave us the Rules of the Road lecture each day. At this stage, we were the information receivers; we complied, skimmed and scanned for answers to literal questions, and filled in bubbles and blanks. We were able to retell the steps to changing lanes, backing around corners, and parking up a hill. As the class moved from classroom learning to on-the-road practice, we were able to sit in a real car and begin to merge our thinking with content by reacting to a re-created road route with real cones, railroad crossing signs, and plastic cutouts of families heading to school in a crosswalk. We could visualize and begin to infer the real road and start to acquire knowledge and see why things matter. We could learn, understand, and remember facts in this stage of the class.*

Later, when my father took me out to practice, I felt the real learning begin. He would remind me of the literal information I needed to remember and check for some understanding, but he would really act as facilitator. He had been modeling driving for me since I was a little kid, of course, but now I looked at his driving much more intently. I watched his hands on the wheel and his feet on the pedals, I peeked at the speedometer, and I watched where his eyes went as he made decisions.

When I took the wheel, he was patient. He allowed me to make mistakes in a safe place, provided options for me to make choices ("You can try using the side mirrors for reversing as well"), questioned some of the decisions I made to push my thinking ("Why are you going over the speed limit?"), and let go of the control he naturally would have as a parent and driver ("Just think to yourself about that"). He allowed me to actively use knowledge that I had about the rules of the road and apply them in a real-life, everyday setting. He was the best teacher I could have asked for as I sprinted to the DMV the morning of my sixteenth birthday with confidence. I passed with ease, having my father's voice in my head the entire time. He showed me. We did it together. Then I did it on my own.

From our early days as learners, we wonder, we view, we learn to read, we wonder some more, read for answers, and ask questions. We expose ourselves to print and cultural information every day, and ask ever deeper and harder questions of the world. This does not cease as adults. As teachers, we have to model our own inquiry each day of our learning lives. We have to share, in a natural way, what we care about and why we care about it as curious, informed, and vigilant citizens in the community.

This is how we get our students ready for the driver's seat. Sharing your curious life with kids opens for them a comfortable space where they can ask their own questions and feel safe about not knowing everything (for even the most precocious of kiddos). It also leads to a tremendous rapport with the students. When they know of your investigative passions, it opens up doors for them to connect with you and each other. It also demystifies you a bit as a teacher, and makes you more human to them. We want this to happen in its most organic, natural way.

> Sharing your curious life with kids opens for them a comfortable space where they can ask their own questions.

What we said earlier about having your students know a little piece of who you are applies to your intellectual life as well. One of my favorite professional development moments was at an in-house session my first year at Burley. Michele Timble, a great mentor and friend of mine, stood up and shared what was on her "nightstand": a YA novel she was reading along with a novel her sister, Debbie, recommended to her, a couple of professional texts to read over the summer, and an Us Weekly magazine. She quickly quipped about her personal life's connection to each text. I was in love, not only with Michele, but with the way this immediately opened up her life to us a reader, a teacher, and a human being. In that very short lesson, she modeled being a learner, a mother, a sister, and someone who appreciates mindless news just as much as me. She was disarming and sincere, and gave us all the confidence to then turn to each other and do the same. And I still can't cancel my subscriptions to mindless magazines to this day. Thanks, Michele.

Yourself as a Human Being

SARA: Nearly ten years ago, I was asked to create an identity web for myself at a Facing History and Ourselves workshop in Chicago by a man who is now one of my life mentors, Chuck Meyers. It was not easy.

I became pretty emotional during the exercise, because I realized that no one had ever asked me to think about how I identify myself. It has always been either lovingly impressed on me by

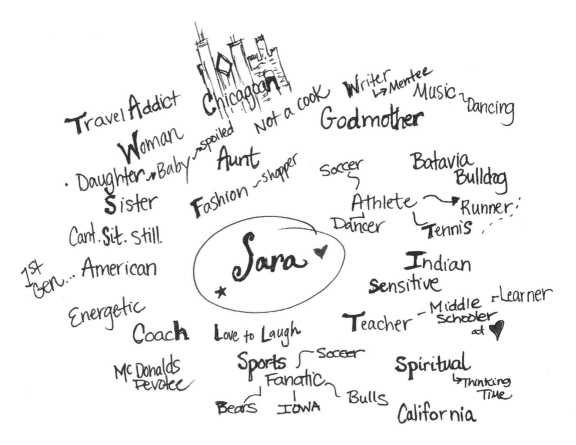

Figure 3.1 Sara's identity map.

my parents (religion and culture) or subconsciously given to me by society (we don't see you as anything but "white"; you're just like us). I also realized as we began to share our thoughts during this discussion that I was not alone.

I realized in that moment that I will never be able to teach kids to wonder or care about history or literature, or any subject for that matter, if they can't identify and honor who they are as both learners and human beings. It will be impossible to understand why choices are made in history or in fiction, why they look at math and science problems the way they do, without having a sense of the layers of personal identity and history behind those choices. It was the single most important thing that I discovered about my philosophical approach to teaching, and myself.

SMOKEY: *But in the summer institutes I did with colleagues for 19 years, we used mini-identity webs as name tags; sticking this to your chest is the greatest conversation starter of all time! Today, mine would look like this (tomorrow, probably a little different).*

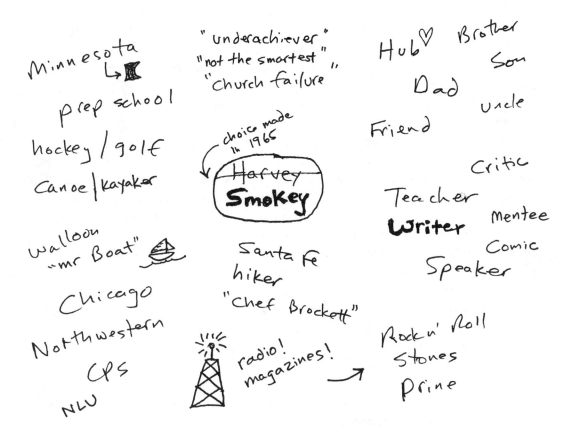

Figure 3.2 Smokey's identity map.

OUR TEACHING BIOS

While knowing yourself as a human being is essential to being really present with your students, understanding your identity *as a teacher* can also help you to think about your experiences in a new way. As examples, here's how we frame our professional identities.

SMOKEY: *If my math (never a strength) is correct, I seem to have been a teacher for forty-five years. I have taught every grade level from kindergarten through college—some of these for years, others for just a day as a visitor. I have written or coauthored twenty books on schooling, literacy, literature, reading, writing, and inquiry. For some years I worked as a professor and researcher, but these days my main job is sharing ideas with, and stealing ideas from, fantastic teachers around the country. Last year, I pursued these endeavors in twenty-three states. Over my whole career, Idaho remains the only state not to benefit from my services. Calling Boise!*

I started teaching at George Westinghouse Area Vocational High School on the west side of Chicago in September of 1969. I was twenty years old. This was at the height of the Vietnam escalation, and I had just spent my undergraduate years at Northwestern as a nonviolent antiwar activist. In spite of an initially promising draft lottery number (ask your grandfather what this means), I was promptly hauled in for an army induction physical and put on the fast track for Vietnam. Then, a painful but fortuitous car crash took me out of soldiering, and I turned the rest of my life's attention to becoming a teacher.

It was an explosive, idealistic time in education. The big book of 1969 was Teaching as a Subversive Activity, in which Neil Postman and Charles Weingartner entreated us teachers to decentralize our classrooms, to stop controlling our kids with lectures and with our leading, right-answer questions. I gobbled up their every word, reached out to them personally, and was lucky enough to have Neil Postman become a mentor to me for decades to come. I was also fortunate to have some amazing local mentors. My doctoral professor Wallace W. Douglas was the uncredited precursor to Donald Graves. He taught us that kids' writing (always British-leaning, he called it "composition") was vital, real, important, personal, and a tool of thinking and learning—not to be bled over with red ink and hurtful marginalia. Rae A. Moses brought me from a kid who argued with her in class, to become her colleague in the linguistics department, and then guided my dissertation on the fraud of bidialectalism—the systematic punishment of black kids for the way they spoke (and still speak).

At Westinghouse, we beginners could try any crazy teaching method we wanted because there was zero accountability for anything. The principal was so terrified of the all-black student body that he never left his office except when guided by one of his African American assistant principals. They in turn seemed deeply embarrassed when assigned to escort duty and rolled their eyes when he wasn't watching.

On one of his rare excursions into enemy territory, Mr. Mulligan walked past my door and spotted my senior English class arranged in a circle. He did a Looney-Tunes-worthy double-take through the window, and then ripped open the door. He strode into the room and silently rearranged all the desks into straight rows—with the thirty-two astonished students still sitting in them. This took some time; when he was finally done, his face was dark red and he was gasping for air.

Throughout this bizarre redecorating process, his guide Mr. Lane leaned against the door frame, gazing at me with an expression that said, "Hey, I can't believe this shit either." Then Mulligan dragged me into the hall and shouted: "What do you think you are doing in there? Don't you ever let me see those kids in a circle again! Straight rows make straight lives." (Yes, he actually said this.) As he pressed his spittle-spewing face ever closer to mine, he was also pushing me against a rolled-up wrestling mat against the wall at knee level behind me. As he finished his rebukes, I slowly tipped over sideways, and watched him retreat to the stairwell.

Undeterred, my friend and social studies teacher Norm Spear and I continued running simulations, mock trials, and the independent reading of YA novels. We found an empty classroom and used it to move all sixty of our kids in there for special events. Like every day. We found an awesome book called Creative Encounters in the Classroom and pillaged its *experiential, student-centered lesson plans. We were the idiots savants of teaching. Inspired by our heroes—Postman and Weingartner, John Dewey, John Holt, Herb Kohl, and the open educators of Britain—we were doing progressive pedagogy by the seat of our pants. We were probably also doing terrible, retrograde stuff that I have conveniently forgotten. There may have been thousands of worksheets. Still, I love that I only remember the progressive practices that we somehow managed to emulate from books.*

SARA: *My journey as an educator began at the University of Iowa (Go Hawks!), where I was primed with all the greats—Lucy Calkins, Don Graves, Nancie Atwell, and Steph Harvey, and serendipitously, my now mentor and fearless coauthor, Smokey Daniels. Iowa had a student teaching program that allowed students to travel abroad, and I jumped at that chance as soon as I could. I loved to travel and I welcomed the experience of an international school much different from what I grew up with. I landed in Dublin, Ireland, at a two-room schoolhouse where I taught junior infants to sixth class (pre-K through sixth/seventh grade) in all subjects. I also ended up being their inaugural PE teacher, which was perfect for me, as we played soccer and basketball every day. I returned home to Chicago where I taught seventh-grade language arts in U-46, the second-largest urban district in Illinois. I got my first taste of public education budget cuts that year and was laid off along with three thousand other nontenured teachers. A bit disenfranchised, but hopeful, I contacted my headmaster back in Dublin. She offered me a long-term sub position for the upcoming school year, and I was on a plane back to Ireland that summer. My heart wasn't done with the Emerald Isle just yet.*

I ended up coming home that next year, hoping to land in the Chicago Public Schools, where my desire for urban education needed to be fulfilled. I spent the next nine years teaching in fifth- to eighth-grade classrooms, learning alongside and coaching the greatest city kids in the world. I fell in love with Burley School and its community, headed by Principal Barbara Kent, who nearly raised me for those eight years. The faculty's dedication to literacy, professional growth, and the love of reading shaped the way I view education today. My class sizes ranged from around twenty-five to thirty-three, and reading levels spanned four grade levels in a classroom. I taught all subjects and when I finally moved into a middle school classroom, I co-created a humanities block with my super-supportive team, because we did not see the value in separating language arts/reading and social studies. To us, they went hand in hand.

One of my favorite parts of my teaching day became the outdoor classroom—the track, the field, and the basketball court. Together with my colleagues, we built a sports program that was supported by the whole school community, validated the middle schoolers as student-athletes, and built role models for our primary grades. More than anything, it strengthened my rapport with sometimes hard-to-reach kids and kids who wanted to be recognized for more than just their academic achievement. Chicago was my introduction to Facing History and Ourselves, an organization whose spirit embodies so much of the work in this book.

I now find myself at The Bishop's School in La Jolla, California, where the months of November through March are far more pleasant than in Chicago. Bishop's is part of the National Association of Independent Schools. Classes are about half the size of my classes at Burley or in U-46, and we are located in an affluent area of San Diego. After nearly ten years of teaching, I still felt like a brand-new teacher in my first years at Bishop's, but I was supported by some of the greatest professionals I have ever had the pleasure of teaching beside. The middle school team works tirelessly to create an experience for the kids that sets them up to succeed on a large new campus, alongside eighteen-year-old seniors. Leaving the public sector and moving into the private school world pulled on my heartstrings quite a bit and was not an easy move, especially as my friends in Chicago went on strike the year I left. I love Chicago and my family and friends dearly, but when asked in my interview why I wanted to move to California and San Diego, I told them that in fifth grade, I did a state report on California, and my heart had been set on the Golden State ever since. That sealed the deal, I think, and I am now a sixth- and seventh-grade teacher.

⬆ How to Respond to the Common Core and the Corporate Reform Movement

Of course our own personal and professional identities are not the only factor influencing how we work with young people. We teach in a hugely complex social-political climate that steers and moderates and channels our teaching selves. The Common Core State Standards (or state mandates very much like them) have now arrived in our classrooms, often with a bang. Your life as a teacher is being changed before your eyes. The new rules may require you to make learning harder, restrict what kids read, and hold students (and yourself) strictly accountable for narrow but measurable outcomes. The watchwords of the day are "raise the bar," "increase complexity," and "plan with data." The word *rigor* (dictionary definition: "The quality of harshness, sternness, and inflexibility") has been refurbished as a classroom compliment. And an ever-expanding schedule of standardized tests ranks kids and teachers alike, with even tougher ones right around the corner.

Also present in your classroom today are two or three dozen young human beings, who are definitely not data. Data don't smile, squirm, or think. These are vibrant, distinctive, and potentially creative persons, moldable minds, waiting for you to ignite their curiosity, imagination, ability, and desire to read the world. Depending on how we respond to the standards initiative, they could end up "college and career ready," prepared to quietly accept their allocated place in a flawed society; or they could become "citizen ready," with the tools, the discernment, and the ethics to struggle for themselves *and others*.

Is there any connection between educational standards and social justice? Does one rule out the other? Are there opportunities here, or just oppositions? Many progressive colleagues whom we respect have devoted themselves to fighting, boycotting, discrediting, or undermining the standards, and especially the high-stakes tests attached to them. We've joined in at times. Thousands of teachers have now entered into an unspoken coalition with conservatives who see national standards and tests as a federal intrusion into state prerogatives. Together, these unlikely allies have had an impact that few would ever have predicted. As this book goes to press, the standards and testing movement is fragmenting into something far less unanimous than its inventors were seeking.

But, politics notwithstanding, when we get up every day, we are still mainly teachers. That's our job and our calling. We plan to work with kids for many years to come (though the actuarial tables are more on Sara's side). So, while we will always save a percentage of our energy for local and national political work, our day-to-day commitment is to students, one kid at a time. For Sara, that means her middle schoolers in California. For Smokey, that means the kids in schools where he visits, demonstrates, and models progressive classroom practices.

It's in this context of everyday work with young people that we have created this book. How do we not just live with the standards and tests, but find opportunities in them? Convert them, transmediate them, transgress them, surpass them? These systems were made by billionaires seeking a docile work force that's educated enough to follow an order, eager to consume and waste, and fearful enough to keep quiet. We can do better, and teachers can lead the way.

The Space

If you want to teach middle school, you must co-own your space. Working along with the kids, you create a new and unique classroom every year. Week after week, you gradually build a highly personalized environment together that optimizes community, support, and learning. The goal is something more like a *family room* than a classroom—with all the metaphors and connotations that word entails.

While there are many healthful room arrangements for young adolescents, you need a gathering area where the whole group can sit up close and personal for minilessons and discussions, and a separate work area with tables or desks where kids can work in small groups or on their own. You need to set up your classroom library, organizing and displaying books, magazines, and other resources. You must figure out how to best give kids access to the technology in the room. Maybe you also set up a couple of small nooks in the corners for quiet reading and reflection. As the year unfolds, the walls gradually fill with the student work and co-created anchor charts. It is almost impossible to undertake this kind of creation if, like most high school and many middle school teachers, you have to share a room with one or more colleagues.

SMOKEY: *In my second year of teaching I had to share a classroom with a somewhat difficult colleague. One day, I hung up a poster in our room during fourth period. Janet tracked me down during fifth and told me to take it down by sixth. This commenced a monthlong series of* negotiations that I eventually abandoned. It turned out that she liked the walls bare, the room neutral and devoid of personality. The takeaway for me was a long time coming. But years later, when a group of us started a new high school in 1996, one of our founding principles was that all teachers would have their own room, no sharing, so everyone could co-create their unique environments with the kids.

SARA: *Setting up a space where the students have ownership and space to think and collaborate takes constant tinkering. It starts with my own work in the summer, before the kids show up, constantly rearranging the furniture, desks, and materials to establish an initial setup that's welcoming, methodical, and accessible. Then, after the first few days of school, the kids become architects of the space as well. We realize that some things don't work; desks are facing awkward directions, supplies are not in the most efficient path. It really is not until students' bodies, backpacks, and countless supplies are in the room that we truly discover how we can function in our environment together. It's a blast living through this process; there is nothing better than a co-created space (see Figures 4.1–4.4).*

Figure 4.1 Students working in the classroom.

Figure 4.2 Whole-class minilesson on rug.

Figure 4.3 Students working in beanbags.

Figure 4.4 Students reading on couch/floor.

Sara's Classrooms

While I have actually taught in eight different classrooms, the last two have been the ones where I could most fully develop the space with my students. Here are overhead maps of my rooms at Burley School in Chicago (eight years) and The Bishop's School (three years) in Figure 4.9.

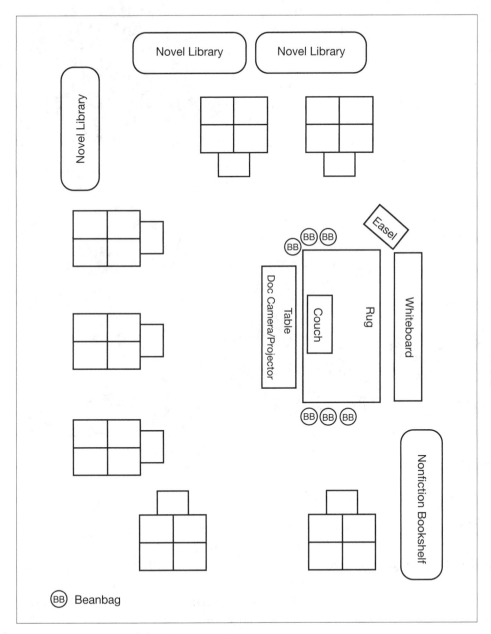

Figure 4.5 Burley classroom map.

BURLEY SCHOOL

My classroom was large and airy, with lots of light. It was the perfect space for thirty-plus seventh or eighth graders who need lots of room to move around. I went through many arrangements at Burley, but this was one of my favorites. It showcased the students on the rug as soon as you walked into the room and gave the kids plenty of space to transition from place to place. In this room you will notice that the projector and doc camera are behind the rug and couch. In some cases this meant that the kids' backs were to me if I was projecting something on the screen. That is fine, as I don't always want to be the focal point of the room. I would often move between a "leading from behind" position to the anchor chart easel by the whiteboard. See Figures 4.5 through 4.8.

Figure 4.6 Cluster of desks with nonfiction library.

Figure 4.7 Presenting from behind; kids on couches, beanbags, and the floor.

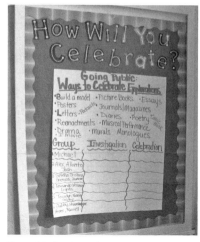

Figure 4.8 Anchor chart on ways to go public.

THE BISHOP'S SCHOOL

At Bishop's most classrooms are small, but I was fortunate enough to be assigned a converted library space the year that I arrived. See Figures 4.9–4.12. You will notice the significantly fewer desks, which just means there was more room for gathering. So I created two rug spaces, one with technology and one just homey, with the standard clusters of desks in between. The kids shift among these three main spaces almost every day; we are always moving. The library is organized in three sections—magazines, nonfiction trade books, and novels.

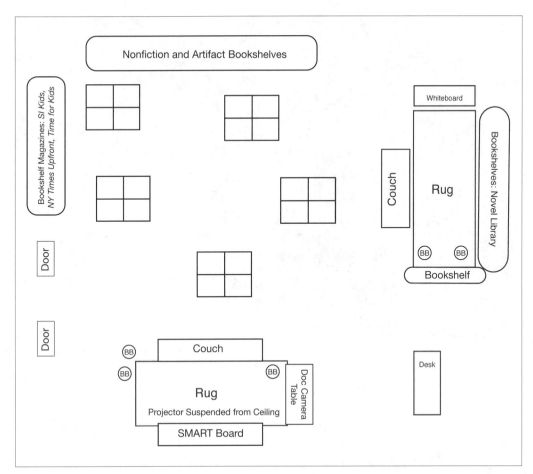

Figure 4.9 Bishop's classroom.

Figure 4.10 A soft start in our reading library.

Figure 4.11 Taking notes on iPads.

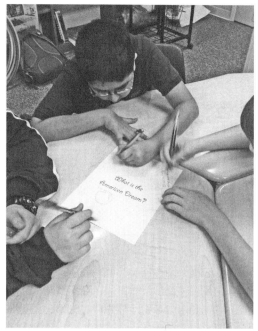

Figure 4.12 In small clusters of desks, kids can collaborate easily.

DESKS OR TABLES

Our desks are always clustered in groups of three, four, or five, depending on the size of the class and our goals. (If I had tables, I'd put four kids at each one, and be thankful that the movable chairs make it easy for kids to quickly rearrange into groups of three or five.) No matter what, we never put kids in rows, because we want them to be able to quickly look up and work with one or more partners, depending on the work at hand. Rows insinuate that the teacher is the only audience, the focal point of the room, and the only person who can help or collaborate with kids—and none of this is true. We want kids to be interdependent as well as independent.

Desks are students' own workspace for the time they are with us, and thus need to be thoughtfully arranged. We need to ensure that the desk formation speaks to kids in a way that says they are in charge of their own learning. They are not positioned to face forward and listen to a droning voice at the front of the room. They are positioned to listen, discuss, share, and to have an eye-line to many parts of the room at once. See Figure 4.12.

TEACHER DESK

For a long time, we had a trend in Chicago where we got rid of the teacher desks in our classrooms. They are generally large, cumbersome wood monstrosities that suck all attention toward them. None of us sat at them while we had kids in the room, and we wanted to make space for couches, collaborative tables, rugs, and bookshelves instead.

If we did have a teacher desk, we would hide it in a corner and just use it as storage for filing the endless papers teachers receive. So we are not saying to throw out your desk, but to position it to function best and send the right messages. Just like the students' desks, it should be thoughtfully located to show kids that the room is a space mostly for them.

RUGS

Some people think that rugs are for elementary kids only. So wrong! Yes, even eighth graders sit on a rug, and they love it. My former principal, Barbara Kent, would come around to our rooms in the summer to check in while we were cleaning and arranging, and to also thank us for spending our summer days working to have a welcoming space for the kids when they walked through the door in August. My favorite part about these drop-ins was her question, "What do you see when you first walk in the door?" Read: the rug and library really need to be the focal points of the room. That question was always enough to make us reflect on the setup of the room. Rugs are available at Home Depot, Ikea, business catalogues such as Demco, and on willing parents' floors everywhere. The parents at Burley knew we were always willing to take clean, well-maintained rugs off their hands. If this was not an option, some of us would check college dorm room displays and Craigslist (selectively). Rugs are comfortable during minilessons, independent reading, small-group work, whole-class meetings, and mental breaks! With any functional workspace in the room, there are norms at the rug. We set these up together:

RUG NORMS—OUR BODIES ARE POSITIONED TO:

- turn and talk
- work independently
- participate in the minilesson
- be comfortable
- be in our own space
- learn the best way we can

Maybe you remember from Chapter 1 how the idea for my shoes-off classroom started with trying to preserve a brand-new rug. I'm not saying you should try this, but for me it keeps the classroom clean, and there is something zen about it. The kids are also in favor of it. They literally kick off their shoes the minute they come in the room and grab their books to read. "It feels like home," as Helen puts it.

COUCHES

Couches are also an ingredient in home-like classrooms. They go hand in hand with the rugs. They generally frame the rug area and provide more space for big kids to congregate when they come together. We also used to beg, borrow, and barter for these in our classrooms.

One of my dear friends lived across the street from Burley and when he and his roommates were moving, they generously called and donated a couple of couches. A team of us walked right over, cleaned them, and carried them across the street. They were his mother's old couches and she was thrilled they found a new home! The rug norms also apply to couches. Kids need to be aware of their personal space.

SMOKEY: *Are norms enough? Many middle school people spend their whole lives trying to keep the kids' bodies from touching in any way.*

SARA: *For sure, I have heard so many people question having teenagers "sit this close together" because they can't handle it, or it may be inappropriate. As spring rears its lovely head in middle school, budding romances are bound to blossom. As with anything, we want kids to be vigilant and aware of the fact that the couches are indeed a learning space and not an opportunity to cozy up to someone special.*

ANCHOR CHARTS

One very visible way in which the classroom environment evolves is in the ever-growing collection of co-created anchor charts hanging on the walls. See Figure 4.13. You may think of these tools as more for elementary classrooms, but we think middle school teachers should steal and use this powerful idea more often.

Figure 4.13 Co-created anchor charts from the first weeks of school.

An anchor chart is a list of ideas that we create together with kids, and then save in a visible spot for future reference. As Stephanie Harvey says, "Anchor charts help us connect kids' past learning to today's teaching" (Harvey and Daniels 2009). These can be lists of academic procedures or strategies, or ways of addressing community problems in the classroom. Typically, anchor charts get created with the whole group sitting in the gathering area, having a brainstorming session. We put the topic or problem at the top of a piece of chart paper and then invite kids' input, discuss, and scribe it. Sometimes we are just looking for a single list of points or ideas; other times we'll set up a two-column chart labeled "advantages/disadvantages" or "looks like/sounds like." Here are close-ups of a few.

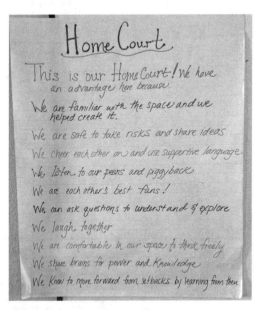

Figure 4.14 "Home Court" anchor chart.

Figure 4.14 is an anchor chart we make at the beginning of the year. We start by thinking about the reasons why sports teams win more games at home than away. Then we take those ideas and turn them into ways of making our classroom our own "home court." You will see more of this lesson, originally developed by Smokey and Nancy Steineke, in Chapter 6.

The chart in Figure 4.15 gets us ready for an inquiry mind-set. In a short five-minute minilesson, I ask kids who have a little brother or sister at home, and what that sibling's favorite question is. They all say, *Why?* Everyone has a story. And with this, we begin thinking about our thinking: Why do we ask questions?

With the type of anchor chart shown in Figure 4.16, we don't gather everyone at once. Instead, the teacher poses a question and leaves the chart on the wall for kids to add comments over a set period of time. When everyone has had a chance to weigh in, the last kid to post brings the chart to the gathering area, and we invite students to discuss what they noticed *other* kids saying.

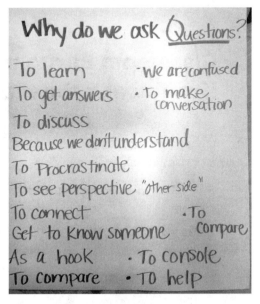

Figure 4.15 "Why do we ask questions?" anchor chart.

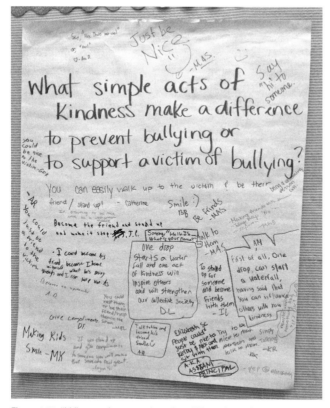

Figure 4.16 "What makes a safe school?" anchor chart.

⬆ Classroom Environment Reflection (for You and the Kids)

After the first couple weeks of school, I give my students a quick survey to see if the learning environment is working for their learning style and sense of safety. I can deliver this on paper or electronically via email, SurveyMonkey, or **Edmodo**. Some of the questions I include:

1. What type of space do you need to get schoolwork done?
2. Where do you do your homework at home? Are there resources or conditions there that we could replicate here?
3. What do you like about the way our classroom is set up?
4. Do you have any changes you would make to the room?
5. Do you feel safe in the place where you are? You can tell me on here or see me privately if there is a concern.
6. Can you see yourself in the walls of this room?

 69 ‹

This type of survey gives me a good idea where kids are on their environmental needs. Then we have a quick discussion the next day, where I first report the survey results to show them that I honor their learning space. Then we negotiate any helpful changes together.

I don't just ask kids how they think our space is working. I have my own reflection checklist that I use both in my initial setup of the room and again now, when I give the kids the survey. This checklist in Figure 4.17 was adapted from the incredibly thoughtful curriculum team at Burley School, representing primary, intermediate, and middle level classrooms.

Descriptor	Comments
Can your students "see" themselves on the walls/shelves? (photos, writing)	
Is student dialogue represented in the room? (quotes, wonderings, writing)	
Are there areas of peace? (quiet spaces to confer, discuss, work out conflicts)	
Is this a safe space to take risks and ask questions?	
Are materials easily accessible and labeled for students?	
Are there routines as students come in and/or leave the classroom? (homework turn-in, paper handouts)	
Have you established norms/expectations for the classroom space?	
Is there literature (fiction/nonfiction) available for students? (promoting a reading life)	
Are there cozy features in your room? (rugs, lamps/lighting, pillows)	
Have the students co-created the organization of things?	
Do the students have ownership of the room as well?	
Is your own (interesting, reading, active, curious) lifestyle displayed in a thoughtful way?	

Figure 4.17 Checklist for reflecting on classroom environment.

Forget that old advice about how you should dress on the first day of school. Your classroom environment makes a far more powerful first impression on your new kids. (OK, you should wear a nice outfit, too.) Kids notice everything. This is your first opportunity to let them know that this is their space too, and when they are here, they are cordially invited to read, wonder, listen, collaborate, take risks, care, and have fun. Classroom environments should be deliberate and thoughtful. They are mindful of the developmental needs of the kids. If we are all going to be in these spaces for the better part of our day and year, let's make them comfortable and enjoyable for everyone.

The Toolbox

Coming up in Chapters 6 through 10 are detailed descriptions of many inquiry topics that Sara and her kids have deeply explored. While each story is unique, under the surface you will notice that Sara constructs every unit out of a fairly limited collection of learning structures, stringing them together in recurrent patterns.

For example, across all these inquiries, students repeatedly turn and talk with a partner for a minute or two, then share these ideas back with the class. The teacher routinely models her own thinking process before asking students to try a new strategy. Kids keep research journals with defined sections and purposes. They annotate the texts they read, leaving tracks of their thinking. They join in structured discussions online and on wall charts. They share their findings with others who behave as attentive audiences. All these are basic structures for active investigation, and they are used, with fine variations, over and over.

To put it another way: Sara's diverse inquiry units aren't spun out of magic, with each one simply being an inspired one-off. Instead, each inquiry is deliberate and crafted from a toolbox of structures that can be assembled and repeated in countless ways. One of the terms for this inventory of instructional routines is *best practice*; these teaching structures are outlined by Zemelman, Daniels, and Hyde (2012).

So before we launch into the inquiries, we want to review the most fundamental of these structures and the language that goes with them.

THE TOOLBOX

There will be few surprises here. Seeing these structures will probably validate much of what's already happening in your classroom. Indeed, most of these tools are not new, and they're not secret. But they may have somehow failed us in the past, and dropped out of our teaching over the years. We are inviting you to reconsider some ideas you may have previously entertained, but discarded under the pressure of time, mandates, standardized tests, and everything else that seems to narrow our instructional range.

Most importantly, we hope that reviewing these basic instructional building blocks will help you see the common deep structures of inquiry with young adolescents. And in turn, that should make it easier to translate and adapt these lessons for your own classroom.

ANCHOR CHARTS   (pages 50–52, 86, 94, 95–96, 97, 99, 100, 111, 158–159)

As we mentioned in Chapter 4, anchor charts create a record of kids' thinking about subject matter or classroom processes. As we refer back to them, they foster independence, responsibility, and choice. To include everyone, charts are usually co-created during whole-class discussions. They capture words and images that remind kids of concepts, structures, norms, or thinking strategies that we return to and refine. They are a springboard to help create rubrics for assessing student work and for helping students to assess their own work. Rubrics that are based in familiar anchor charts ensure that there are no surprises for the kids regarding what you are looking for while assessing.

Preparation

In planning for anchor charts, think about what their purpose will be. Are they helpful for collaboration or social skills? Or do they convey unit objectives and essential questions? Charts are a visual reference to help kids in future lessons, so consider how the students will use the charts independently after you have co-created them.

With the Kids

Bring kids to the rug with their journals. Most charts that end up on the wall act as a snapshot of a minilesson that students will also copy down in their journals as well, as shown in Figure 5.1.

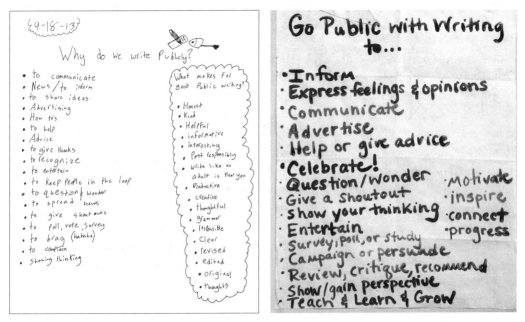

Figure 5.1a, b Student journal and accompanying chart.

This particular lesson comes early in the year, before we begin publishing on Kidblog, Edmodo, and Twitter. I begin the discussion by asking, "Why do writers write publicly? Why do the authors of your books, your magazines, newspapers, and social networking sites write? What is the purpose of writing? The *so what*?"

We grow a list from the kids' journal responses, which then serves as a chart for choice and direction all year long. When kids are writing, they should be thinking about their audience, genre, and the "so what" of their writing, so they know if they are getting their message across and their voice heard. They can always look up at this chart and target a purpose for their writing and an audience. This list becomes an ongoing reference for when kids ask, "What should I write about?"

BACKCHANNELING (page 89)

Backchannels let kids have a real-time online conversation during class, similar to the way adults might have real-time conversations on Twitter about the State of the Union speech or the series premiere of their favorite show while watching those broadcasts. Teachers can check into this conversation during or after class to get a window into what students are thinking. You can also project it for all to follow, even as the lesson continues.

Preparation

There are many tools that you can use to open a backchannel in your classroom. We use Edmodo because students are familiar with the platform and because of its strong privacy features. In workshops with teachers, we often use Today's Meet, which is super simple to set up and use.

With the Kids

In *Connecting Comprehension and Technology* (2013), a companion to Harvey and Goudvis' *The Comprehension Toolkit)*, Stephanie Harvey, Anne Goudvis, Kristin Ziemke, and Katie Mutharis describe how their students have backchannel discussions during read-alouds. As the teacher reads, the kids are on iPads or laptops, responding to what they hear, see, and think as the story unfolds. The teachers are purposeful in when to give kids time to stop, think, react, and type. Student voice is valued during the read-aloud for on-the-spot reactions, and when the digital conversation is over, the teacher has a running log she can read later to see which kids need support during independent practice. You may be thinking (as Smokey is) that backchanneling redefines what "attention" looks like in the classroom. We are inviting kids, at least some of the time, to *not be looking at us*, but to switch between watching what we are modeling and responding on their device. When you think about it, this requires far more active thinking from kids, but at first, it can feel like you have undermined kids' focus—*on you*!

 BLOGGING (page 127)

The audience for students is no longer just the teacher: kids are writing for many other readers in notebooks, on phones, on blogs, and on social media sites. It is their right, once they clear the age restrictions of the Internet (thirteen for Twitter and Instagram), but it is our job to help them with their new responsibility. Like Edmodo, Kidblog is a safe venue for student voice. This time, kids are the architects, writers, and editors of their own blog site. In today's world of blogging and social media, audience matters. We want kids to be ready to be heard while practicing the new social skills of writing their thoughts and feelings for a public audience.

Preparation

While there are many blogging platforms, Sara's classes use Kidblog: the account setup is a few easy steps, just like Edmodo. The only information the kids need to input is their name.

Next, find two or three mentor blogs. Scour the Internet for engaging, kid-friendly blogs. You might look for blogs by Young Adult authors, athletes, or kids, or for blogs about topics that are a part of your learning life: cooking, collecting, or fitness, for example. Then, consider the qualities of the blog posts that you like: Are they funny? Is the topic something important to you? How does the author use point of view effectively? What's the style of the piece? What is the length? Who is this blogger writing for?

To model this, prewrite a blog you can show your class. Choose a mini-inquiry wonder of your own. Conduct your mini-inquiry sifting through books, articles, or the Internet, and taking notes in your journal. Using your new knowledge and feelings about it, write your first blog post for your audience: your students.

With the Kids

Bring kids to the rug with their inquiry journals and project one of the blogs you chose as a model for yourself (travel, cooking, gardening, or sports are typically good choices). Introduce the idea of a blog and get a feel for students' familiarity with the genre—have they read or seen one before? Walk kids through the blog, the same way you would with any text, marking characteristics you notice together along the way. When you are finished, you will have a pretty good list.

Then let them in on the process of blogging: share your preparation and finally reveal your own Kidblog. Let them know that they are going to become bloggers as well and that they will be in charge of their own blog page. Also note that along with your blog come reactions, thoughts, feelings, and the need to self-monitor your sharing.

Let kids consult their wonder lists then conduct research for their first blog post. They might organize the research in a two-column chart in their journals, with one side listing the information learned and the other showing their thoughts or opinions about the new information. When they are ready with this chart, or even have a draft in their notebook, kids can get set up with their Kidblog accounts and be approved to blog.

GRADUAL RELEASE OF RESPONSIBILITY

The Gradual Release of Responsibility (GRR) instructional model was originally developed by David Pearson and Meg Gallagher (1983) and later classroom-ized by educators like Stephanie Harvey, Anne Goudvis, Debbie Miller, Regie Routman, Ellin Keene, Susan Zimmerman, and Cris Tovani. It provides one of the key metaphors of middle school teaching. Independence is essential in growing upstanders, and as we gradually release responsibility for learning to our kids, they move toward independence. If we model what we are asking the students to do, exposing what our own thinking really looks like and even letting kids watch us struggle the same way they might, we have a captive audience—an audience that is more willing to take risks because we have just modeled the same.

A cycle of GRR teaching looks like this:

I do it, you watch. Teacher models or demonstrates her thinking for students. The baseline version is a *think-aloud,* during which the teacher reads a text aloud, stopping periodically to share her thinking as she goes.

We do it together. Teacher invites kids to chip in their thinking during her demonstration. The classic example is *shared reading*, where the teacher reads a text aloud, pausing for kids to contribute their connections, questions, and reactions. A common variation: have the kids assist you at first, then let the kids take the lead, and you assist them.

You do it with my help. Teacher releases kids to practice on their own, with her close support. Typically kids meet as individuals or in small groups, while the teacher visits around to confer and lend help. The kids support each other in taking this step toward independence.

You do it on your own. Now the teacher turns kids loose to do all the reading, writing, or researching they have been practicing. She is still available to help, but now in a facilitator and coach role, not as a lesson-teacher.

THINK-ALOUDS: I DO IT, YOU WATCH (pages 141, 167, 194, 200, 209)

We've failed for years to *show* kids how smart readers think. It is not enough to merely assign or command reading, we must demonstrate it first, ourselves, especially with complex text. Think-alouds are a pure instance of a teacher modeling her thinking for her students. We don't do this for long, maybe two or three minutes, after which we often shift to a *shared reading* where we invite the class to think along with us and chip in their great ideas. But the brief doses of true thinking aloud are really important examples for kids of what the actual cognitive work of reading looks like. Note that this kind of modeling works for other thinking processes too: teachers do "write-alouds" where they compose text in front of kids, while vocalizing their thought process. And they do "search-alouds" (see page 200) where they demonstrate going online and conducting a thoughtful search for information.

Preparation

Select an engaging text and preread it, selecting some stopping places and developing some teaching points that target the strategies that are the focus of your lesson. Sometimes, you might also want to think aloud a text that you have *not rehearsed* or even read carefully. This way, kids will get to see you making meaning right at the point of utterance—which, if you think about it, is the job that they are asked to do on high-stakes tests. To put it another way, kids need to see their teachers encounter and grapple with unfamiliar text, as well as passages they have rehearsed and are to some extent "pretending" to read fresh. Make a copy for each student; you will be reading and looking at it together. Using a document camera is a great way for students to follow what you are saying and for you to jot your thinking in the margins as you go.

With the Kids

As you begin, tell kids about any prior knowledge you have about the title, the topic, or the author. As you continue to read, stop to share your reactions, connections, questions, and inferences. At each stopping point, whether it is planned or spontaneous, jot a quick note in the margin to flag your response. After the think-aloud, kids can have small- or whole-group discussions, trying to notice what you did as a reader.

Different think-aloud texts lend themselves to different comprehension strategies in beautiful ways. Linda Hoyt's *Interactive Read-Alouds* for grades 6 and 7 (2009) provides a fantastic list of read-aloud titles and companion texts, aligned with today's standards.

SHARED PRACTICE: WE DO IT TOGETHER (page 115)

A shared reading can use any piece of text that you want students to experience, literary or informational. A math problem, a hypothesis or challenge in science, the rules of a game in PE, or a dialogue excerpt in a foreign language would all be fair game. You can also use shared reading to help students dig into texts that might be more challenging than you would expect them to read independently.

Preparation

Select a text and preread it to develop teaching points that target the intended outcomes of your lesson. Make a copy for each student; you will be reading and looking at it together.

With the Kids

During the lesson, you will read out loud while the kids follow along with you. You'll stop periodically and invite kids to share their thinking; sometimes they'll just burst out with a reaction or connection, which is fine. Scribe these kid comments in the margin of the text just as when you are doing a teacher think-aloud. In effect, everyone is pooling their thinking to develop a better understanding of the text. Using a document camera is a great way for students to follow what you are saying and for you to jot in the margins as you go.

GUIDED PRACTICE: YOU DO IT WITH MY HELP (pages 143, 147, 167)

Guided practice is a structured opportunity for individualized and small-group attention. After the teacher models on the rug, and perhaps shifts to a shared reading as well, kids can head back to tables and desks to try out a thinking strategy on their own. They work as individuals or small groups, while the teacher visits to provide close support.

Preparation

Knowing your kids and your content ahead of time is the key preparatory work for this structure. Predicting and noting who may need your support during guided practice will make for a smoother transition from think-alouds and shared reading.

With the Kids

After you've modeled a strategy or skill and given students opportunities to interact on the rug, students return to their individual workspaces to give it a go on their own. They bring with them all the language from the think-aloud, your annotation of the text, their pair shares with a buddy, and the rich group conversation.

Now you can gather small groups of kids who need the same kind of support in a formal guided reading (or writing, or researching) lesson. Or you can move throughout the room, conferring with individuals. It is important not only to meet with the kids who need support, but also to check in with the kids who easily "get it." You still want to give them individualized attention and enrich their experience. Even simply pushing them to ask questions that stretch beyond the text selection is a valuable interaction.

INDEPENDENT PRACTICE: YOU DO IT ON YOUR OWN (page 143)

In guided practice, we were choosing which kids to support at what time, and planfully visiting groups and individuals to be sure everyone gets the help they need. But now, during independent practice, the kids decide when they need your support, and it is mostly up to them to seek it. At this point, they are working on longer-term, often individualized or small-group projects, and you have "fully released" them to take responsibility for their own learning. At this stage, you are serving as a consultant, advisor, coach, expert researcher, or content-area expert.

Preparation

There is less preparation when kids are working independently, because they are often pursuing different tasks and topics that they have chosen. Chances are you will not be an expert on every topic or have a ready answer for every question a kid might have. You have to be in the flow. So, while this stage of GRR takes less advance preparation, it requires you to be highly flexible, to think on your feet, and to make smart game-time decisions, one after the other. We envision this as working side by side with kids, exploring and learning with them, in real time.

With the Kids

In every inquiry lesson in Chapters 7 through 10, you'll see Sara working the kids through the whole gradual release model, all the way to independent practice. Each unit, whether it is about civil rights, immigration, globalization, life after death, or soccer equipment, begins with teacher modeling and works its way toward increasing student autonomy and responsibility.

At this stage of learning, the kids are working either alone or in small groups, following work plans and calendars they have made (page 195). They are making the decisions about what to work on when, whom to connect with, what resources they need, and what will happen tomorrow. They are using their journals to record notes and observations. The teacher circulates through the room, available to help anyone who seeks her. Some teachers post a daily sign-up list where kids or groups can request an appointment to confer over some puzzling research, a stuck point, or a management issue. Zooming out from this productive hubbub, what you are looking at is a true *workshop*—where a master craftsperson assists apprentices in creating real works for the world.

 HOT SEAT   (page 152)

This strategy gets kids into character so that they can understand and even empathize with literary characters and historical figures. Hot seat can be a great way to help students analyze the issues behind a particular historic event or controversy. When it is enacted, a hot-seat session looks a lot like a TV interview show.

Preparation

Identify the people students will be portraying and line up chairs panel-style for the students who will bring these people to life. Taping the names to each chair makes it feel "real."

Give the class time to prepare questions that they might ask the characters. Questions about a particular event or about choices the people have made are often a good starting point. While students are doing this, select or take volunteers for the actual roles. These students will prepare by anticipating the questions others may ask them and considering how the person they are portraying might answer these questions. Name tags and props are always a hit, as well.

Set up expectations by sharing with the kids some things that you will be looking for. Ask them to co-create a quick list or simple rubric with you to clarify expectations. You can use these for student self-assessment or more formal assessment. Here are a few items that we see time and again on these lists:

- Eye contact
- In the role
- Deep questions/questions that get more than a yes or no
- In the Zone body language
- Thoughtful answers that show an understanding of the text and event
- Friendliness and support

With the Kids

After the actors take their seats and the other students begin asking their questions, take anecdotal notes on participation. Guide the conversation if needed, and model asking follow-up questions to help kids sharpen their queries and monitor their own listening.

IDENTITY WEBS (pages 80, 82, 84, 118, 161)

Identity webs are at the heart of empathy and inquiry in the middle school classroom. These webs are visual representations of how an individual sees himself and how others see him. Identity webs can easily become a go-to strategy with your kids: they help students to understand themselves better and to activate their critical thinking and empathy.

Preparation

If you haven't made identity webs with your students yet, read Lesson 1 (Exploring Identity) in Chapter 6, which outlines how you can get students started. The first step is for you to model making your own map, so consider what elements of your life, personality, and personal history you'd be comfortable sharing.

With the Kids

Use pages 78–85 as a model for showing students how to create an identity web and then supporting them to make webs for their own identities.

You can use identity webs to give students a new lens for looking more deeply at a person: authors and characters in literature, scientists in science, mathematicians in math, and role models in any content area. For a shared reading on the rug, you might have kids begin a web in their journals that is focused on a character or person in the reading. As kids become more comfortable with the use of these webs, they make connections between ideas and begin to ask questions—great springboards for inquiry!

INQUIRY JOURNAL (pages 168, 186, 194)

In the inquiry classroom, kids need a tool to keep track of their thinking, reading, and exploring. Sometimes called a *reflection* or *explore journal*, this trusty tool gives students a consistent place to write down their wonders and manage their research.

Preparation

Each person's journal is unique. If you keep an inquiry journal yourself, sharing it can help students imagine what theirs might look like. It also gives you a chance to introduce your life as a reader and as a curious human being. If you haven't kept a journal before, you can begin your journal alongside your students.

With the Kids

Introduce the inquiry journal as a place where you can wonder, sketch, make notes, save articles and clippings, and try out ideas. Journals can be divided with Post-its or tabs for specific inquiry topics or units, and each section will include places for *wonders* (kids' questions), *research* (new information), and *resources* (publication info).

Model and share for kids the first page of an inquiry journal: *My Wonders*. Build excitement for using this journal by letting this page and a few pages after be a space where they can write anything they are wondering about. The page can be set up as a two-column chart for questions relating to yourself and questions relating to the world. Model some questions you are wondering about yourself and your life (What happens to the clothes I donate to Goodwill? What is the best pair of running shoes for me?) or bigger "world" questions (How long has the conflict in Ukraine really been going on? How does the Red Cross spend its donation money?). You'll notice that some "self" questions could easily be "world" questions, and vice versa. That's no big deal. The value in listing these two types of wonders is simply to help kids pose questions widely, from both near and far. You can see Smokey model these kinds of questions on pages 185–186.

As kids independently come up with some of their own self and world questions, let them turn and talk to generate more ideas. Keeping a running, public list in the classroom is particularly useful, especially when a good question comes up that the class doesn't have time to work on right then: you can ask one kid to "go and post it on the class wonder chart so we can come back to it later."

As you move through an inquiry unit, have students use the research and resources sections to keep a record of their findings, the specific resources they have consulted, and ways in which their thinking has developed.

MIND MAPS/CONCEPT MAPS (page 161)

When we make a mind or concept map, we are trying to draw what our thinking looks like, to show our understanding of a topic in graphic form. This allows us to represent all the cognitive work—visualizing, inferring, connecting, questioning, synthesizing—we are doing when we read a text.

Preparation

Choose two similar, short texts: one to model for students and another they can use for independent practice. For the text that you will demonstrate with the kids, think in advance about what your mind map might look like.

With the Kids

Ask the students to pay special attention to what your mind is doing as you read the text aloud and then draw your mental representation of it. Your map does not need to be a piece

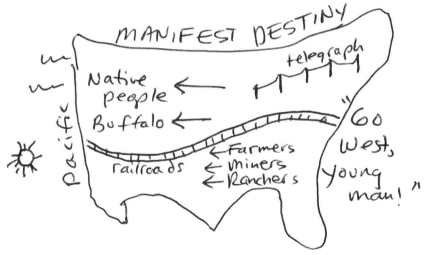

Figure 5.2 Mind map for a text on westward expansion.

of art; it can be a web, a simple flow chart, a time line, a cartoon—whatever best describes the way your mind sees the text. Let the kids see you referring back to the text and hear you talk aloud about how you're choosing ideas and structures.

Now pass out the second text for kids to read independently, leaving your own mind map model on the document camera as a baseline. Release kids to try out mind maps either individually or in small groups. Then call everyone back to share some of their creations on the document camera. Celebrate different approaches to mapping, and discuss how this graphic process can help us crystallize and leverage our own thinking.

⬆ NOTETAKING FORMS

Notetaking is a process of determining importance that can be difficult for kids. If taking notes is not modeled, our young readers will record somewhere on the spectrum between random words and straight-out plagiarism, missing key ideas of the text.

ALPHABOXES   (pages 112, 121)

Alphaboxes are a notetaking gift from Linda Hoyt's *Make It Real* (2002). The form has twenty-six small boxes on a page, each labeled with a letter of the alphabet, in order. As kids read new material in class, they use this sheet to write down key words, in the alphabetically appropriate box, which helps them recall the main ideas later. With alphaboxes, kids are not just regurgitating the words on a page, but identifying key words and storing them in a format they can use to find the term later, when they need it.

Preparation

Read the selected text for your upcoming lesson and fill out your own alphabox page for the words you think are essential for understanding the passage. That means as you read, you'll enter terms, numbers, vocabulary, people, places, and dates in the appropriate alphabox.

When you have finished reading the passage, see if you can recall the words on your alphabox page and determine their importance to the big ideas or goals of the lesson. This preparation will help as you model for kids.

With the Kids

Pass out blank alphaboxes (Figure 5.3) and project the sheet on the doc camera. Before you even begin to read the passage, have kids use the alphaboxes to record any words that are part of their schema or background knowledge on the particular topic. Model one or two yourself to show kids how you place terms in the appropriate letter boxes. Next, read the passage and continue to lift words from the text as you determine importance. After students have added a handful of terms, practice using their notes to recall the text in front of them. How is each word on the alphabox sheet important to the text or the big idea of the lesson? Give the students time to finish their reading and notetaking during independent practice.

Alphaboxes: _____ Name _____ Date _____			
A	B	C	D
E	F	G	H
I	J	K	L
M	N	O	P
Q	R	S	T
U	V	W	XYZ
Dates & Numbers	Sketches/Wonders:		

Figure 5.3 Alphaboxes

SEE, THINK, WONDER (pages 115, 161)

See, Think, Wonder is a notetaking tool that helps readers dig deep into text, seeing more than surface meanings. It also activates curiosity and works as a mental springboard for inquiry work. Gradually, the Wonder section fills with questions kids can independently explore. The visual thinking focus of See, Think, Wonder is a comprehension approach widely used by Harvard's Project Zero, Stephanie Harvey, Linda Hoyt, and many others. It was reintroduced to Sara by her teaching partner and science teacher, Cory Logan, who uses it throughout the year to teach kids strong observation and inference skills.

Preparation

Prepare copies of a See, Think, Wonder sheet: one for you to use as a model and one for each of the kids. If you haven't used the See, Think, Wonder sheet before, use your planned selection of lesson text or images to fill out a blank thinksheet (Figure 5.4) for yourself before class.

With the Kids

Using your preparation for this lesson, you will guide the kids through the same thought process you experienced and jotted down. Have them use copies of the template or fold paper in their notebooks to make their own See, Think, Wonder pages. Tell kids: "In the See column, list the literal things you see, without making any inferences or predictions. These can be as simple as color, words, pictures, details, a person, and so on. List everything your eye notices right away."

Stop to turn and talk or share out the first column. If there is any confusion about what is literal and what is inferred, you can address it at this point. A helpful way to begin is to

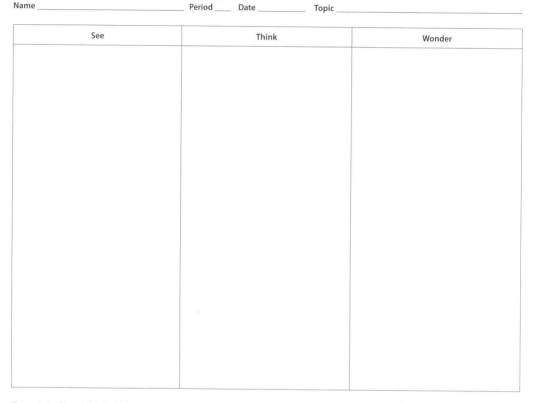

Figure 5.4 See, Think, Wonder sheet.

share one or two literal See's from your own list. Kids may think it is silly to write down such obvious items, but will soon realize that every item leads to further exploration. Now, move kids to the Think column. "Write down what your mind is thinking about each observation. You may be making inferences, predictions, judgments, and connections beyond the surface qualities of the material. When you are ready, move on to list questions for the author, photographer, artist, or object in the Wonder column. What do you want to know more about?"

ONLINE COLLABORATION
(pages 5, 25, 52, 89–91, 117, 120–123, 128, 129, 138, 149, 190, 200)

With the help of technology, kids can continue collaborative work beyond the four walls of the classroom. While Edmodo is the app that Sara uses with her classes, it is not the only tool of its kind. Your school or district probably gives you access to some similar service.

Edmodo is a free, familiar online platform. Sara calls it "Facebook for school," as it runs nearly the same interface: kids can post, comment, and share; they can add photos, links, or cheer each other on. Each class and individual student has their own wall. Small groups can be made within classes for inquiry teams and lit circles. Polls, mini-quizzes, and homework can be scheduled in advance and posted on the schedule.

Preparation
Set up your account and individual classes before having the kids sign up. Edmodo's website will walk you through the process in a few simple steps, then give you join codes for each of your classes. It has all the privacy locks a teacher or parent could ask for. One of its greatest features is that kids cannot post to the individual wall of another student; a post has to go through the class wall or the teacher. The focus is on learning, and there is no room for cyberbullying or peer conflict.

With the Kids
Edmodo doesn't require students to give away any personal information, email addresses, or even their last names. Kids use the join codes you obtained for them to add classes to their account, storing passwords somewhere they can access them when forgotten. It is important for kids who are using this platform as an educational tool to be aware that the things they say are now public to all of their peers and teachers. (See page 98 for lessons we teach about protecting your "brand" while online.)

Edmodo allows kids to continue dialogue begun in class and can even serve as a conversation tool for homework that they can access remotely in real time. Kids practice the same discussion skills they use with the whole class and small groups, and they now have the entire discussion transcript in front of them, live. It is a great way to gather anecdotal data for assessment purposes as well.

READ-ALOUD (pages 81, 88, 140, 157)

Read-aloud is a sacred time not only for primary children, but for everyone—including big kids and adult kids. A read-aloud on the first day of school builds community and begins to set norms for the rug, the couch, and the social skills we will build all year long. Read-aloud is a time for guided instruction in conversation, fluency, and critical thinking. Through modeling and interaction, kids build comprehension, listening, speaking, and writing skills.

Preparation

Choosing read-alouds that match the units you teach is a great way to start. For his civil rights literature circles, Ben Kovacs at Burley School complements the kids' novels with articles, primary sources, and picture books. Some of his rich title selections include *Harvesting Hope* by Kathleen Krull, *Sit-In: How Four Friends Stood Up by Sitting Down* by Andrea Pinkney, and *Delivering Justice* by Jim Haskins. Make sure to read the titles you choose ahead of time so you can flag those just-right moments for kids to turn and talk. The justly celebrated *Read-Aloud Handbook,* Seventh Edition, by Jim Trelease (2013) gives great guidance for selecting and performing works that really engage students.

With the Kids

The first level of reading aloud is to just do it! We *Homo sapiens* seem to be hardwired to love stories and chronological narratives, especially ones that recount our common adventures, our ancestry, our people—as well as far-off, imaginary times and places. As teachers and story-readers, we are always working to make our performance of these texts as powerful and evocative as they can be—worthy of the ancient fire circle. Sometimes the greatest service we can give to young people is to just read a text, uninterrupted. Or we can merge into think-alouds.

 SILENT DIALOGUE/WRITTEN CONVERSATION (pages 91, 104, 136, 149, 161, 162)

Silent dialogues (sometimes called *text on text* or *written conversations*) present kids with short readings or visual images, and ask them to respond and interact with each other entirely through writing. This kind of conversation invites students to take and support a position, instills the habit of pausing to think about your thinking, and allows for more introverted kids to take an equal part in discussions. Kids slow down and focus on the views of others. The final "dialogue" is also a visual representation of all student thinking that can be revisited later.

Preparation

Choose the short text and/or image students will be studying and discussing. Glue this material to a much larger sheet, like chart or butcher paper, providing big margins for students to write in. You will need to make several of these charts: one for a model and one for each group of three students. Bring a set of multicolored markers or pencils for each group so that each student can write in a different color.

With the Kids

Begin by talking about the norms of discussion. What do good discussants do? Listen carefully, make connections, ask questions, respect others' opinions, disagree agreeably, make eye contact, smile, and nod. Introduce the idea of silent dialogue now, where students are still responsible for these qualities, but they display them silently, on paper. No, they don't make eye contact on paper, but they can draw arrows from someone's text to their own. They can't smile and nod, but they can support a comment by writing "I agree" or "Good point."

Have your model chart ready and have a volunteer come up to the board or doc camera with you. Both of you will read the focus text at the same time and take your time to comment on it, in the form of a written question, a connection, a reaction, or a new idea. While the rest of the kids watch, read your partner's comment, use your discussion norms, and respond to your partner in writing to begin a conversation. Once kids get the hang of this, talk to them about the importance of silence so everyone has a space to think and respect the comments of others. Let kids go off on their own if the materials are hung on the walls, or back to their tables if the materials are there. As the charts fill after eight to ten minutes, bring the kids back to the rug and use the charts to spark discussion and to debrief the process.

These are great charts to keep up on your walls for anyone to read. You can also try written conversations inside notebooks, where kids write letters back and forth to one another. We often have written conversations on our Edmodo pages as well, often as homework; the kids can have discussions at night, from home. Smokey and Elaine Daniels' book *The Best-Kept Teaching Secret: How Written Conversations Engage Kids, Activate Learning, and Grow Fluent Writers, K–12* (2013) is a great resource for the many ways to conduct this kind of dialogue in class.

⬆ STANDING DISCUSSIONS: MINGLE, GALLERY WALK, AND HUMAN CONTINUUM (pages 91–92, 159, 163, 178, 191–192)

Kids don't have to spend all their time in their seats. In fact, if they do, you run the risk of energy blackouts, overloads, and major short circuits. As the renowned educator (and authorial spouse) Elaine Daniels puts it: "Kids need to wiggle." Never more true than with young teens. So we need to get kids moving around the classroom, dissipating some nervous energy, but also plugging into the curriculum while they do it. We want students to productively circulate, interacting with each other about ideas, research, interpretations, and points of view. We call this family of activities the "up and thinking" repertoire.

Preparation

The key here is to decide how you want kids to meet up, what they will talk about, for how long, and what the accountability will be. With all these activities, kids form partners or threes and discuss an issue, often jotting notes, and then re-form with new partners to continue and broaden the conversation. It's like speed dating, but with knowledge building, not weekend plans, as the objective.

With the Kids

In Chapters 7 through 10, several different standing discussions are used. In an open *mingle* (pages 191–192), kids quickly pair and re-pair, so that in just a few minutes, they get to chat briefly about a curriculum topic with six to eight classmates. In a *human continuum* (page 163), students line up according to their opinion or interpretation of an issue. First they talk with people standing beside them in line, who agree with them; they take turns sharing the specific evidence that has led them to take this position. Then, we fold the line so everyone is opposite someone who disagrees, and the debate is on! In a *gallery walk* (pages 91, 159, 178), individuals or groups post a chart or drawing of their learning on the wall, and then others circulate through, studying these artifacts and leaving written comments on Post-it notes. Students typically cycle through three or four posters before returning to join in a full-class discussion of the poster highlights.

TEXT ANNOTATION (pages 141, 167)

Leaving tracks of your thinking, marking the text, and jotting marginal annotations are all ways kids show us their thinking during independent work, whether they write directly on the text or on Post-its. This ability to interact with the text is vital in inquiry: as kids read and do research, they need to be able to learn from, understand, and remember what they read.

Preparation

Prepare a text to use as a model and also to give to kids. Pulling out an old novel, cookbook, magazine, or college text you read as a student with copious notes in the margins is also a great example to show what real readers do and to share your reading life. But you also need to annotate a text "live" so kids see where all those marks came from.

With the Kids

Explain that expert readers often mark, or *annotate*, texts as they read. We need to "stop, think, and react"—to pause during reading to capture and jot our responses, so we can remember what we were thinking about the text at that moment. We can do this thinking with highlighters, written notes, or quick codes, which we'll try below.

Before you begin to think aloud through the article, work with students to make some codes they can use to signal different thoughts. A few starter ideas:

√ = I already knew that
! = something important
? = question or confusion
C = connection

Hand out the article to the kids and begin to read a few lines of text, modeling how you stop, think, and react, using the appropriate codes. Then invite them to try it out for themselves. After a while, let them turn and talk with a buddy to share their thinking. Once they have the hang of it, kids can head off to leave tracks in their independent work. These text codes aren't the only form of annotation we use, of course; often we ask kids to write words or phrases in the margin, or search for and mark specific text features or evidence.

TURN AND TALK (pages 79, 80, 81, 98, 115, 116, 119, 187)

Also known as "pair share," this is the baseline of student interaction in the classroom, and we start using it on Day 1. When we invite kids to turn and talk, we are requiring them to put ideas into their own words, to listen carefully to the ideas of others, and to go public with their thinking in quick and comfortable ways. To ensure engagement, master teachers have kids turn and talk very frequently—three, five, seven times an hour.

Turn and talk gives you a live assessment of how kids' thinking is unfolding. It is a wonderful classroom management tool as well: we often find ourselves getting frustrated when kids become squirrely during any lesson, but soon we realize they are really signaling, "Hey! Quit talking and let us discuss! We have so much to say about this!"

Preparation

Make sure partners are in an optimal, one-to-one talking position; shoulder to shoulder, eye to eye, or ear to ear. Kids should sit so that they are focused on each other and can "screen out" the visual or auditory distractions of other nearby pairs. Having a designated area like a rug or groups of desks makes it easier for kids to interact: thoughtful and deliberate proximity is important for collaboration.

With the Kids

The activity is as simple as it sounds—while you're working with the whole class, you take a minute and ask kids to turn and talk with a partner, usually for no more than a minute or two, and then volunteers share their ideas in a whole-class conversation. Give kids the responsibility to look around and make sure that everyone is included in a pair or trio. The topic can be anything about the curriculum—sharing initial thoughts about a story we just read, naming takeaways from a science experiment just completed, or solving a math story problem. So often, a quick turn and talk reminds us that two heads are better than one.

Choose spots in a story or topic that make great opportunities for kids to share their thinking: it may be a place of great excitement or possible confusion, an intense moment in the plot, or a point where there might be multiple solutions to a problem. This will become natural as you notice kids' faces and body movements signaling when they are bursting to talk.

*

PART 3

OPEN HEARTS AND INQUIRING MINDS

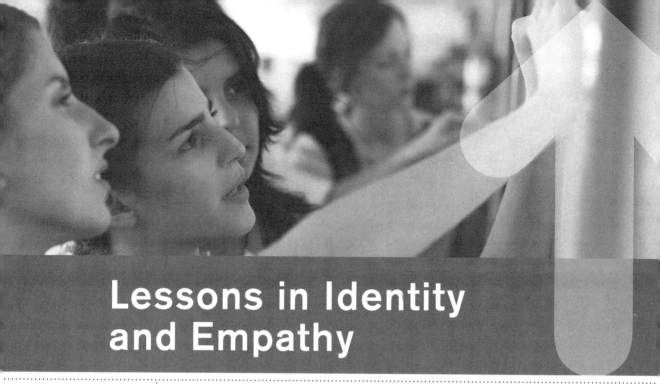

Lessons in Identity and Empathy

chapter 6

I'm a kid who is shy, but if you get to know me, I'm pretty cool.
(EVAN B.)

I consider myself kind of a nerd.
(HARRY H.)

I am a unique, special girl, and I'm proud that there is no one else like me.
(SIMRAN D.)

I've wondered more than once what it would be like to live as a "typical American."
(YEA P.)

I am the girl who has never had insanely curly hair and now straightens it to somewhat resemble "white girl" hair.
(KIARA J.)

*I don't understand "family first" because some of my friends are
100% more important than my family.*
    (CLAIRE L.)

I am a girl obsessed with Justin Bieber, so I guess I am Layne Bieber.
    (LAYNE F.)

I tried to be an overachiever. But I am no overachiever.
    (VAL F.)

My art is not the best, but it is mine.
    (LOREN I.)

So far we have been talking about the kids, our own teacher selves, the learning space we create, and the structures we use. Obviously, the curriculum—weeks and months of meaty, engaging content—is where we will put all this thinking and planning to work. But in an upstander-growing classroom, there are a couple more ingredients we need to develop early: identity and empathy. This doesn't mean kids aren't learning *any* subject matter in the early days of school, but we are definitely frontloading issues of personhood, reflection, and community.

SMOKEY: *For sure, the importance of this identity work is huge. But as a teacher, what if I am reading this book in January, a whole semester into the year? What if it's too late to frontload? And what if my class is bombing interpersonally? Do I have to wait for a new set of kids to arrive in August and try again?*

SARA: *Definitely, just give up. Every man for themselves! No, you know what I'm going to say. Of course the beginning of the school year gives us unique moments to work on our human relationships; for sure, first impressions provide important opportunities. But, the best day to start working on identity and empathy with your kids is the day you wake up thinking: things have got to change—I need to know my kids more, we have to become closer as a community. And then you start with the kinds of lessons and experiences in this chapter, whether it is April 23 or Halloween or graduation day.*

SMOKEY: *Thanks for making that official.*

Before we can really dig into our course curriculum, we need to help kids build the necessary skills to be collaborative, metacognitive, and responsible for their roles in our community.

Coming up in this chapter are six lessons that have been Sara and/or Smokey's go-to community builders, no matter what age level or subject matter we are teaching.

1. Exploring Identity: *The Bear That Wasn't*
2. Empathy/Bullying: *Not My Fault*
3. Risk-Taking: Home Court Advantage
4. Working in Groups: Team Behavior
5. Disagreeing Agreeably: Framing Friendly Challenges
6. Responsibility: Building (and Protecting) Your Brand

The first two are transformational multiday lessons that help grow successful, interdependent, and caring learners for an entire year. They directly address issues of identity, empathy, upstanding, bystanding, and bullying. You will revisit them often throughout the year. The last four are steps toward a collaborative, collegial classroom. They take less class time and are more easily described, but are no less important.

LESSON 1

Lesson 1. Exploring Identity *(45 minutes)*

Text: *The Bear That Wasn't* by Frank Tashlin (1947)

For an abridged version, please see https://www.facinghistory.org/for-educators/educator-resources/readings/bear-wasnt

SARA: *I normally teach this lesson on the first day of school, right after I have led the kids through our first "soft start" (pages 13–17). This experience is adapted from the resources of Facing History and Ourselves and is foundational to working with identity. It's based on a great read-aloud that kids immediately relate to. In the story, a bear wakes up from hibernation and realizes his environment has drastically changed. Trees have been replaced by factories, animals have been replaced by humans. When he goes to explore his new habitat, he deals with a series of confrontations where he questions his own identity because others attach labels to him.*

Group Brainstorming

The kids come in and after we go through the pleasantries of taking off our shoes and enjoying some independent reading, we get down to business. I ask them to bring their new journals over to the rug and I write the word *identity* on chart paper or a whiteboard.

"I am writing a term that is very important to history on the board. Can you write it down with me in your journals, and then just think in your mind for a moment as I write these questions?"

What makes up a person's identity?
What defines your identity?

Hands go up right away, but I ask them to put them down and just think for a moment, in their minds only. If they need to write down their answers first to get their thinking out, they can also do this. I introduce **turn and talk** by saying: "Turn to someone next to you, just say hi, and tell them how you feel about these two questions." Make sure everyone has a buddy to talk to.

I hear an assortment of answers: hair color, it's who you are, identity theft, what you like, personality. So we share out in the big group and come up with a great list and some fruitful discussion. See Figure 6.1.

Arman says, "How you treat others."

I push him to help us understand.

"Arman, can you tell me what you mean by that?"

"Yeah, well, how you treat other people says a lot about who you are. If you are nice, or mean to them."

"Why do you guys think I would be asking you about this word in history class?"

Gavin: I was just wondering that!

Me: Why on earth would I ask about identity—or you—in history class?

Bobby: Well, all of that stuff on the board is our history. We wouldn't be here without history.

Dash: Some of those things are from our parents or grandparents and they are our history. Our ancestors.

Figure 6.1 This chart stays up all year, and provides a working definition for identity that we add to as we share more experiences together.

Me: What if I said, to really understand history, you have to understand yourself?

Blank stares and confusion . . . and soon, a few "ohhhhs."

"I am wondering if it is easier to understand history if we know how we would treat people, or want to be treated . . . and how we would react to something. Or what role religion or skin color may play in that moment in history. What if it was us in the pages of history we read this year?

73 "If I haven't totally confused you, **turn and talk** to your buddy about this. Can you see any part of your identity in history? Or if you are confused, talk about how you are both confused."

I listen in . . .

Sydney tells her partner that since she is a girl, she can vote now because of some women in history and that she can play any sport she wants.

Isabela says that she read *Number the Stars* and the characters who were Jewish, like her, went through things she knows older generations of her family did. Some other kids are still confused and that is OK. It is the first day of school. This is a seed that we will be nurturing all year long.

As I watch the kids talking, I'm getting fired up for the year to come. I gather the class back together: "You guys, the cool thing about identity is that it's not just connected to history either. To understand the way you solve math problems, or science, the way you read and respond to novels or your own writing, or how you play out on the field or court, you really are trying to understand your own identity. The way you see things is because of who you are, the way you think about your own thinking."

64 ## Identity Webs

"I am going to do my best to use our chart (see Figure 6.1) and make connections to myself." I draw a blank web on the board and write *Ms. Ahmed* in the middle. "Well, I'll start with some easy ones. Family: I am a sister, aunt, daughter, godmother. Gender: I am female. Job: I am a teacher. Nationality/ethnicity: well, that is fun for me because I am American and I was born here, but my parents were both born in India and that is part of my ethnicity and why I have some of the physical features that make me, me." See my web in Figure 6.2.

Figure 6.2 My own identity chart serves as a model that will connect ideas as the kids work independently.

"Can you guys go ahead and try your own web independently? I am going to keep going on mine up here." This gives anyone who is feeling stuck an opportunity to look at my web and see if it sparks anything for them. They can piggyback off my web to add to their own.

I give them two to three minutes for some independent writing time on their own webs. When they are ready, I have them **turn and talk**, sharing one unique thing (that isn't necessarily obvious) about themselves with a buddy next to them.

Then I bring them back to the whole group.

"3, 2, 1 . . . Thanks. I want to hear from the whole group. Before we share out, I want you to know that this space for us is so, so safe. This is a space where I can share ideas and you can share ideas and we will work really hard to be good listeners to one another. We will talk about this a lot as the year goes on. Is there a brave volunteer who is willing to share something really unique to their identity? Something more than just the color of your shirt?"

A few courageous hands go up. I ask them to say their names as they share, because it is so early in the year and not all the kids know each other.

SMOKEY: *I am interested that you are naming the fact that it takes some courage to put yourself out there, especially on the first day of school.*

SARA: *Calling them brave gives them the permission to own it before they share something that could potentially lead to a vulnerable moment. If I call for a brave volunteer, it is an invitation to take a risk.*

Kids continue to work on their webs, as shown in Figures 6.3 and 6.4:

I am Chinese.
I love to surf.
I have grandparents that came here from Egypt.
I am a twin.

"You are developing some great webs! Can you all do me a favor and circle two of the most important pieces of your identity? The two things that really mean so much to you. That reflect who you are, every day."

I do the same on my own web on the board for them.

I circle *teacher* and *Chicagoan*.

Read-Aloud

 ⟩ 70

"OK, hold on to those two things for a while. We are going to read a great story together about identity. This is called *The Bear That Wasn't.*"

There is in fact, a bear in the story and he is having a really hard time with his identity because everyone keeps telling him that he is not a bear. He keeps on insisting that he is, but no one believes him.

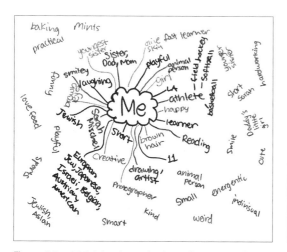
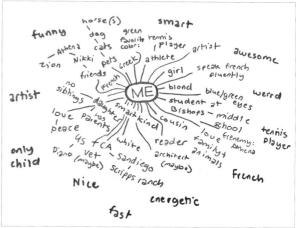

Figures 6.3 and 6.4 Identity webs from Sarah and Grace. The darker items represent a second round of entries.

Theo pipes up. "Well, doesn't he look like a bear?"

I respond, "Exactly, Theo. He looks exactly like a bear. But wait till you see what they tell him he is.

"Before I begin reading, can you all draw one more blank identity web, like you did for yourself earlier, in your journals? This time, write *The Bear* in the middle.

"We are going to use our same Identity chart we created together (see Figure 6.1) to try and make an **identity web** for the bear. That may seem silly to you, because he is a bear, but you will see pieces of his identity come out as we read. We are going to read with these questions in mind: How does the bear see himself? How do others see him? We are going to use our list and write everything we observe about him on the outside of the circle."

Game-Time Decision

There are different ways of getting this story into kids' heads, and I have tried them all with different classes. Sometimes I just read the picture book aloud and have the kids make identity webs for the bear as they listen. Other times, I have done a shared reading where we all have the text in front of us and I read from the doc camera. I have also asked kids to mark their text as we go and then we do a web on the board together. We stop to turn and talk and I chart what they are saying. The decision comes from assessing the needs of my readers, the size of my class (the picture book is small), and the time of day in regard to their energy levels. All variations are interchangeable and can have valuable outcomes in terms of comprehension, digging deep into identity, and collaboration. This lesson can be done with any biography picture book.

I begin reading the story aloud. We watch as the bear encounters a foreman, who is convinced that the bear is one of his workers.

> The Bear replied, "I don't work here. I'm a Bear."
> The Foreman laughed, "That's a fine excuse for a man to keep from doing any work. Saying he's a Bear."
> The Bear said, "But, I am a Bear."
> The Foreman stopped laughing. He was very mad.
> "Don't try to fool me," he said. "You're not a Bear. You're a silly man who needs a shave and wears a fur coat. I'm going to take you to the General Manager."
> The General Manager also insisted the Bear was a silly man who needs a shave and wears a fur coat.
> The Bear said, "No, you're mistaken. I am a Bear."

The story continues as author Tashlin leads us through the bear's struggle to stand up for himself and declare his bear-ness to all the naysayers who are telling him otherwise. His identity is vulnerable and he must hold strong to who he really is.

As we read through the book, I stop periodically and give the kids time to practice turning and talking with one another and sharing ideas as they fill out their webs for the bear. Some write annotations while I am reading; some wait for the opportunity to turn and talk. As we finish the book, I see their webs are filling up steadily from all the ideas they generated on their own and in pairs.

We do a quick go-around for any words they added to their webs and I jot these quickly on the board, helping any readers/listeners who may have missed something. Next, I pass around a basket of skinny markers. They have all been writing in pencil and I want their new thinking to be in a different color.

One theme of the story is that people are defined both by how they think of themselves and by how others perceive them. I work with kids early on to make this distinction, or at least begin to grapple with and discuss it.

"OK, with your new color, I want you to pay close attention to something. See if there are any words you wrote down that may not be how the bear sees himself, but how others see him. Circle those words.

"I'll start us off with an example. I think some people see him as 'a silly man who wears a fur coat and needs a shave.' He didn't see himself that way, so I would circle that."

The kids all laugh because that is exactly what the foreman and everyone tells him. I flip through the book again, telling kids to simply look at the pictures. This helps to activate their memories as they are working through the different terms with each other. The "picture walk" stimulates kids to recall the story and lift any words they can from the images they see again.

"If you don't already have something other people said about the bear, you might think of something now. Go ahead and add it in this new color as well. So, by the time you are done, all the words that show how the bear views himself are in pencil and the words that others use to label him are in a color." They talk with their partners and come up with some great terms: *a man, liar, not a bear, factory worker, less than they are.*

Quick Write

"At the beginning of this story we thought about how the bear sees himself. Then we looked at how others viewed him. Why might both those things be important to someone's identity?

"I am going to ask you to write about this topic for a few minutes. Can you find a space in your journal after the webs and write down your thoughts about this? Why might how others see you affect your identity? Why isn't your identity only how you see yourself? Your notes can be in sentences or bullet points."

I move around and read upside down and over shoulders. I see lots of responses that reflect their developmental stage:

> People care about what others think about them.
> I know who I am, but sometimes people tell me things and it makes me think.
> No matter what people say, you should always have self-confidence and just be yourself.

Identity is in constant question at this age. Kids are asking who they are and who they will be. They are hyperconcerned with the way others view them, and how they see themselves is continually evolving. We want them to work toward recognizing how the choices we make are grounded in our identity.

I don't expect kids to share this personal writing with the whole group, but I do ask them to summarize if they feel comfortable. In some classes the kids shared and in others they did not. I am OK with that because I was observing them as they wrote and checked in with kids who needed a quick conference. Again, I salute them for being brave by doing this kind of thinking and taking the risk to share in front of their peers.

64 Identity Webs Go Home

"For homework tonight, you are going to continue to examine the Identity chart we just brainstormed together (Figure 6.1). You are going to actually give your parents or any adult you can find some homework. Go home and ask them to list ten things they think of when they describe their own identity. Show them the list we made in class so they have some terms to help them.

"Then have your grown-up circle one or two things that are most important to them. Ask them to either explain to you why and you write it down, or have them write it right in your journal. Be sure to tell them the two pieces of your own identity that you chose to model for them.

"Do you like the idea of giving your family homework?"

Smiles all around.

"Me too; have fun."

This lesson serves as a cornerstone of our year. We revisit this chart, we revise our identity webs, and we refer to the bear when we experience others telling us who we are. I want kids to continue the discussion of identity at home, because I'll explicitly share that theme with parents at our Open House, and it is something we will be working on all year.

This lesson is a great way to help families communicate at home. I often hear parents say, "I have no clue what is going on because when I ask how school is, they just say, 'fine!'" This identity work is one way to open up the lines of communication. In case there is no parent at home, I always offer the option of talking with another adult or teacher around the school, or even an older sibling. Parents always respond to this lesson by thanking me for talking with the kids about their selves and their family roots. I even hear from some parents that their students will not speak their family's first language at home and only want to speak English. I offer my empathy, as I went through this myself as a teenager. So now as an educator, I pledge to keep the home/school connection and dialogue open.

Viewing an Identity Video

We continue our exploration of identity with a powerful TED talk, "The Danger of a Single Story," by the remarkable African writer Chimamanda Ngozi Adichie. (For this resource, see http://www.ted.com/talks/chimamanda_adichie_the_danger_of_a_single_story.) As Adichie explains, "Stories matter. Many stories matter. Stories have been used to dispossess and to malign, but stories can also be used to empower and to humanize. Stories can break the dignity of a people, but stories can also repair that broken dignity." Adichie explains how we often assign identity to others: we tell single stories that create stereotypes, which then become the only stories that are told and believed. So much of the work we do with middle schoolers is centered around their complex identities, so they, like the bear, are not reduced to a single story, a simplification, or a stereotype. We want them to examine their identities and own who they are. And we affirm with them that they are the only ones who get to do that.

Students consider their own personal identity webs and also create an identity web for Chimamanda Adichie. Then, they journal about the following questions:

What is the danger of the single story according to Chimamanda Adichie?
According to you?

After journaling and discussion, the kids were motivated to make a video public service announcement as shown in Figure 6.5 about the dangers of a single story, the single story that they feel others have assigned to them, as well as their view of themselves. This was an out-of-class project a small group of students did on their own time. They came up with a storyboard, dialogue, and filmed around school.

Figure 6.5 Screenshots of the seventh graders owning their identity from their single-story PSAs.

Empathy/Bullying *(1hour)*

Text: *Not My Fault* by Leif Kristiansson (1973, 1999)

I write these four terms on four pieces of chart paper or sections of the board:

Perpetrators, Victims, Bystanders, Upstanders

When kids gather at the rug, I ask them to try defining these terms in their journals. Since I often notice nervous and blank faces at this moment, I prompt kids with a question. "Who can raise their hand to just say, I have seen this word used, but am not totally sure what it means?" I explain that *defining* can mean all sorts of things—trying to write out exactly what it means, offering a few synonyms, connections, sketching something that would describe it, or guessing. But they have to try to write something.

I push students to look for clues in all parts of each word to help them figure out the meaning. As they write, I walk around and look over shoulders and listen.

Annika and Rachel are making great text connections to *The Watsons Go to Birmingham, 1963*.

> **Annika:** The four girls in the church bombing were victims.
> **Rachel:** Ya, totally. But did they find the perpetrator of that?

 I hand them sticky notes to post this thinking on the appropriate **chart**.

Craig and Annie connect to other terms:

Craig: I have heard the word *innocent bystander* before.
Annie: I know that means they weren't part of the crime.

We take a few more minutes for kids to place Post-its on one of the four charts. Next, I have volunteers read aloud a Post-it that really stands out to them from any one of the four charts. Or kids can ask a question to probe a definition they haven't figured out yet. I ask them to write down anything from these charts that will add to their understanding of the terms. In both of these steps, kids are learning from kids. Up until this point, I have not shared my definition of any of these words. I really emphasize that they listen and observe the work of their classmates so the transfer of knowledge is not continuously from me to them, or from textbook to student. I am no match for their brainpower as a group!

Craig: Well, something Annie and I put up there, is up there a few other times and that is the word *innocent* under bystander.
Meghan: I noticed that some people put *dead* for victim but that doesn't necessarily mean they are dead. They can just be bullied.
Me: What do you guys notice about the word *upstander*? I notice that there are not a lot of Post-its on it. I know that it is new to you, so let's look at anything in the word that may help us.

Jack immediately notices that it contains the words *stand* and *up*.

"Whoa! Let's talk more about that," I say.

Quinn connects to the words. "Well, if *bystander* is standing by, then maybe *upstander* is standing up for someone, like the victim."

"Jack, Quinn, thanks. Let's move into today's read-aloud and watch these new words come to life."

Thus, we have begun our working definition of these four roles in society. This is what Period 4 came up with:

Victim: Person, sad, 4 girls from [Birmingham] bombing, target, JFK, MLK, affected by the crime or incident, harmed, killed

Perpetrator: Suspect, caused harm to victim, law breaker, violator, traitor, did a bad act

Bystander: Witness, somebody who stands by an event without doing anything, choose not to act, coward (sometimes)

Upstander: Strong say in the situation, influential, helping out, tries to fight/help, acts/chooses to help. Stands up. Bystander that stands up and defends the victim

When you have multiple classes, it also helps to save these charts and combine all the data.

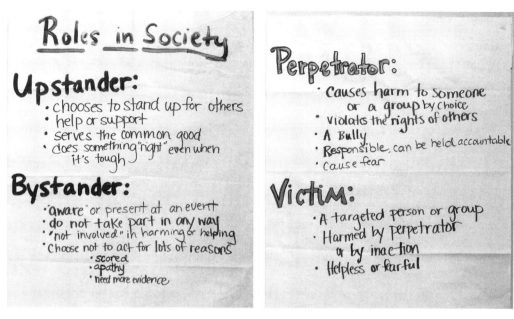

Figure 6.6 Anchor charts with our shared definitions of roles in society.

70 ◄ ### Read-Aloud

I introduce our upcoming read-aloud, *Not My Fault* by Leif Kristiansson. You can find this 32-page picture book on amazon.com. "Today we are going to read a story where all four of these roles show up. The setting of this story will be really familiar to you because it is on a school playground. As I read, I want you to try and identify the perpetrators, bystanders, victims, and upstanders in the group. It is a short book, so just listen and stay with me; I'll give you time to prove you know who they are." I begin reading:

> It happened after school.
>
> I hit him too
>
> But it doesn't matter,
>
> Everyone was hitting him
>
> So you can't blame me.
>
> He should have called for help!

As I read, the kids can't resist. Some are muttering "victim," under their breath. Some are shouting out "perpetrator" and tapping the kids next to them for reassurance. I keep on reading because they are so engaged, but I also stop a few times to let them point to the book and show me who is what. Some classes make a very keen observation that the bystander actually changes on each page. See the charts in Figure 6.6 that we created.

Online Collaboration (Backchanneling)

I prepare to read the story again, but before I start, I have students log onto **Edmodo** on their iPads and get ready to **backchannel** or digitally chat with each other as I read aloud. This form of silent dialogue allows kids to converse while they are listening to a story, and gives everyone a voice right in the middle of the reading. For kids who may be experiencing "meaning breakdown" as they read (or listen to) a text, their classmates' backchanneled comments often clear up misconceptions and keep their comprehension rolling. As with any lesson, this is adaptable to the age group and classroom climate. I have used different versions of this lesson for different classes at Burley and at Bishop's, in eighth grade and in sixth grade. My colleagues Kristin Ziemke and Katie Mutharis (2013) have done awesome work elaborating the varieties of backchanneling in their primary and intermediate classrooms.

69

58

SMOKEY: *I know you love hearing me say that this kind of multitasking just risks us doing a crappier job at two or three things at once.*

SARA: *Yeah, can't get enough.*

SMOKEY: *Something in my ancient teacher DNA says you are diluting kids' attention when they can choose to either listen to your read-aloud or chat about it simultaneously. The same thing is happening at teacher conferences I attend. Audience members used to look at a speaker during workshops, but now half the faces are buried in iPads. I keep thinking they are just playing Candy Crush or checking their retirement portfolios. Backchanneling sure changes what "attention" looks like in the classroom.*

SARA: *You really are a dinosaur. First of all, I still love the authentic, uncontrollable blurt-outs from the kids as I read. Of course, my class could also join in small-group discussions at tables after the read-aloud, or convene for a whole-group conversation. Both work well, but it does change the dynamic of the response. Kids can notice and share things right away in a backchannel discussion without disrupting the power of the story being read aloud. I do pause page by page as I observe their fingers typing vigorously.*

SMOKEY: *That pausing makes a big difference, I think. When you look at it this way, backchanneling starts to resemble old-fashioned note-taking, in many ways. We teachers never objected when kids bent down to copy down our precious words, even through this was a form of multitasking, I guess.*

SARA: *Now you're getting it. There are also opportunities to turn and talk on every page of this story, but the book is extremely short and powerful. I have tried stopping often, and it changes the momentum of the story. For sixth graders, who can also manage backchanneling, two read-throughs has been a good balance. (See Figure 6.7.)*

Sabrina F. • Sep 4, 2013

They talked as if it was his fault

Quinn R. • Sep 4, 2013

If everyone does it than they think its okay for them to do it too

Annie C. • Sep 4, 2013

The boy also didn't stand up for him so we can blame every person because they are all doing it

Elizabeth S. • Sep 4, 2013

A bystander is talking in the beginning, doesn't know what happened. Scared. Bystander, A kid is crying because something happened, probably a bully he was a victim. The bystander is acting innocent but really he should've got an adult. Everyone hit him even the bystanders! He's going from a bystander to a perpetrator. He's innocent then guilty! He thinks if he gets picked on he should blame himself. Why? Thinks he's a crybaby. It's not fair to this boy. The bystander was afraid to be an upstander. Everyone didn't do anything when he was cring. He hit him too but apparently we can't blame him because others hit him also. That's so mean to him. less . . .

Adam M. • Sep 4, 2013

Deep down feels guilty but is resisting

Matthew C. • Sep 4, 2013

It's still his fault it's everybody's fault even if they didn't hit him they still didn't go tell a teacher

Adam M. • Sep 4, 2013

they all bullied him in one way

Jack H. • Sep 3, 2013

The bystander who is also a perpetrator is really mean and doesnt want to help the victim.

Grace B. • Sep 3, 2013

I think that everybody had a part in this story. Even though by themselves it didn't look like anything overall, it makes a difference

Figure 6.7 Edmodo backchannel for *Not My Fault.*

Aaron B. • Sep 3, 2013

why didn't anyone help him i mean they all saw the thing and they new it was bad. they're all coldherted idiots.

 Sydney C. • Sep 3, 2013

He didnt have to yell for help Stand up for kids around you. You may not want to deal with it if you don't know what its like. ive had experiences and I WANT to stand up for others. Help people around you

 Margaret B. • Sep 3, 2013

You should always ask what's wrong when someone is crying or looks like is having a hard time. Insist that you want to help, and just by showing that you care it could help the victim. And if you feel like you can't do anything to help, you HAVE to get a teacher.

 Logan S. • Sep 3, 2013

There is one victim. Many perpetrators. And no upstanders. That's what I think based on what I think the definitions of the words are

Figure 6.7 *continued*

Silent Dialogue Walk

Now is a good time to get kids up and thinking, moving around while armed with thoughts and a writing utensil. Before the lesson, I have prepared nine sheets of chart paper, each with one question (below) reflecting the big ideas in the story. We will use these to begin our yearlong discussion of bullying, bystanders, and strategies to help students navigate this ever-present epidemic, both "live" in schools and in digital form on social media. ❯ 70

SILENT DIALOGUE QUESTIONS ON CHART PAPER

Can you define the term *bullying*?

How can bullying be carried out by an individual and a group?

Why are some people more likely to get bullied than others?

Why do you think people bully?

What choices do the bystanders have in bullying?

What advice would you give someone who is being bullied?

What can be done to prevent bullying?

How can bullying connect to bigger problems in the world?

How are you responsible for bullying?

Papers are hung around the room, on tables or desks, or out in the hallway as gallery stations where kids can stop, think, and react to the question with their writing tool of choice. I offer them skinny colored markers for variety and to make sure that separate comments "pop" visually. The kids love it because the charts are really colorful when they are done. (So do I, really.) At other times, I have posted direct quotes from text or images on these charts instead of questions and invited students to simply comment.

In this lesson, I have kids circulate *individually* through the different charts; other times I have the charts travel and the kids stay in teams. In either case, kids are to be silent and I caution them about bunching up at one or two charts. The silence allows for time to think and to let new concepts settle. Other norms include pausing to think before they write or respond to another person's comment. They need to spread out evenly, so each chart has a roughly equal and manageable number of kids working on it at any given time. They also need to sign all their comments, so we can talk later about who raised what points (and I can assess the level of participation and thinking from each kid).

This silent walk is great for getting students up and moving, but also for teaching them to pause and carefully study others' thinking before they write. And when they do offer comments, they are displaying their many comprehension and discussion strategies—connecting, questioning, inferring, determining importance, synthesizing—right on the charts.

Kids walk around our question gallery for eight to ten minutes, spending some writing time at each chart. I participate also, modeling how to connect to others or react to comments, and pushing the thinking of some kids who just want to get it over with by writing a quick response. They are easy to spot; you can follow them inconspicuously.

When kids think they are finished (or I think they've rushed through), I always suggest that they go back and see if someone responded to one of their own comments. This is not a hard sell, as kids always want to know who is "listening" to them. They'll go, "Oh yeah!" and scurry back to a chart across the room. And when they find that note, it is a natural time to add yet another comment to the conversation.

At the end of our time, I ask volunteers to bring all the charts over to the rug, where we hang them on the board and debrief the process as a whole group. I lead with: "What did you notice?" "Were there people who agreed with you? Disagreed with you?" "Were there new ideas or things that you never even thought of?"

Kids give answers ranging from the colors on the poster (as expected) to the connections they made with others. Nikial noticed that a lot of people shared his thinking, because he was drawing arrows to lots of comments. Maddie loved the colors that showed everyone's thinking; Ian added that when people really wanted to make a point they wrote in all caps or exclamation points, kind of like getting louder.

This discussion goes on for about five minutes, and then I show them the ending of the book.

"OK, I didn't mention this before, but this book is not over."

"What?! You mean they beat up on this kid even more?" asks an exasperated Alex.

"No, the story part is finished. But the author wants us to think about a very important question."

I show them an all-black page with white text: **Does it have nothing to do with me?**

The last few pages display real and infamous images of war, conflict, famine, nuclear explosions, and social conflict from our world's history. It is a delicate instructional decision whether to show all the disturbing images the author chose, or to limit which ones to share, depending on your class. In my different schools, I have carefully chosen which images to show, censoring or editing them depending on my audience and community.

With a class that can handle the gravity of these images, I have shown the book in full and connected the images to history. As I flip through them, I ask the kids to keep thinking about this question: Why did the author choose to include these in a book about playground bullying? Their homework assignment is to write their thoughts about that topic in their journals.

As an alternative culminating experience or as an extension, I have also asked kids to write in their journals about this: The victim in this story never speaks. Why do you think the author made that decision? It is a profound challenge for kids to connect big-world realities to things they experience around their own school. It helps kids to make sense of the roles individuals play in conflict and in everyday situations, and to choose what their own role will be.

Along with Lesson 1, using *The Bear That Wasn't*, this lesson serves as a landmark in our inquiry classroom. It sets the tone for the year, and builds critical thinkers who begin to notice whose voice is represented and whose is not in the stories, news, and events that surround us.

The goals of the lesson are to plant these seeds and build the upstander language so we can have this in our conceptual vocabulary all year. The chart with the words *upstander*, *bystander*, *victim*, and *perpetrator* is not wallpaper; it is a living, breathing tool we use time and time again. Yes, it is about bullying, but it is also wider than that: it gives students a sense of obligation to one another and (we hope) to the greater world around them.

Building Social Structures

As we previewed earlier, the next four lessons are shorter than the first two. These are more targeted to specific skills kids can use to connect, collaborate, empathize, and share their learning with others. Before our first group inquiry projects of the year in September, we talk a lot about the experiences kids have had working in small groups. This does not just mean past school research projects, but real-life small-group experiences like playing board games, joining in camp activities, playing on a sports team, or just hanging around with different groups of kids. We draw on these experiences in lessons that help kids construct lists and charts that support collaboration all year long.

LESSON 3

Risk-Taking: Home Court Advantage *(45 minutes)*

Students need to be friendly and supportive toward each other so that they can pursue engaging activities all year long. Everyone needs to feel safe to take intellectual risks, make mistakes, and try again. This cannot happen when classmates' banter borders on "cut-downs" or harassment, or in a worst-case scenario, when students are outright mean to each other. There is an analogy here to sports teams, which tend to win more games on their home field or court than they do away. In school, we need to be each other's best fans and supporters, not "boo-birds" mocking from the bleachers.

The lesson begins when I hand out the team standings from some pro sport. (I usually do this lesson in the fall, when the baseball season is finishing up, and abundant home and away stats are available.) I ask kids to read the standings and speculate with a buddy about why teams usually win more games at home than away. Then we make a whole-class list of possible reasons. Typical entries: your fans are there, everyone is cheering for you, you play harder, nobody puts you down, you know the field. Then I ask, "How could we have home court advantage here in this classroom?" So we make a second **chart** (see Figure 4.14 on page 51) that translates from sports directly to our classroom and serves as a compact for the entire year.

56 ⟨ 🧰

To finish off the lesson, I ask pairs of kids to make colorful posters about what *home court* means to them. Then we post these on the walls for all to see—and for the continuing reminder they offer that in my room, we all enjoy home court advantage every day. (See Figure 6.8.)

Sports analogies often work in your favor with middle school kids. This year I even found myself extending it to the dance floor, the dojo, and the recital stage. I heard the words *home court* echoed in class and in the hallways all the time.

Figure 6.8 Students create their own home court posters in small groups to hang around our room, so they are surrounded by support.

I am grateful to Nancy Steineke's book, *Reading and Writing Together* (2002), for this lesson. There is also a helpful video of Nancy doing this with high school kids in *Best Practice Video Companion* (Zemelman and Daniels 2012).

LESSON 4

Working in Groups: Team Behavior *(45 minutes)*

We've all seen what happens when group work isn't really teamwork. Recently, my students were part of a retreat in which the organizers assigned them to assemble cardboard boats that would carry their teachers across a pool. (And, yes, some teachers really did get volunteered for this.) Unfortunately, the situation didn't set the kids up for success: they had little guidance, no opportunities to test out ideas, and little time. While I was supposed to be observing the kids and hearing about their action plans as they worked, I found myself in a role more like a World Wrestling Entertainment referee. Kids were shouting, blaming, and tattling instead of working together, making collaborative plans, or talking through conflicts. The building materials became toys and even improvised weapons. We saw exasperated red faces, withdrawn kids, and even some tears.

After most of the teachers made it safely ashore (thanks to duct tape), we decided as a teacher team that the kids were not prepared well for this type of work. When we came back to the classroom, the kids and I took some time to reflect on what went well and what didn't. We turned and talked about what actions or attitudes can make any small-group endeavor fun and interesting—and also, what behaviors can throw it off track. We gradually built an **anchor chart** on "What Works" and "What Doesn't Work" (Figure 6.9).

› 56

Notice there's nothing about boats in here; these insights apply to almost any team situation. Like many of our other anchor charts, this one stays up in the room so we can refer to it later, either as problems arise or as we simply refresh our understandings of these pros and cons. Sometimes we literally make a pledge to, as best as we can, not revisit the right side of this chart.

SMOKEY: *With this lesson, as so many others in this book, there are different possible times to introduce it. Before group work starts, you can have kids make these lists and hopefully prevent some of the common pitfalls. Or, you can wait for a teamwork breakdown to occur, and then teach this lesson as a fix-up. You probably won't have to wait too long for an opportunity.*

Now, this is not a joke. The fact is, we have to plunge kids into doing real group work long before we could possibly "cover" every possible collaboration skill. If we wait until all imaginable lessons are taught, it might be April! David Perkins of Harvard's Project Zero points out this phenomenon (2010). Kids have to join in authentic, "whole game learning" every day, at whatever developmental stage they have achieved. Meanwhile, we teachers observe, and then follow up with lessons that help kids solve problems, develop alternative strategies, and get better. So, after observing the kids' efforts, we teach many social skill lessons to provide the next steps they need to grow as collaborators.

Figure 6.9 Our co-created anchor chart on group behaviors.

Group Work

What Works
- sharing ideas
- communication
- initiative
- shared leadership
- a common goal
- a good attitude
- nice tones & words
- checking in
- listening!
- shared responsibility and accountability
- celebrating talents & thoughts
- deep breaths
- support for team

What Doesn't
- Bad attitudes
- Being bossy
- procrastination
- arguing/yelling
- getting off track
- Not listening or sharing
- panic mode/rushing
- Being an "island"
- Not stopping to check in
- "My way or the highway"
- blaming others
- lack of communication
- not establishing goals or tasks

LESSON 5

Disagreeing Agreeably: Framing Friendly Challenges

(30 minutes)

If adults know anything about group work, it is that we don't always see eye to eye with the people on our teams. We can help kids be prepared for this reality with some verbal and nonverbal tools that will support them in these moments. Continuing the conversation about collaborative group work, we can revisit some areas of the right side of the previous lesson's chart, or ask kids what disagreeing looks like and name some strategies to get through it.

I gather kids on the rug and talk about how in school we will have literature discussions, group work in math, lab partners in science, teams in PE, all kinds of groups—each with the potential for conflict or disagreement. I get the truth out of them first.

"What do you guys do when you really disagree with someone? A brother or sister? Your parents? Partners in school?"

I start the honesty train and share that as an adult, I sometimes disagree with one of my friends about politics or current events. I used to get really frustrated, roll my eyes, or try to think of something sarcastic or kinda mean to say back. But I learned over time to do a couple of things before I let myself get to that point, so we could still have these conversations and keep our friendship. One of them is listening to everything the person has to say first.

Kids admit to doing the same as me, sometimes slamming bedroom doors, and crying.

I meet them halfway for their bravery in sharing. "Oh man, me too!"

I tell them that we all need to find better ways to disagree because as they get older, they are going to start forming their own strong opinions and ideas, and they will want more freedom to do what they want. I really hook them when I let them know that these secret strategies will also be the key to getting along with their parents as they become tweens and teens. I share that the first step is to *listen* when we disagree with someone. Then, we go from there and brainstorm productive ways to disagree.

I lead them with questions that help us problem-solve before the big blow-ups or slamming of doors.

 ⟩ 56

"What are some strategies we can use when faced with a challenge?

"How might a behavior like stopping or pausing be helpful if you disagree with someone or are about to boil over with anger?

"In the story that I told you about me, what could I do better when I disagree with my buddy?

"Can you guys think of other productive ways to talk to someone whom you may disagree with?"

Now I give kids some time to brainstorm ideas in pairs, jotting down quick notes. Next, we regroup to co-create a list of the most promising and practical strategies. Figure 6.10 shows one class' ideas on how to handle a disagreement so no one gets hurt.

Figure 6.10 One class' anchor chart of strategies to use when disagreeing with someone.

Responsibility: Building (and Protecting) Your Brand *(60 minutes)*

Every one of our middle schoolers is constantly—consciously or unconsciously—"building a brand" for themselves. That emerging image can change day to day, or even minute to minute, depending on whether the kid's cortex or amygdala happens to be in charge. We have to guide them through this, and let them make their own choices, but also help them predict potential outcomes and build the very difficult skill of foresight. What will happen if I release the words that are bubbling into my mouth right now? How will all the different receivers be affected if I just push Send or Publish? Who will I hurt? What does this really say about me and the brand I am building for myself?

Step into any middle school in America, and you're likely to hear kids exclaim, "I was just play-ing around!" as they try to defend saying something they should not have said. And *would* not have said if they had been thinking about their thinking and pausing purposefully in their interac-tions with others. This lesson aims to help students recognize the power of language and to use it with care.

I gather kids on the rug, and begin by asking them to think about the stories we have read so far this year, and recall any hurtful language exchanged by those characters. Or, I continue, think of insults, stereotypes, or negative language you've heard around school or on social media, and write them down. The kids all give me the "Are you sure we can write this?" look. Once I provide the green light and the assurance I won't rat them out, they are happy to write any profanity, slur, or insult they have heard or read. Some of them smile while they do it; others cover up the words as they write them.

Then I ask them to do a two- to three-minute quick write on these questions. The questions are on the board, but I also say them aloud as they write.

- How does it feel to *hear* this language?
- How does it feel to *be the target of* this language?

Some of the kids ask right away, "Are we going to have to share this?" Planning this lesson, I know their writing might not be authentic if they know they must share their thoughts aloud. And of course, nobody will be compelled. But I point out that their discomfort with these words should tell us something about the impact this kind of language has. I invite them to **turn and talk** about these questions if they are comfortable. If not, I ask them to just reread their writing while others share.

Next, I ask kids to go back to their writing and stop, think, and react to these three questions in writing. What does this language say about the person *using* it?

- How do they think it feels to *say* this language?
- What should they think about before and after they use it?
- What does this say about them?

I give kids another two or three minutes to respond to these prompts. As they write, I observe to make sure three minutes is long enough. I look for signals from them on this—eye contact with me, turning and talking to a buddy. If they are still voraciously writing, I give them more time.

I then tell the kids that first we looked at how this language affects the *victim* in the situation, and that is very important because there can be intent to hurt the person. Then, the questions that they wrote about helped us to looked at the *perpetrators* and how they can be perceived by others. Thinking of these two perspectives, all these words we wrote down and all the language we see, hear, and read every day, we can really see the power that language can have.

Then I say: "You don't have to share the insults you wrote down earlier with a partner or with me, but let's use our journals and the way we are feeling to just help us answer this question: What power does language have? In other words, what power do the words you use have?"

I walk around and am reading over shoulders as the kids write. The kids are able to articulate that language can separate people, that we can use mean language to bully, or that our language can identify us as an upstander or a perpetrator. See Figure 6.11.

 56

It's bad enough to use potentially injurious language in our "live" classroom community. But at least here, a student can immediately apologize (or at least claim that they were only kidding). But once that student hits Send in a wireless world, his or her comment is now public property. It doesn't take much searching on Google to find tweets, Instagram posts, or Facebook posts that are crude and unkind, and perhaps received tons of negative public feedback. The consequences for digitally disrespecting others can be dire and long-lasting, and these lapses are usually impossible to take back.

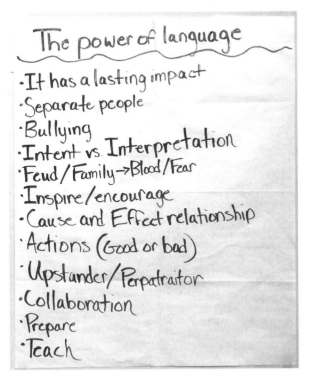

Figure 6.11 Kid-scribed anchor chart about the power of language.

I project a few screenshots of these kinds of public embarrassments; showing the destructive aftermath of each one sends a loud and clear message. One striking example concerns Hollister, a clothing brand that many of the kids are loyal to. The company was forced to publicly apologize after some of its fashion models had tweeted, "Hahahahaa, they *rrrruuhhhvvv* it!" on a trip to South Korea for a store opening. The models were quickly fired.

As I share the screenshots with the kids, some of them are laughing; others are in shock. "People say that stuff?!" they shout out. In the case of Hollister, we talk about how the hundreds of thousands of Hollister's followers saw these tweets and how it can be so offensive to many groups of people. And hurt a brand.

Unlike any previous generation, today's middle school students have access to social media that can make their thoughts and ideas public domain forever. While today's adults might have been able to apologize in person for an unfortunate comment made when they were younger and then forget about it, what today's kids say could follow them for years to come. Students are not likely to be thinking about the digital footprints that they're leaving behind as they connect online, but more and more colleges and places of business are looking to find just that. It's our job and their parents' job to help them "protect their brand" online—and in person.

I explain that we will be using blogs and Edmodo in class this year, and that the concepts we're talking about are just as important when they use these tools in their personal lives. To help students be mindful of what they're saying online, I ask them to join me in co-constructing one more list: "Questions to ask ourselves before we make our comments or images public."

In our brainstorming, I can tell from kids' comments that many of them have already addressed this issue at home, or have gained plenty of background knowledge elsewhere.

"My mom always says to my sister, if you can't say it to me, don't put it online."

"Some people I know write something online, then regret it like thirty seconds later and go to delete it."

"Ya, and someone could have screenshot it in those thirty seconds and sent it out to other people."

Figure 6.12 shows what our list looks like when we have put all these thoughts and experiences together.

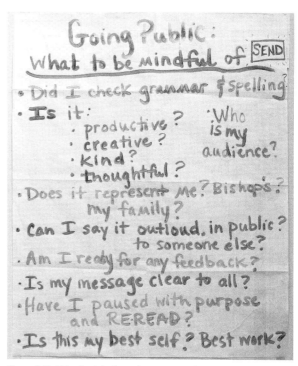

Figure 6.12 We decided to always use this checklist to make sure we are ready to go public on the Internet.

56 <

We keep the list in a prominent place in the room and refer to it before we submit online comments, questions, or images—or respond to others. And, yes, my room will be festooned with all sorts of anchor charts by mid-September!

Conclusion

The six lessons in this chapter are groundwork for what you and your students will be building in your year together. Before we can begin to sprint down the curriculum road, we must first walk with the kids. It's our job to get them ready to talk, wonder, listen, post, see difference, celebrate difference, be reflective, feel empathy, agree, disagree, and be critical readers, speakers, and authors of the world.

PART 4

*

A COMPASSIONATE AND CHALLENGING CURRICULUM

Mini-Inquiries

chapter 7

Monday morning. Kids pour into the room, kick off their shoes, and beeline for their usual spot, a pillow or beanbag to curl up with a book for a few minutes. A few of them stop dead in their tracks as their usual morning routine is interrupted by something displayed on the rug. "Eeew, oh my God, what is that!?" Marley and Zion emit in a respectfully quiet shriek. Another one or two follow with unified gasps of horror and wonder. They squeal, "Ms. Ahmed!?" almost as if I don't know something is there.

"What is it, guys?"

"That is what we are asking you!"

"Well, check it out and let me know what you think."

A few of them lie down on the floor for an eye-level view of it. Others have no clue there is anything there because they are already in the Zone with their books.

On the rug, I had set down my breakfast leftovers from the past Saturday morning. A sea urchin. I had it in a plastic container set on a piece of chart paper, where kids could write their wonderings and reactions, and get up close and personal with our new friend as shown in Figures 7.1 and 7.2.

They did just that.

70 ‹

104

Some of them smelled it, asked if they could touch it, and stared for minutes. Others wrote *gross* and *weird* on a Post-it and walked away. Still others had some background knowledge from seeing an urchin on restaurant TV shows, on vacation, or at the same market where I found it. Questions began to pop up, so I told them they could spend their reading time discovering some answers and I would share its story when we came together on the rug in a few minutes. A few of the boys who had been in the Zone left their books facedown to quickly check out the creature.

Figure 7.1 "Wonderings About Sea Urchins" chart and specimens.

They were mostly interested in viewing more images of sea urchins and their natural habitats.

"Ms. Ahmed, you killed this thing?!"

"They serve it in restaurants that have sushi!"

"Can you can get stung by them in the ocean?"

A couple of kids ran back and forth between their computers and the urchin to double check some new findings.

When we came to the rug, I brought our urchin with me. "So I have a quick story to tell you about my weekend. I had my own little mini-inquiry at the farmer's market on Saturday and

Figure 7.2 A student getting right in, touching the spikes of the sea urchin.

I had to share it with you!" I tell them the story of how a vendor at the local market offered me a taste; how he opened the urchin and exposed the bright, grainy inside; and how it took all of my courage to try it. The kids looked, listened, and passed around the urchin some more.

"I was so excited about this little creature that I knew I had to share it with you guys. After my cousins and I tasted it, I asked the man for a bag to put the remainder in and asked if it would last until Monday to show you. I actually observed it in my refrigerator this weekend from time to time and noticed that the color began to change to this green. I wonder why. It was pretty dark on the inside when we first opened it."

I passed my phone around with a few fun pictures of the inside and of my cousins and me enjoying the delicacy. A few of them shared their initial thinking.

"So, I just wanted to share that with you because it was such a cool moment for me to venture out and eat something I normally would not try, and I loved it! I also realized that I did my own inquiry. I observed something, activated some background knowledge, asked questions, did some research by trying it, discussed my new discoveries, asked more questions, and shared out with all of you. So awesome! Let's get him back in the container for the next class and continue with our day. If any of you try one, see one, or find out more about it, let us know, OK?!"

Types of Inquiry Projects

The sea urchin adventure was what we call a *mini-inquiry,* a quick exercise in honoring our curiosity and finding out information about things that puzzle us in the world. This inquiry, which took only about ten minutes of class time, is one of four types we share in this book.

SARA: *Smokey, maybe you better introduce the next four chapters, since you and Steph Harvey basically wrote the book on inquiry.*

SMOKEY: *Yeah, we invented inquiry, just the two of us. Don't you remember that the book has tons of your lessons in it? Steph and I were mostly documenting the practices of great teachers like you.*

SARA: *Aww, shucks, Smoke.*

SMOKEY: *But sure, I'll give a little background if you like. In* Comprehension and Collaboration: Inquiry Circles in Action, *Steph and I identified four different types of small-group inquiry projects that we saw great teachers across the country using.*

MINI-INQUIRIES

These are short investigations of simple topics posed by either kids or teachers. Mini-inquiries typically take from a few minutes to one day to complete. They offer kids practice in noticing the fascinating questions that come up, in and out of school, and in forming pairs or teams to seek some information about them. In this chapter we share two more examples and the steps for managing them with any topic.

CURRICULAR INQUIRIES

This is the most frequently used inquiry model in today's schools. We take mandated curricular topics, from photosynthesis to manifest destiny, but instead of relying on teacher and textbook presentations, we help kids form teams that each investigate the topic, or a key part of it, through jigsawing. Given that curricular inquiries often tackle major, complex subjects, they can last for days or weeks. In Chapter 8, we show generic steps and lessons that you can use for any topic, and we share a detailed sample unit on immigration, globalization, and child labor.

LITERATURE CIRCLE INQUIRIES

Most American students these days get chances to join in ongoing book clubs or reading groups commonly called *literature circles*. This structure allows kids to pick their own books and their own group members, and therefore to take significant responsibility for their own learning. When they have finished their books, we ask students to identify their lingering questions, and then re-form into inquiry circles to learn more about the issues the books raised for them. In Chapter 9, we show you the key lessons needed to support these groups—and recount a lit circle inquiry based on the powerful historical memoir *Warriors Don't Cry,* about school integration in the 1950s.

OPEN INQUIRIES

We think these are the most fun investigations to teach, because now we say to students "What do *you* want to learn about for a while?" We help kids list and winnow promising topics of curiosity, form them into groups by topic similarity, and then support them through the whole inquiry process. For some understandable reasons, many teachers save open inquiries until the end of the year, when the testing season has finally passed and, as we say, "Now we can really learn something." But the example we share in Chapter 10 was done in October, as a way of getting kids psyched to do inquiry of all kinds, all year long.

Exploring Mini-Inquiries

Mini-inquiries often begin spontaneously. A spark of curiosity pops up in class, or some amazing/thumb-sucking question just jumps out of a kid's mouth. Or you, the teacher, bring in a puzzler you've run across yourself. Like a sea urchin! Here are a few others we've addressed in our classes.

Do animals have friends?
Are dragons real?
Who came up with pi?
When did newspapers get color?
Why are adults addicted to caffeine?

What teams did Magic Johnson play for?

How do you get picked to go up in space?

What are Skittles made out of?

Where does the Rockefeller Center get its 76-foot Christmas tree?

Why are there so many jellyfish off the coast of Japan?

Figure 7.3 Inquiry PicCollage: Do chocolate chips have caffeine?

Ava really wanted to find out if all that chocolate she eats makes her wired. Yep, it does.

When kids come up with questions like these we happily set aside our agenda for a few minutes because *nothing is more important than honoring and nurturing kids' curiosity.* So off we go to scratch that itch, to get that answer, to solve that puzzle. Other mini-inquiries can be instigated by the teacher as a way to model and demonstrate the habits of the curious life. When we want to lead kids through the inquiry cycle of curiosity, investigation, and sharing, we can begin with topics that puzzle or plague or intrigue *us.*

Mini-inquiries might last two minutes (grabbing a factual answer), ten minutes (gathering some background information on a public figure), or at most, chunks of a couple of days (researching a more complex topic). Diving into these questions also shows kids how necessarily messy inquiry can be; some topics are "quick finds" and yield satisfying answers within minutes, while others explode in unexpected complexity, and still others yield no reliable answer now, and may never.

From the outside, these kid-driven mini-inquiries can look like digressions or sidetracks. Far from it. When we make the game-time decision to step out of the day's lesson plan, we aren't letting the kids off the hook or offering them some kind of nap. What we are saying to kids is, OK, let's go on a research break together. Talk about a teachable moment.

During these mini-inquiries, kids practice what grown-up researchers do: they pose and refine questions, seek out information and corroborate it across sources, create public reports, and join with others to share and process findings. And guiding this inquiry process is the teacher as Master Researcher, modeling the strategies that lifelong learners use to pose and get answers to their own questions.

Standards Skills:
- Ask open-ended research questions.
- Conduct short research projects based on focused questions.

Chew on This

Sammie knew just what to get her pal, Isabela, for a Secret Santa gift. She tossed it at her, shouting, "You're definitely gonna like this one!" Tearing through the bag, Isabela squealed at the delicious sight of a humongous bag of her favorite hot chips.

"Oh my God, yum! Can I open it now, Ms. Ahmed?"

"No, it's 7:30 in the morning."

Isabela nods her head in agreeable disappointment and puts it away.

"I can't believe you eat those as much as you do to begin with," Sammie comments.

"Why? They are amazing! You've eaten them too!"

The bell rings so I am saved from mediating a tough debate.

Later, in history class, because we have a modified schedule and winter break is approaching, I have planned for the kids to have a mini-inquiry day. I bring them to the rug and they see what I have already written on the board: *What are you wondering about today*?

"So, you guys, our vacation is coming and everyone is so excited, I thought the best way to send you off is to be curious about life." Blank stares. "You are going to see family, go to the beach, and see new places, and the best way to see all of that is through curious eyes. You guys love to ask questions—you ask me a hundred questions a day about homework and classwork and my life—but now let's find some answers to what you are curious about today."

I model my own thinking first. "For example, I am super curious as to why ginger supposedly has anti-inflammatory healing powers. You guys know I hurt my wrist and I don't like to take a lot of medicine, so everyone keeps telling me to use ginger as a natural way to calm down the swelling. I want to know why it is so magical! Will it work for me?

"What about you guys? Turn to the inquiry section in your notebooks and let's start making a list together of what we are all wondering about. While you are writing down the date and lesson title, go ahead and turn and talk with a buddy and come up with some great lists together. If you are stuck, remember that there are all our nonfiction magazines and books around us, and that you can also pull from a cool story you recently read."

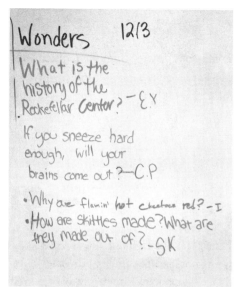

Figure 7.4 Mini-inquiry wonders list.

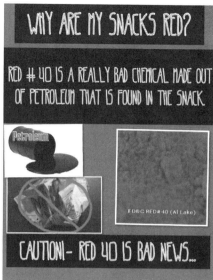

Figure 7.5 Isabela's mini-inquiry PicCollage.

Isabela turns to me and says that she is interested in her hot chips. I tell her I know she is, but then ask her what specifically about the snack she is wondering.

"I want to know why they are red," she replies.

I assure her that is a great mini-inquiry question and that she also may not want to know the answer.

When we are ready to share, hands go up with great enthusiasm. Figure 7.4 is the beginning of a list we created over the next few minutes:

Isabela had a tough time finding out why her hands were always dyed red after she ate an entire bag of chips. The manufacturer's website wasn't making it easy to understand what the ingredients actually were or why they may dye fingers. But after a while, Isabela's first audible gasp rang out across the room.

"Ewwww! Tar!"

Her horrified yelling echoed through the room for the next twenty minutes. After class she walked over to Sammie and apologized for seeming to diss the gift.

"Sammie, thanks for the present, and I am really sorry, but I am never eating those things again."

Making Mini-Inquiries Work in Your Classroom

1. Model. Model. Model.

Always take time to be *you* with your kids, and share your curious life. Let them know how questions pop into your mind. Tell them how you drive by the same statue, marker, construction site, or store every day and have always wondered what it was, and you finally took time to stop and investigate. Tell them you go on walks and notice the nature around you—birds, flowers, plants, trees—and want to know more about the specific species in your community. Show them pictures or lists of your wonders in your own journal, iPad, or Kindle. Have a running list of everyone's wonders on chart paper in the room, which the kids maintain and write on as they feel necessary. Start it off yourself, and get in on the fun as well.

 ❯ 56

2. Make time.

Mini-inquiries can take two minutes, ten minutes, a class period, or a day. They can happen in a teachable moment. Set aside a time that is right for you and your students. It doesn't need to be another thing in your busy agenda, but as you begin to value and model your own curious life, opportunities will pop up in your curriculum. I often plan for a day or two during a unit where I can give the kids time for this. The mini-inquiry can be about our content area, one of the thousands of questions kids always have bubbling in their minds, or from postings on our class wonder wall. It is a moment for them to take initiative in the classroom, but we are also teaching them the research procedures that come with this type of investigation.

> Rather than making "enrichment" worksheets to fill this extra time, allow kids to do mini-inquiries.

Some especially good moments for mini-inquiries include:

- When we are introducing inquiry learning
- Special schedule days (assembly, report card conferences, late starts/half days)
- When we end a unit just before a break and it doesn't make much sense to start something new
- For enrichment if some kiddos finish their independent work early
- Grandparents' or Visitors' Days

One of the most opportune times for mini-inquiries is when you hear kids complaining: "What do we do when we're done?" Rather than making "enrichment" worksheets to fill this time, allow kids to do mini-inquiries, grabbing a topic from their ongoing personal lists. That way, instead of busy work that you are responsible for assessing, copying, and storing, kids are in charge of their own learning. "Spare time" is allocated to their wonders, their research, and their new learning. Then they can share their findings in the empowered voice of a budding specialist.

3. Keep doing it.

66 ‹

As students become more familiar with mini-inquiries, they are growing a repertoire of ways to ask questions and gather information. Among these tools are **alphaboxes** and other "thinksheets," past anchor charts we have made, and the inquiry section of their journals, where throughout the year they keep a running list of questions they are wondering about. As you get to know each kid better, you can help them choose topics that match their curiosity and learning style, and that will keep them engaged and accountable. It gets easier and easier to slot in time for both whole-group and personalized mini-inquiries.

Apert Syndrome and Mary Cate

SMOKEY: *The mini-inquiries we've shown you so far are pretty brief, but remember what we said earlier: mini-inquiries can sometimes stretch over a few days, especially if you find that your kids are immersed in powerful work. That's what happened when Sara noticed an area where her kids needed to grow and shared a rather urgent and heartfelt question of her own.*

SARA: *In middle school, kids are at a crossroads about their identity. They are not sure where they stand on the continuum of childhood to adulthood, and they are constantly aware of everyone else around them. They make choices, good and bad, based on the reactions and reassurance of others and all too often, it can be at the expense of a peer, buddy, or someone even closer, like family.*

Early in the school year, I was reminded of some of the bad choices I saw kids making while I was coaching cross-country. We were about four meets into the season. Most of the same nearby schools participate in every meet, so we see a lot of familiar faces each week. There was a young lady from a competing school who ran every single race. And every single race, she came in dead last. She would be cheered in long after all the other girls were finishing and even as the boys were already lined up to go. She would never quit. Never stopped to walk for a second. She smiled every race she ran and finished with grace. This young lady was overweight for her age, especially in comparison to the young runners around her.

One race in particular, my girls and I were looking for her to cheer her in and I overheard two boys from another school spot her.

"Here she comes . . . soooo slow . . . sooo fat."

"Oh, I can't move any faster, I'm too big."

They were feeding off each other, laughing the entire time. My girls didn't hear a thing.

We have all had that teacher (or parent) moment. The instant where, in public, you want to reprimand someone else's unsupervised child. What they are doing wouldn't fly in your classroom or your home. This was my moment. I let it go for a few minutes after the runner came by. Then I turned to the boys and asked them what it was about her that made them say the things they were saying? Both of them quickly denied saying anything. I asked them, wouldn't it be great to recognize and realize how hard she works to finish every race? Harder than anyone else out here?

It was still bothering me days later. Too often in middle school, kids are targeted for their physical appearance. Kids are not born mean; it is learned behavior. It's also possible for kids to learn new, healthier behavior, especially if they have a better understanding of who the "other" is. I didn't share the story of the runner with the kids—that might have felt accusatory. Instead, I thought of someone else I know who is working to combat the reactions that many people have to someone who looks different. This became my way of championing a dear friend, her daughter, and kids like her daughter who will grow through life with this battle.

This lesson accomplishes many of my academic goals for my students: they synthesize information from a variety of sources—texts, interviews, visuals, and more. They read these sources closely and consider the texts' reliability and value. They work collaboratively to develop and hone ideas. They present their findings in writing and speaking. I can be confident that I've met any necessary standards. However, what feels most important to me about this work is how it takes students beyond the standards: the young people in my classroom are asking, over and over again, "So what?" They are articulating how the work they are doing affects their thinking and their beliefs. They are taking action in the world. And they're doing all of this while working through the grit of stigma and stereotype to become more compassionate and aware human beings.

Day 1 (60 minutes)

For this two-day lesson, I started with the kids "cold." I gathered them on the rug and began like this:

"I want everyone to take a minute and close your eyes; if you are not comfortable doing that you can just look down and think in your mind. I want you to think about something, an experience you have had when you encountered someone who is or was different from you. I want you to picture what this person or group looked like in your mind. What made them different? Now I want you to be honest with yourself, how did you react either on the inside or outwardly to this person? What were you thinking? This is a very private thought, so we won't be sharing them. OK, open your eyes.

"Can someone tell me what *different* could mean? It doesn't have to be about your private thought. I'll give you an example—different can be skin color. What else? If you feel safe checking in with someone next to you, do that first."

tip!

Ways to Go Public with a Mini-Inquiry

We always discuss the many different ways to share knowledge in our class. We can make objects or displays, write reports, or—most enjoyably for everyone—have researchers share their findings aloud with the group. But on days where our time is limited, or only a few students may be working on mini-inquiries, they are other great ways to go public without requiring a whole class sit-down meeting. Watch the next few tip boxes.

Some hands go up . . .

A group of boys calls out: Height!

Matthew: Disability.

Me: Can you tell me more about what you mean by disability, Matthew?

Matthew: Yeah, like some people are in wheelchairs or have mental disabilities, like my cousin has a pretty severe one.

Me: Oh, thank you for being brave and making a very personal connection for us.

Gabbie: Clothing.

Me: Can anyone describe why clothing would appear to you as different?

Bobby: Well, different cultures and traditions wear different stuff, or even just fashion.

A few more hands go up and we have a pretty good list: hairstyle, fashion and accessories, tattoos/piercings (lifestyle), languages we hear people speaking.

"OK, thanks guys, we all have reactions to things that seem new or different to us, don't we? It's human nature."

I pass out the **See, Think, Wonder** sheets as shown in Figure 5.4.

When kids are reading an image, this tool helps them to begin with what they literally see, and then dig deeper. See, Think, Wonder sheets give students the ability to compartmentalize their thinking in a way that allows them to first observe without judgment. From there, they are able to synthesize old and new learning to form hypotheses and analyze material with a critical and curious eye.

Seeing

"I am going to show you something that I want you to just look at for some time. Try and think in your mind about what you 'see' and keep those thoughts private at first.

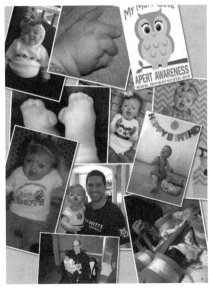

Figure 7.6 Mary Cate PicCollage. Images drawn from www.mymarycate.org.

🧰 ❯ 67

🧰 ❯ 61

'See' meaning, I see a Happy Birthday sign, or I see an owl. Name the literal objects or words you see. Then when you are ready, you can begin to write what you see. Let's give everyone some time and space to think. Ready?"

I project the PicCollage in Figure 7.6 on the screen and just watch and wait for thirty to forty-five seconds. The time really depends on how the kids are responding. I shared this image with several classes and their reaction times varied widely. There are a lot of soft, yet audible, *awwwws, oh wow's, she's so cute, I'm sad.* A lot of them want to ask me questions right away, so I turn them to their buddies next to them for shared thinking power.

"I know you are eager to talk, so when you feel like you are ready, turn and talk with someone next to you about what you see. If you join forces, you can write down your thinks and your wonders as well.

"Remember, in your Think column are what you now infer or may understand about all the objects you just listed, so your judgments, opinions, thoughts, and feelings. Your wonders are still your thinking, but now in the form of a question. For example, why do her hands

tip!

PicCollage: This is our class favorite right now. The app provides you with a blank canvas, access to photos on the web, and different design tools to show what you know. Our parameters for this are: title in the form of your question, images to support what you learned and want to teach others, and captions for all photos that will help audience members gain knowledge without you having to explain over and over again.

- Integrate and evaluate content presented in diverse media and formats, including visually.
- Use comprehension skills to analyze how words, images, and graphics work together to impact meaning.

look like this? Anything that you are wondering. Make sure everyone is included in a partnership by turning both ways and asking who is with you if you need to. Ask someone to join your partnership if need be."

SMOKEY: *I am appreciating how Sara just took an extra five seconds to have kids make sure everyone is included. This kind of constant, mindful social maintenance is what sustains a high-morale classroom.*

I listen in and move around, and with every question I get—"Who is that, Ms. Ahmed?" "Do you know her?" "What happened?"—I redirect back to their partners so they can share perspectives together. "Can you guys talk it out? What makes you wonder that? Write it down in your wonder section and I promise I will do my best to answer it in a while."

I can assess kids' engagement level by the way they are pointing at the screen to defend or show the evidence of their thinking. Pencils are flying up as pointers and some kids even walk to the screen, eager to cite their evidence. After about two minutes of **turn and talk** time, I bring the group back together by counting down, 3, 2, 1.

"I would like to hear from you, but if I call on you, be ready to share something your partner shared with you, so I know that you were being a good listener during your collaboration."

SMOKEY: *There she goes again, strengthening social skills, this time by ramping up the mutual accountability of partners.*

"What did you and your partner see, think, and wonder? I want to remind you that when you share in this way, you can say, 'Something that Matt noticed that I didn't before was . . . Or, my partner wondered something that I did too. We both want to know. . . .'"

As hands go up, I already see kids going back to their sheets and the image to help them back up what they are about to share. I tell them they can go up to the screen and point if they would like to show us precisely what they discussed. Some even look to their partner's sheets as a reminder, because they will be sharing what they heard and learned from them.

> **Sammie:** I see a baby girl.
> **Nikial:** I see a birthday sign.

Jack: I see a baby that has deformed fingers and toes.

Me: Thanks. What is your thinking right now? And that can be in the form of a think or a wonder.

Lousie: Well, I feel sad.

Johann: I am wondering what Apert is because I see it up there.

Ki: I am thinking that this baby might have Apert or something wrong with her because she looks like she is in a hospital in that one picture.

tip!

Edmodo: Kids post what they have learned and peers can ask questions or discuss.

Some kids are pointing and some kids physically get up and go to the screen. It is important for them to be grounded in the image as they navigate their new thoughts. I also know that, for some of my more "active" learners, getting up to go to the screen or board, if even for ten seconds, is helpful for their minds and bodies.

"OK, all of you have something to say, but I want to share a little bit of her story with you so you can get to know her a little more."

I have also loaded the PicCollage image onto **Edmodo**, where they can get a closer look.

 〉 69

Game-Time Decision

With some classes that day, I had kids go directly to it on their iPads as I told the following story. In others, I just kept their attention on the screen and me. With an added piece of technology, their focus shifts dramatically. When we have the projector screen in front of us, we are all accountable to one another. It is powerful to all be in the room together as one shared experience. But for this specific image, there are lots of tiny details the kids could better see on their iPads, zoomed in. So, I did it differently with different groups.

"This is Mary Cate. Mary Cate lives in Chicago and as you can tell, she loves to smile and laugh. She is almost two years old and she was born with something called Apert syndrome. You may have inferred some things about what Apert syndrome means, like it affects her craniofacial features, fingers, and toes. Mary Cate was born with this very rare syndrome and she is the daughter of my very good friends Kerry and Chris. That's Chris in the picture with her. Mary Cate's nicknames are M.C. and Mar and as of this July, she is a new big sister to baby Maggie! The older gentleman in the other picture of Mary Cate is a priest. I know that Kerry comes from a religious background and this is a piece of Mary Cate's identity."

Thinking

64 ⟨

"So we have been talking a lot about identity. From the pictures and my story, if we were going to make an **identity web** for Mary Cate, what are some things we could put on it, based on what you've seen and heard about her so far? Use our identity chart paper on the wall to help you or your minilesson notes in your notebook. Turn back to your buddy and see what you can come up with together."

After some work time, I bring them back as a whole group by counting down and I again ask kids to report what their partner said. "Tell me a piece of Mary Cate's identity that your buddy shared with you or that you came up with together."

I hear all kinds of things: family, birthday parties, blue eyes, happy, Caucasian, she is a big sister, she has Apert syndrome, family, she must be Irish!, her hands and feet may not allow her to walk so well.

"Great list, guys, I like how you were able to notice other things about who she really is, other than her physical differences, because we know that isn't the only part of what makes Mary Cate, Mary Cate!"

Wondering

"Now can you go back to your wonders and really see what kind of list you have. Make sure that everything you are curious about is down there. I'll give you a minute to quietly do this because you just received a ton of new information from everyone around you. If you are stuck on a wonder, I will be around and you can also ask someone near you if they can listen to one of your wonders."

Kids write, look, and confer for another minute.

"OK, great, share out a couple of wonderings with the group."

> **Mila:** I am wondering what her surgery was for in that picture?
> **Margo:** Can she talk?
> **Rocco:** What actually is Apert syndrome and how do you get it? Can anyone get it?
> **Alex:** Will she grow out of it?
> **Me:** You are going to get a chance to find out the answers to all of these questions and to know Mary Cate a little more in just a minute, but first I have a really important question for you. This question is going to take a lot of honesty and bravery on your part. Are you up for the challenge?"

Sharing in a Safe Space

"I want you to think about your true, first reaction to the collage I showed you. What was it? I want you to be honest with yourself, and if you are feeling safe and want to be honest with us, I invite you to do this when you are ready. This is your space where you can share and not be judged for what you are thinking."

SMOKEY: *You're asking kids to take a pretty big emotional risk here. Are they ready for this?*

SARA: *Yes, if we don't rush it. From early in the year, I work to help students to feel safe in our classroom with lessons like Home Court Advantage (pages 94–95), and day-to-day attention to our supportive climate. I also work to get students (and myself) OK with silence. Many of them are quick to put their hands up and blurt something out. But I often tell them to put their hands down and just think in their minds for a while, and then explicitly tell them to raise their hands after about fifteen seconds. At this point in the year, they know to take some time and just be with their thoughts. In the end, this patient approach seems to evoke more thoughtful self-disclosure.*

Some brave hands go up.

> **Matthew:** I immediately thought of my cousin.
> **Catherine:** I felt pretty sad at first looking at her hands and feet.
> **Gabi:** It creeped me out a little at first.

There were a few nods after Gabi said this.

> **Max:** Ya, it makes you uncomfortable to look at.
> **Alex:** Look at that cute baby!
> **Joshua:** Honestly, I didn't even notice it at first; I wondered why we were looking at pictures of a little baby. Then I saw her hands and feet.

"I can't thank you guys enough for sharing. That's tough stuff to admit, but this is the reason why Mary Cate's mom, Kerry, would like to raise awareness. When Mary Cate was an infant, Kerry had an upsetting moment at a park one day when a few kids were being insensitive about the way Mary Cate looks. She knows that people react this way, and that they will for Mary Cate's entire life, but she is working so hard to share Mary Cate's story with classrooms and communities all over in hopes that

tip!

Turn and Talks: If we don't have time to create something to share, we come back to the rug. Kids tell their learning to a buddy next to them, and then I ask each partner to share with everyone what their partner told them. This structure gives kids practice at actively listening to, honoring, and summarizing what others say. When my students are so excited to share some new learning they can get crazy with "me! me! me!" and this helps them chill out and listen.

Mary Cate can be accepted for who she is, not what she looks like. Kerry invites dialogue with her and Mary Cate. Knowing what you now know, you guys are the ones who can continue this work for Kerry and for kids all over like Mary Cate. Rather than looking away or making private comments, you might have some better ideas about how to interact with people who look different."

Beginning Our Inquiry

69 ◀ 🧰

"I posted some links for you on **Edmodo**. One is a blog link called mymarycate.org, and it is a personal blog written by Kerry, Mary Cate's mom. She takes the time to write about their experiences as a family and all about Apert syndrome. Like I said, Kerry is really thoughtful about her audience and works really hard to raise awareness about Mary Cate and other children with Apert syndrome.

"Can anyone share with the rest of us what it means to raise awareness and why Kerry might be working so hard to do this?"

> **Annie:** Maybe she wants people to know about it, so they aren't mean to Mary Cate.
>
> **Me:** Yeah—and that connects back to the story of the playground, as well.
>
> **Mila:** She wants her to have as normal of a life as she can.
>
> **Alex:** So other kids aren't mean to her and get to know her on the inside.

Johann O. • Sep 22, 2013

Aperts syndrome is a very rare defect that can either be transferred from a parent that has Aperts to the child or it can be a or it can be a fresh defect. When someone has Aperts Syndrome the, the effects are that their toes and fingers are binded together. Another mutation is that the skull does'nt grow quick enough to hold the size of te brain. Aperts Syndrome is named after a french physician named E. Apert who first discovered it.

Connor K. • Sep 22, 2013

Apert syndrome is a very rare birth defect that can be inherited or just a fresh defect. Aperture syndrome causes problems to the heart, eyes, figers etc... When you have this your skull is unable to grow and your toes and fingers are fused together. Surgery can be done to separate the fingers and the toes. Also research shows that it is more likely to happen wit an old male.

Rachel L. • Sep 23, 2013

Apert syndrome is a rare birth defect that occurs once out of every 160,000 to 200,000 people. It's a genetic defect/mutation. It affects your cranium/skull, face, fingers, toes ect... Sometimes when your toes are fused together, it affects how you walk. Mary Cate had to get surgery done on her feet so she could walk properly. Also, since your skull plates are fused together and not loosely separated, your head can't grow to its adult size, but the brain keeps on growing. To relieve the skull, you get surgery at an early age to separate te plates in your head. The syndrome is named after E. apert, who described the syndrome less...

Figure 7.7 After viewing the PicCollage and Kerry's blog, kids report their initial findings.

Sydney: Well, we take a lot for granted and always want more, but others don't have what we have, so that's important.

"Awesome. You guys are really starting to think the way Kerry may have in these moments. Let's help her with that work, OK?!

"I know that you are thinking about more things you may want to research from your wonders column about Apert syndrome. I posted a folder of resources for you on your Edmodo accounts, including blog entries, comments, pictures, and videos for you to explore.

"There will be lots of new terms that we learn about Apert as we read. For homework, your goal is to read through some entries on Kerry's blog in addition to one other link about Apert syndrome, and share Mary Cate's story with someone at home. Record what you find out about Apert and Mary Cate in your journals or on **alphaboxes** and also comment right under the links I sent you. This will continue the discussion. You have ten to fifteen minutes now to get started on it, so I can walk around and help you get on the blog site and confer with anyone who needs help with all of these new medical and biological terms."

 › 66

 › 69

Making **Edmodo** available for them to show their new learning is also a way for me to monitor what they were doing at home.

With high-interest, intense work like this, I am reminded of the power of the amygdala. Kids want to do this kind of work because of their high levels of compassion and curiosity. When I assign tasks like research, conversations at home, and reading, I give students time in class first, to ensure their engagement. Of course, I didn't have any trouble getting them into reading Kerry's blog because it is thoughtfully written and designed, with lots of images of Mary Cate and her activities. Kerry also explains a lot of the medical procedures at an understandable level for all

Figure 7.8 Student researching on iPad.

Logan S. • Sep 22, 2013

At first I was shocked. I didn't know what or who I was looking at. As I began reading the article and studying the picture, I realized that this Girl was named Mary Cate and she had Apert Syndrome. I learned that Apert Syndrome is a genetic disease that gives you a fused cranial skull, fused toes, fused fingers and other defects. From their blog, I learned how easy my life is and how much effort her and her family have to accomplish normal tasks. She is one tough cookie. Reading about her made me stop thinking about her as a victim of this disease, and more of a hero more...

Grace B. • Sep 22, 2013

When I first saw the photos I was a little confused. I didn't know what had happened to her or anything about her, like her age. When Ms. Ahmed explained who she was and what happened to her I understood. Now, I sympasize with her and understand that she is just like any other child and that people shouldn't judge her on what she looks like.
I definitely agree with @KateR because she is unique and special she is not weird or different than other people. Everyone is different than each other.

Ava D. • Sep 23, 2013

I remember when I first saw the pictures of Mary Cate. Before I understood Apert Syndrome and how happy and cheerful she was, (don't judge me please) I was a little grossed out by her fingers, toes and facial features. Once I began to read about her and understand how hard her life was, I felt pity. One story on the site was that they were at a park, and 2 little boys said "What a weird and strange baby," Then Mary Cate's mother started to cry. I felt REALLY bad. Now that I have learned about her, and I know that she looks different, I think that we and other people shouldn't just judge a book by its cover. In this case, don't judge Mary Cate because of her Apert Syndrome. less...

Margo L. • Sep 24, 2013

@Sydney I think that she is unique and pretty too. I felt bad too when they boys came up. I also felt bad for them mother

Meghan B. • Sep 24, 2013

Yes Kate I totally agree with you, because you describe Mary-Cate's situation very well.

Maddie C. • Sep 24, 2013

@GraceBoyer On how you said you were confused, I totally felt that way too. and how you said she is just like everybody else and people really shouldn't judge her, which is so true. I just loved what you said and it really seemed like you connected with her and how you understand what is going on with her life.

Nakial C. • Sep 24, 2013

I agree with you Aaron Benedek, Mary Cate she takes it positively

Andrew B. • Sep 24, 2013

@ian lee I was a little freaked out, like you, at the beginning. I like how you said that it was cool that she was unique. I would have never thought of it that way.

Kate R. • Sep 24, 2013

@Meghan Behr I think you explained that really well. I like how you used references from the blog. I also agree with you when you said when she's happy I'm happy and when she's sad I'm sad I feel the same way.

Figure 7.9 Kids posting about their emotional responses to Mary Cate and moving into an active conversation about difference.

of her readers. Now I am comfortable that when the kids go home, their interest is already piqued and there is no uncertainty about where they are going next. Over the next few weeks, I got plenty of comments from parents about how Mary Cate was a big topic of conversation at home.

Day 2: Building Knowledge (45 minutes)

As kids come back to class, there is a good buzz building about Mary Cate and their new knowledge. Some of the kids tell me that they read the blog with their families at home. Others are talking about how many surgeries they realized Marcy Cate has had already. Then there are the few who found the stories that Kerry shared about some unpleasant encounters, such as the playground incident, and were wondering, "How can people be so mean?" At the rug, we talk about all this and I give them a chance to share with a buddy some new knowledge and how they are feeling after reading everything they did the night before.

Thinking About Our Thinking

"I have already heard some great things and I am going to give you a chance to share your thinking about all of this. Can you give me a thumbs-up signal to let me know if your thinking has changed from your first reaction to now?"

Thumbs go up and some go sky-high. "OK, thanks! We are going to show how our thinking changed with some writing on **Edmodo**. I know we all want to share, so this is the best way we can do it and listen to one another at the same time.

"How did your thinking change from first 'seeing' Mary Cate then to reading more about Apert Syndrome and getting to know her family? Be honest but thoughtful about your public writing."

SMOKEY: *I love online discussions too, but you could use other platforms—like pencil and paper—to hold this conversation, right?*

SARA: *Sure. We do this type of dialogue in multiple ways. We can sit down in a circle and have an out-loud group discussion; we can have a written conversation*

Standards Skills:
- Conduct short research projects based on focused questions, demonstrating understanding of the subject under investigation.
- Use technology, including the Internet, to produce writing and to interact and collaborate with others.
- Gather relevant information from multiple print and digital sources.
- Students clarify research questions and evaluate and synthesize collected information.
- Read closely to determine what the text says explicitly and to make logical inferences from it; cite specific textual evidence when writing or speaking to support conclusions drawn from the text.
- Analyze how two or more texts address similar themes or topics in order to build knowledge.

 ›69

on paper, taking turns writing back and forth to partners or small groups; or we can have a silent dialogue on big pieces of chart paper hanging around the room, where I've posted a few guiding questions, and the kids respond quietly on their own, using different colored pens.

For this particular conversation I chose an online discussion, because I know that everyone wants to be heard. I can listen in to everyone at once, and support individuals through conferring as others continue to work. I can assess what they have learned over the inquiry time and how their thinking has changed by reading their entries right then and there, and help those who really need a nudge on how to put their synthesis of knowledge and compassion into words. Everyone has a space and time that they can use to be thoughtful and honest. In this mode, there are no dominant voices, nor the apprehension that can come with speaking while looking a whole group in the eye. Everyone's writing is visible, so all perspectives are heard and the kids become the ultimate facilitators of the discussion.

Kate's response (Figure 7.10) is what every educator in the world is looking for in terms of synthesis of learning. In a short paragraph, she was able to:

- Review the characteristics of informational text.
- Monitor her comprehension.
- Make connections.
- Draw inferences.
- Recognize underlying messages of text to find a theme.
- Take an active role as discussant.
- Go public with her writing.
- Articulate and consider the way her own beliefs, behavior, and thinking changed over time.

This is what I teach for. (Also see Figure 7.11.)

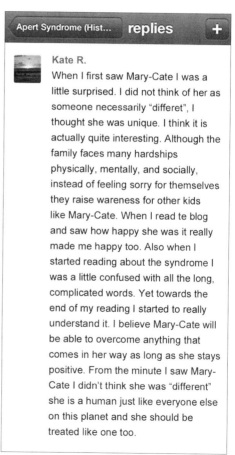

Apert Syndrome (Hist...   **replies**   **+**

Kate R.
When I first saw Mary-Cate I was a little surprised. I did not think of her as someone necessarily "differet", I thought she was unique. I think it is actually quite interesting. Although the family faces many hardships physically, mentally, and socially, instead of feeling sorry for themselves they raise wareness for other kids like Mary-Cate. When I read te blog and saw how happy she was it really made me happy too. Also when I started reading about the syndrome I was a little confused with all the long, complicated words. Yet towards the end of my reading I started to really understand it. I believe Mary-Cate will be able to overcome anything that comes in her way as long as she stays positive. From the minute I saw Mary-Cate I didn't think she was "different" she is a human just like everyone else on this planet and she should be treated like one too.

Figure 7.10 Kate's response.

Reflection and Celebration

We come back to the rug and I have the word *compassion* written on chart paper. On the screen is the feed from their Edmodo posts the night before. I talk to them about how proud I felt to read their posts and how I even shared the screen shots with Kerry.

"After reading and listening to your new knowledge from your inquiry, I have a new word that I think we are all really demonstrating right now: compassion. I want you to turn and talk to a buddy or trio near you about this word. Thinking about Mary Cate: What is it? What do you notice about the word itself?"

After a few minutes of work time, we reconvene. "3, 2, 1, let's bring it back and share what your groups talked about . . . I am going to make a list on the board with some keywords I hear you say."

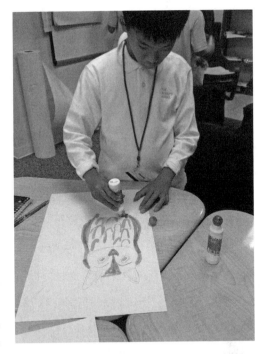

Louise: Well, the word *passion* is in the word *compassion*.

Aaron: To care about someone or something.

Me: Your thinking is right on, guys.

Figure 7.11 Kids spending some time celebrating Mary Cate.

Annika: We can show our helpfulness.

Annie: Well, I think it is like how we felt first and now. Before it was like, we felt sad or bad for her, but now we love that we know her just as a regular kid. We can basically be kind to everyone and not treat them different because of the way they look.

This is our final list from all the classes:

Compassion

    Caring about something or someone

    Passion

    Helpfulness

    Support: Fund raising, walks, bike ride

    Stand up

    Raise awareness

    Runs

    Be friendly!

    Listen!!

    Ask questions

    Be kind

    Don't judge

    Be sensitive

    Empathy

I ask if anyone has any final thoughts. Ava shares from her Edmodo post that she realized when she first saw Mary Cate she felt a little "grossed out" because of the differences, but now she feels like she knows her and that we should never judge a book by its cover.

I ask for a show of hands—who else can honestly say that their thinking changed over the last two days? At first many had an uncomfortable feeling, a feeling of pity, of uneasiness to the eye and heart. But as they took the time to explore their discomfort with inquiry and understanding, their thinking changed—which is what we are always working toward with kids. They did the groundwork for empathy and compassion.

This is not an accident. This is a great group of kids, but this learning experience grows from inquiry work. When students are given opportunities to merge their thinking with content, a huge array of skills is activated. They are connecting, inferring, questioning, determining importance, synthesizing, and reacting to lots of new information. They become active learners, gaining new insight and knowledge of how the world works. From here, the sky is the limit and they can connect their hearts and minds to activate their compassion and advocate or take action. They can say, "What am I going to do about this?"

SMOKEY: *I've been in your classroom enough to know that you are not "brainwashing" any students. But so often people think social-justice-oriented teachers* *are simply imposing their own passions and opinions on kids. What would you say if people read that kind of intention into the Mary Cate story?*

SARA: *Mary Cate's story is about identity and the way people view differences. It could be anyone's story. Anyone that has been teased or ostracized for the way they look; the girl at the cross-country meet. Kids began with a judgment or unfavorable reaction, the way many of us do when we see something that makes us uncomfortable; took time to learn, talk, and write; then began to understand. I did not instill or force compassion into them; it was activated by reading and viewing the story of a little girl that could have been anyone of them. They saw firsthand how we react to differences and, with a safe space and time to digest and wonder, were able to say, yes, I felt this way initially because I was unsure, but now that I have learned, I see things differently.*

"Wow! You guys, I am so proud of these two days we have spent growing from a very new experience. That was really tough heart and mind work. I have a small surprise for you. I called Kerry before all of this and asked her permission to share Mary Cate with you, and she was so thrilled for all of you to learn about her and Apert syndrome. In fact, she was so excited, we thought it would be great for you to meet . . . " I can't even finish my sentence.

(Mouths agape.) "Mary Cate is coming here?"

"Well, not exactly coming here, but Kerry and I thought it would be a great idea to Skype with her so you can meet her from Chicago! Would you like that?"

"Yesssss!!!"

It was like everyone just won the middle school lottery.

"I will take that as a yes! OK, the next period we all have together next week, we will Skype with her. By then, you need to be experts on Apert so you can ask some great questions when we talk with Kerry. With the rest of our time and for homework, I want you to use all of your images, research, reading, new thinking, and alphaboxes to start drafting a paragraph showing that you are a new expert on Apert syndrome and can teach others. Let's use **Kidblog** the same way Kerry uses her blog to raise awareness about Apert and Mary Cate. We want to be upstanders for Mary Cate, the same way she is."

Standards Skills:
- Produce clear and coherent writing in which the development, organization, and style are appropriate to task, purpose, and audience.
- Write informative/ explanatory texts to examine and convey complex ideas and information clearly and accurately through the effective selection, organization, and analysis of content.
- Use technology, including the Internet, to produce and publish writing and to interact and collaborate with others.

 58

Louise S.

Aperts Syndrome can cause deformities to a child. Deformities such as, fused fingers and toes, fused cranial structures, and a retruded midface. Aperts Syndrome is very rare as the article states it has been seen in only 86 people. The condition can be inherited by a parent or be a fresh mutation. One little girl, Mary Catherine Lynch, and her family have been affected by the Syndrome. Mary Cate has been through many surgeries to help fix some of the deformities she has. She and her family are very optimistic about her condition. Mary Cate and her family would love if you could spread the word about Aperts.

Matthew A.

Apert Syndrome is a condition that makes the fingers of the hands and the toes of the feet to become fused together at birth, and a retruded midface. The normal skull is made of many plates loosely connected to each other, to allow space for the brain to grow. But Apert Syndrome causes premature fusion of the skull plates, putting pressure on the brain as it ages. This, by the way, is called *craniosynostosis*. All these symptoms, plus many smaller other ones, can greatly effect people and families that have it. One example would be the young Mary Cate and her mom and dad. When Mary was born, her parents were horrified. But they were still loving to her, despite her appearance. Mary underwent many surgeries, which scared her mommy and daddy greatly because she was so young and having operations already. Many normal kids have already said pretty mean things to her when she is playing in the park. It saddens Mary's parents, but it also strengthens them to make the world a better place. As L. R. Knost said, "It's not our job to toughen our children up to face a cruel and heartless world. It's our job to raise children who will make the world a little less cruel and heartless."

> **tip!**
>
> **Kidblog:** A blog site that works in a feed form similar to Edmodo. Students can have ownership of their blog entry, titling it something great, and others can comment on this as well.

Sammie S.

Bravery, trust, and family is what makes Mary Cate. Mary Cate is a baby girl who has a special condition called Aperts Syndrome. Aperts Syndrome is a condition where if you have it is causes deformites, cranial problems, and fused body parts. Mary Cate has gone through a lot. She has many surgeries, and after the surgeries her eyes swell shut. Aperts Syndrome makes it harder for a child to learn things. Mary Cate's family is very supportive of her and they mean the world to her. Aperts Syndrome is sometimes passed on by a parents genetic, or it's usually just random. A parent with Aperts has a fifty percent chance to have a kid that also has this condition. For some odd reason studies show that Aperts is more likely to occur if you have an older father. Aperts affects the family of the kid because it is very stressful, and difficult because they have to accept that their child has to go through many operations and they have to try not to get frustrated with them. They will also probably have to help a lot with regular things. Aperts Syndrome is a condition that gives kids cranial problems and other side affects.

Day 3: Skype Day (20 minutes)

The kids literally come in barrel-rolling over each other to get a seat near the screen to meet our new celebrity. I calm all sixty of them (the whole grade level is with us) and remind them a little bit about how Skype works so they are mindful of sound, movement, and the time difference between Chicago and San Diego. (It was Mary Cate's nap-time, but her mom kept her up for us!)

Figure 7.12 Skype screenshot with Mary Cate in corner.

Mary Cate came on screen in her highchair, ready to meet sixty new friends. I asked kids to develop some good interview questions ahead of time, and had them email them to me. I chose five kids to ask Kerry their question if they were comfortable.

- Is Mary Cate always happy and [does she] love being a big sister?
- What is the hardest part of being a parent of a child with Apert syndrome?
- Do you talk to Mary Cate about her operations?
- What does she like to do and play with?
- What is next for Mary Cate?

 69

Kerry is an expert at fielding questions and making people feel validated for asking them. She is honest, does not hide any information, and is great at making connections with her audience. When kids asked about what Mary Cate plays with, she connected to the kids by saying, "The same things that you played with when you were one and two." She then shared some of her favorite toys. Kerry included Mary Cate in the dialogue as well, sharing her sign language capabilities with us.

Standards Skills:
- Use comprehension skills to listen attentively to others in formal and informal settings.
- Participate productively in discussions, conversations, and collaborations with diverse partners.

After the Skype date, we quickly turned and talked and then shared out:

"I can't believe how good she was; my little sister would never sit still for that long!"

"I think it is so cool that she can sign!"

After the conversation, Kerry sent me a message to let me know Mary Cate kept signing, "Please, please, please" when we hung up. As in, *please* see the kids again.

We all felt the same.

What Did This Mini-Inquiry Accomplish?

My goals for the first few weeks of school are to make sure that the students explore their own identities and connect more closely with others. With that comes a ton of groundwork, and it begins with creating the space where they can be honest in their thoughts, handle strong feelings, and work with others by listening. This lesson certainly accomplished those goals.

However, I also took a risk with this lesson. I knew that if I wanted my students to become upstanders, I needed to address the incident at the cross-country meet. But I didn't know what to do at first, and ended up doing it indirectly with Mary Cate. If I had been playing it safe, I might have structured this more tightly or let the pressure of addressing all of our curriculum, textbook, and testing goals convince me to skip the issue altogether. As teachers, we often wonder, "How will I get through the book? I only get through the end of the Reconstruction every year!" But if we let these worries dictate what we do, we miss opportunities for life-changing learning.

During this inquiry, the students spoke to each other, wrote for a public audience, and listened. I was never their primary audience: they were doing authentic work in the world. More than anything, they responded to each other as human beings. They were honest, they were vulnerable, and they owned it. That can't be measured. They were able to articulate how their thinking changed and how they are better human beings for it. It is a slow and careful transformation to become an upstander, one that we cannot race through. But they are on the journey.

As this book goes to press, we should note that Mary Cate has become quite a national celebrity as she teaches the world to #*ChooseKind*. Coordinating with the Twitter hashtag of R. J. Palacio's YA best seller, *Wonder,* Kerry and Mary Cate have visited over forty classrooms this year introducing Apert syndrome to kids around the Chicagoland area and discussing the novel. Her new baby sister, Maggie, even shows her support by joining her on this mission. Kerry often describes her initial choice: to either hide Mary Cate from the world or to give her as normal of a life as possible. She chose the latter and we are a better society for it.

What About the Required Curriculum?

Inquiry learning can feel so emotionally powerful that we overlook how well it meets academic standards. This lesson is an example of how students are achieving our highest goals for them, with plenty of vigor—and academic rigor to boot. From the minute we began this lesson, students were selecting and analyzing multiple genres of informational text. They were notetaking, comparing, and discussing what they perceive when they listen or read closely, and when they watch. They cited evidence from text, both visual and narrative, and made inferences based on that evidence. Kids were able to integrate information provided in different media as well as in words. In reading a piece of authentic writing, Kerry's blog, they were able to analyze her rhetoric and point of view. They navigated a short research project to answer questions they had, drawing from multiple sources. In their subsequent writing, kids were able to use technology as a means to produce and publish writing, while also collaborating and learning from one another.

I think that when my kids encounter other unique, complex situations—inside school and out—they will be better able to understand, investigate, judge, reflect, care, and act humanely.

Curricular Inquiries

Now comes our teaching bread and butter. Curricular inquiry is the structure we use to transform whole chunks of required subject matter into energizing, kid-driven investigations. Remember we said earlier that inquiry teaching means turning required curriculum into questions that young adolescents cannot resist answering. That's what these content-based units can do.

SMOKEY: *Readers, this would be a good moment to stop and think of a specific unit that's coming up very soon in your own teaching. Your choice could be science, social studies, literature—any topic subject that requires several days to a couple weeks of teaching and learning. As this chapter unfolds, keep your pending unit firmly in mind, so you can see how Sara's ideas might translate to your own planning and teaching.*

We cannot teach everything—and deep inquiry learning takes time. Of course, sometimes we *do* try to teach everything. In fact, American schools have long been trapped in a "coverage" mind-set, where teachers try to cram tons of content down kids' gullets when there is little chance of their understanding or remembering the material. Smokey calls this phenomenon the "Curriculum of Mentioning," because we fantasize that mentioning ideas to children is the same thing as building knowledge. In our hearts, we know that kids will forget most of this "covered" content about one minute after—or sometimes before—the big test on Friday. With the weekend comes oblivion.

So as inquiry teachers, as middle level educators, we have to think carefully and decide scrupulously what's worth kids' time. We need to be picky about what topics we teach and how long we spend on each one. As Smokey, Steve Zemelman, and Arthur Hyde report in *Best Practice* (2012), many prominent subject matter organizations, from the American Association for the Advancement of Science to the National Council of Teachers of Mathematics, have repudiated the coverage model. Instead, they want students to go deeper into a smaller number of topics. The Next Generation Science Standards say that kids should experience a limited number of robust scientific investigations during which they experience how scientists actually think, hypothesize, develop experiments, gather data, and draw conclusions (2013). Students should not just read a single bland history textbook—they should work like historians, triangulating a broad array of primary and secondary source documents, sifting through different accounts, deciding what counts as evidence, and asking whose voices appear in the record and whose are left out.

So what do we choose to teach well and deeply? If you happen to be a fan of Grant Wiggins and Jay McTighe's *Understanding by Design* (2005), you know that they suggest four "screens" or questions to ask when we are deciding what's worth teaching:

1. Does the subject reside at the heart of the discipline? Can you really understand the field if you don't understand this?
2. Is the topic subject to misconceptions? Will learners suffer if they don't have their misconceptions corrected by studying this?
3. Is the subject authentic and relevant to life as we live it?
4. Is the subject interesting and engaging to learners?

We really appreciate that in Grant and Jay's model, all other things being equal, you teach the stuff that's interesting to kids.

SMOKEY: *Sara, how do you decide what to teach, what big units to devote your limited time to? How much freedom have you had in your schools?*

SARA: *Teachers never have enough time, and sometimes, there are too many choices! We have big curriculum maps spanning multiple units, countless objectives, and endless standards we "need to get through" between August and June. We are given district targets, scope and sequence guides, textbooks, workbooks, unit plans, units in tubs, professional texts to model our teaching upon—it's quite an endeavor. In the schools where I've taught, there's been ample room for teachers to take curricular initiative, but only when we have made very intentional choices, backed those decisions with research, and really shown ourselves to be experts in our field.*

I choose my units by planning with my grade-level or departmental teams. For the classes where I am essentially an island, teaching the subject matter alone, I always go back to the kids. I study the units that are designated to my grade level, then I rebuild them to put students' curiosity first.

SMOKEY: *OK, sounds like you are trading breadth for depth, taking your kids deeper into a smaller number of topics. But still, inquiry learning activities take more class hours and days than textbook readings and teacher lectures, no matter how ineffective those are. How do you get everything done?*

SARA: *Sometimes inquiry is infused throughout the unit, as in the example coming up in this chapter. The whole unit is designed around small-group inquiries where kids jigsaw the content and end up teaching each other. As readers will see, I don't spend much time presenting. Instead I truly do* facilitate. *I have to find great materials—articles, documents, images; develop tools, like various planning forms and thinksheets, that help organize kids' investigations; and create structures within which kids can think and learn. And then, when we "go live," I have to manage, counsel, and coach the never-entirely-predictable process of kids' investigations.*

This is a shift from the control and predictability we sometimes prefer in our classrooms, but a far more valuable experience for kids. With some other units, I take a more active information-giving role. I lay out essential ideas of a subject but as we learn together, we carefully keep track of what we wonder along the way. I have already built in time, either along the way or at the end, for kids to address these personal questions and curiosities.

I'll say something like, "Hey! We have learned so much about ancient Egypt, but you guys asked so many great questions along the way that we just couldn't get to! Now, let's take some time to get those answered." Then I give kids the space to be the engineers of their own wonders and research; they have watched me model how to do it for weeks, so they are totally ready! I am careful to document everything kids do, so I can reflect on what worked and what didn't, and adjust my planning for the next time.

So, yes, I do set common goals with colleagues and with the required curriculum, but I also synchronize with the kids. As they develop their inquiries, I try to provide the space they need. If my students want to take action and advocate for other kids in crisis, as they did in our inquiry about Syria, I am going to make time for it, because we value reaching out as a community of learners.

SMOKEY: *Thanks—that's a complicated balancing act for sure.*

SARA: *So to pick up where we left off, yes, I'm down with Wiggins and McTighe's "screens" for worthwhile content. I also have a couple of my own:*

- *Have the kids already posed questions or shown curiosity about the topic?*
- *Is the topic rich and complex?*
- *Can learners disagree or debate?*
- *Are interpretation and analysis required, with different facets to be explored?*
- *Are there moral and social values in question?*
- *Are there decisions to be made? Positions to be supported? Action to be taken?*
- *Can there be multiple outcomes, understandings, or solutions?*

As I planned for our required curriculum unit on immigration and industrialization in seventh grade, I found myself going right down this list and being able to check everything off. Inquiry ready!

Curricular Inquiry: Immigration and Industrialization

Day 1 (60 minutes)

Industrialization, and the social ills that often accompany it, especially for recent immigrants, is a key unit in our history curriculum. While I want kids to learn the broad concepts of these dynamic, interactive processes, I also want them to feel the tremendous impact such changes can have on flesh and blood human beings. Therefore, the key event we'll study is the Triangle Shirtwaist Factory fire in New York in 1911.

Building Background from the Textbook

To begin the unit, I had kids read a section in our textbook (I do use it sometimes!) about population density, poverty, and child labor in India and China. When we gathered on the rug to talk about it, the students immediately personalized the plight of kids their own age (and younger). We started to question the social and moral implications of rapid industrialization. Adolescents have a strong desire to connect events to their own place in this world, and that's just what we began doing. The kids' comments and questions showed both their interest and their readiness for further study. I primed the discussion with a bit of my own thinking:

> ### Standards Skills:
> - Determine what the text says explicitly and make logical inferences from it.
> - Determine central ideas or themes of a text.

"I wondered as I was reading this chapter, are children going to school or just working? I always read articles where it seems some children don't go to school because they need to earn money for the family."

> **Ellie:** There aren't any laws protecting the children, probably.
>
> **Annie:** I agree, I think if that were here, people would wonder why the kids aren't in school and get really upset. I think that's against the law here.
>
> **Layne:** Piggybacking off Annie and Ellie, do you think that there are places in America or Mexico that do it, but secret, and we just don't know about it?

I could immediately see that the topic provoked kids' curiosity and would involve values, decisions, and perhaps even action on their part. Industrialization was ripe for inquiry.

"So we are learning that there are not always protections for workers around the world. Some of you said that we don't have that issue here because we have laws protecting us. Some of you weren't sure if that's true here or not. Well, we do have something called *labor unions* here that protect our workers. There were some really brave people who paved the way for us to be able to work or go to school in safe and healthy conditions. But where did they come from, how did they start, and how effective are they?"

Written Conversation

"I am going to send you back to your tables in a minute. You'll find a collection of images waiting for you: a political cartoon, a newspaper headline, a photograph, and a diagram." These images offer a range of biased and unbiased perspectives, and are good examples of how readers gather research. I show kids how each picture is centered on a sheet of paper, leaving a wide margin for them to write in and then pass around their groups. "You're going to read these images and have a **silent dialogue** around the photos on the paper provided. Everybody use a different color pen so we can see who writes what, OK?"

We have worked earlier in the year on reading images, aka "visual literacy." The same strategies that the kids use in reading literature and nonfiction text—inferring, questioning, determining importance, asking questions—can be used to read images. Now, kids take their colored pen of choice and go to work, observing, thinking, wondering, connecting to one another, and sharing ideas in a written conversation that allows even the shyest of kiddos to share without hesitation.

Game-Time Decision

Depending on the number of students in a group, or class-specific management needs, I have two variations of this activity.

1. All students at a table simultaneously write on one big piece of chart paper, and each sheet rotates from table to table around the room until everyone has seen and commented on each image. See Figures 8.1–8.3. That means there is a single different image on each large poster.

2. The mini-version: I have smaller papers, each with an image (at least one page for each kid at a table and the same set on each table), and kids write their thoughts, then carousel them around the table within their own group.

As they scan through images, kids gradually begin silently writing basic questions and observations on the papers.

- Where is this?
- It is just women and children.
- Was it the fire in the diagram that killed people?
- I notice the cartoon says 'murdered.'
- Was it on purpose?
- Their clothes are fancy.

Figure 8.1 Tana, Val, and Jina examine a primary source during their silent dialogue.

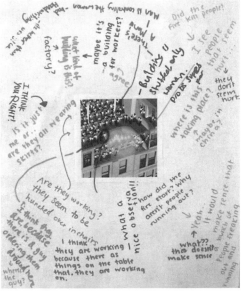

Figures 8.2 and 8.3 By the time groups finish, papers are covered in questions, connections, and thoughtful conversation.

The kids' interest is activated, they have a ton of questions, and they want answers. After about ten minutes, kids come back to the rug. I ask them to share some comments they read or wrote themselves during the silent dialogues.

Layne: So, someone noticed this is New York from the article photo?! Is that what those pictures are? That happened here?

Scotty: So we had factories in the U.S. like the ones we read about in India and China?

69 ‹ 🧰

"While you guys were writing, I walked around and tried to join as many conversations as I could, and noticed you all picked up on the tragedy of the fire and some of you even pointed out the word *murder*. These images and articles are from an event called the Triangle Shirtwaist Factory fire, and yes, it did happen in America.

"Tonight your homework is to investigate a little further. I have posted some articles to **Edmodo** on a new 'Triangle Research Page.' So have a look at these pieces, and then do some investigating on your own. See if you can find some interesting articles and post them to the page as well. This will become a collaborative resource-building page for all of us to share from." (See Figure 8.4.)

SMOKEY: *I love that Sara is basically crowd-sourcing research materials from her class. Sometimes teachers fear inquiry because they think they must find every single article and resource all by themselves, before the unit even starts. Why not let a gang of eager co-researchers help you out? Let the kids do some of the digging. But then, of course, you have to carefully scrutinize and vet what the kids come up with, as Sara models next.*

From the posts I see that evening (and into the next morning), I can tell that the kids were not just grabbing URLs, but scanning and evaluating potential resources first. Kids need to know how to be critical consumers of the resources they are being offered. This searching for articles and resources also helps students surface background information they may already have, preparing them to connect upcoming new information to their existing schema.

Standards Skills:
- Integrate content presented in diverse formats, including visually.

Standards Skills:
- Determine what the text says explicitly and make logical inferences from it.
- Determine central ideas or themes of a text.
- Use technology, including the Internet, to produce writing and to interact and collaborate with others.
- Draw evidence from literary or informational texts to support analysis, reflection, and research.

Figure 8.4 Kids dialogue on Edmodo about their sources and their overall evaluation of them.

70

Day 2: Deeper Reading of Nonfiction Resources (90 minutes)
Read-Aloud

As kids come into class, I am mindful of their questions from the previous days and am prepared with different resources to model how to listen, view, read, and talk about the historic event we encountered yesterday. Students already have some questions they are curious about, so I am ready to show them how to interact with and code text to determine the important details. We meet on the rug and they have their journals and pencils, ready to listen to a read-aloud and then annotate an article with me.

"Good morning, guys. When I first read our textbook chapters about immigration and industrialization, I immediately connected it to a historical novel, Margaret Peterson Haddix's *Uprising*. This book tells of an event that happened to immigrants to America in the early 1900s. There are three girls in this story: One is an Italian immigrant. One is a Russian immigrant. One is a very wealthy New Yorker. The event that brings them together is the Triangle Shirtwaist Factory strike and the tragic event that follows. One of my favorite things about this novel is that the identity of the narrator is a complete mystery. The story is told through one of the girls' perspectives, but the reader doesn't know until the end. Let me read you an excerpt that connects to the images we viewed and wrote about yesterday."

> "He won't talk about the fire," Harriet says. "He'd like to pretend it never happened."
>
> Mrs. Livingston can believe this.
>
> "Read the newspapers, then," Mrs. Livingston says.
>
> There were plenty of stories written at the time.
>
> Mrs. Livingston herself has not read any of them. She couldn't, back them. But she is always amazed at how much other people know because of the papers: girls who were away at Vassar or Bryn Mawr or Smith in 1911, who can recite the exact number of the dead; women who spent their 1911 all but chained to sewing machines in other factories in the city, who can describe exactly how the flames leaped from table to table, from floor to floor. "I've already read the papers," Harriet says . . . "But it's not enough. The newspaper stories are just paper and ink. It's easy to think it's not real. I want . . . flesh and blood."

I put down the book and am immediately attacked with pleas to "keep reading!" (The secret is to stop on "flesh and blood.") I let them know the book is in the library if they want to check it out. One of the kids slyly pulls my copy from right beside my chair and reads aloud the next section. "Civil disobedience!" Then three others call "Next!"

I know the energy is high, but I want to sneak a minilesson in here. I quickly model one of my own text connections, to reinforce their thinking.

"I have a connection . . . I know that Smith, Vassar, and Bryn Mawr are women's colleges because I remember my neighbor from when I was younger went to Smith. She was a sweet older lady that I sort of considered my grandmother, and she had a diploma on her wall from Smith and used to tell me stories about it. I hadn't known there were all-female colleges back then."

I keep it quick because I don't want to take away from their excitement about the subject, but connect to the students by telling them Smith is actually still all-female. "Why don't you guys turn and talk about what you are thinking."

I lean in and eavesdrop on some of their discussions. I overhear talk of the pages I read aloud to them:

Standards Skills:
• Read closely to determine what the text says explicitly and to make logical inferences from it; cite specific textual evidence when writing or speaking.

- Who is Mrs. Livingston? Is she a real person from the fire?
- How many people died, you think?
- The chains reminded me of slaves.
- I wonder what the flesh is all about?
- Sounds like a gruesome fire.
- My great-grandma went to Vassar I think, but I'll ask my mom.

Now we narrow down our curricular inquiry journey to focus just on the Triangle Shirtwaist Factory fire, and all the events, people, and social movements related to it. Of course the big story is about labor, capital, management—huge issues worldwide and throughout history. But I don't want kids to view these issues as just an international problem, about kids in India or China. The fire happened right here in America. I also want them to *feel* as well as understand the event. I draw in their hearts and minds with powerful images, a gripping read-aloud of historical fiction, and high-interest nonfiction articles and images. With their curiosity now activated, we can go deeper.

Think-Aloud with Annotation

When I call the kids back to whole group from their turn and talks, I have an article about the Triangle Fire projected from the document camera, and I also pass out copies. To model good close-reading strategies, I'll do a **think-aloud**, during which I will share my own thinking as I go, leaving tracks of my thinking in **text annotations**. I get kids ready to read the first section along with me, pencil in hand, and later I will release them to practice these strategies on their own.

> 60

> 72

"Hold on to the questions and ideas you just came up with in your pairs. We will be weaving them in shortly. Now, as I read this piece, I'm going to try to notice the language and word choice that the author is using, to question the text, and also to think about the people mentioned in this article—their race, class, gender. I am going to see if there are any heartstrings being pulled by the author as well. You can do the same with your wonders. (See Figure 8.5.) Stop me if something

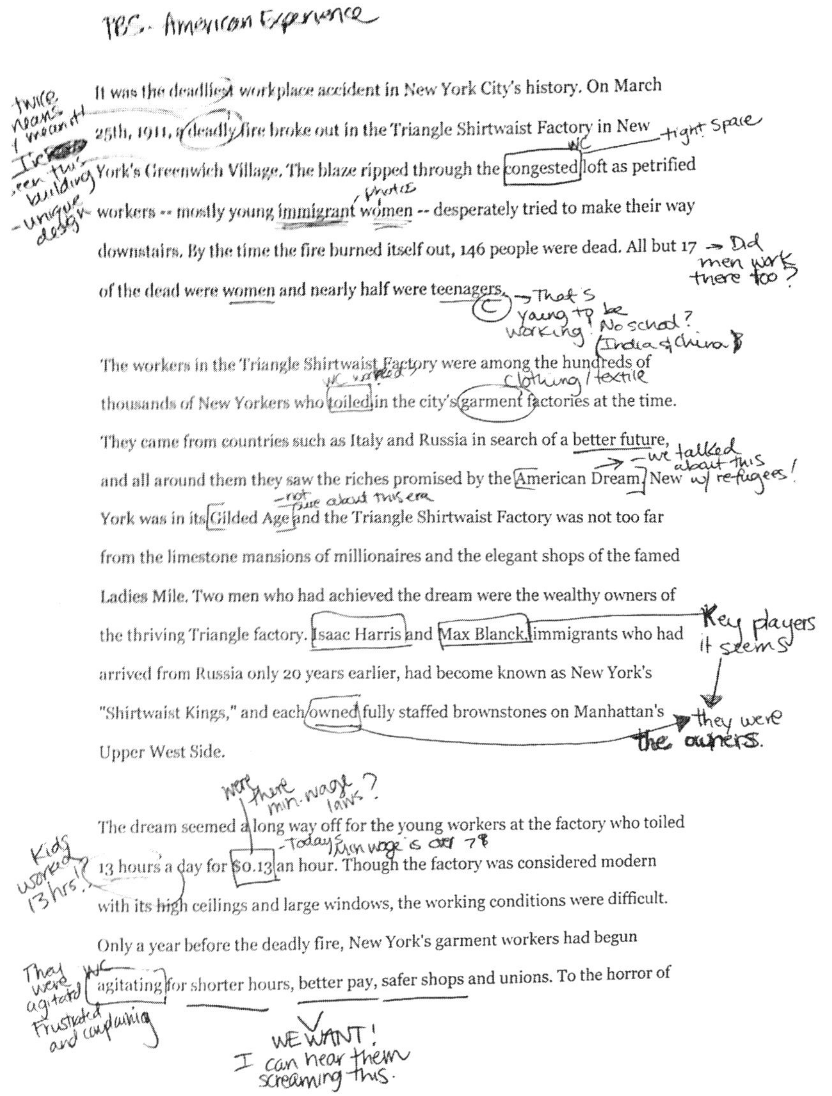

PBS. American Experience

It was the deadliest workplace accident in New York City's history. On March 25th, 1911, a deadly fire broke out in the Triangle Shirtwaist Factory in New York's Greenwich Village. The blaze ripped through the congested loft as petrified workers -- mostly young immigrant women -- desperately tried to make their way downstairs. By the time the fire burned itself out, 146 people were dead. All but 17 of the dead were women and nearly half were teenagers.

The workers in the Triangle Shirtwaist Factory were among the hundreds of thousands of New Yorkers who toiled in the city's garment factories at the time. They came from countries such as Italy and Russia in search of a better future, and all around them they saw the riches promised by the American Dream. New York was in its Gilded Age and the Triangle Shirtwaist Factory was not too far from the limestone mansions of millionaires and the elegant shops of the famed Ladies Mile. Two men who had achieved the dream were the wealthy owners of the thriving Triangle factory. Isaac Harris and Max Blanck, immigrants who had arrived from Russia only 20 years earlier, had become known as New York's "Shirtwaist Kings," and each owned fully staffed brownstones on Manhattan's Upper West Side.

The dream seemed a long way off for the young workers at the factory who toiled 13 hours a day for $0.13 an hour. Though the factory was considered modern with its high ceilings and large windows, the working conditions were difficult.

Only a year before the deadly fire, New York's garment workers had begun agitating for shorter hours, better pay, safer shops and unions. To the horror of

Figure 8.5 As I read the text during our shared reading, I model and annotate my own thinking.

comes up that you just talked about. And remember what we always say, the best readers ask questions. Ask questions of the text, of the author, and the event. We will do this together as well."

Guided and Independent Practice

Now I invite kids to continue annotating this article back at their seats. I remind them to look for powerful language, the people who are mentioned, and the answers to any questions they already have. And of course, to ask even more questions. I move around the room as they work and generally sit with a couple of kiddos, either because they need the extra support, I can tell they are having a tough day, they may need help to stay on track, or because I simply haven't been able to spend time with them lately. Others work on their own.

We come back to the rug and discuss questions that were answered and more questions that arose during the reading. I write on the board as they talk, putting kids' initials right beside their thoughts. These conversations also begin to naturally reveal groups of students who have the same wonders or interpretations about this complex and ethically rich topic. Questions are arising about key figures mentioned in the article, in particular the factory owners, Harris and Blanck. Some of the kids are suspicious.

> **Allie:** How come in the article when it says, "Harris and Blanck were notified by phone and escaped," they didn't tell their own factory workers?! Don't you think they would want to save them, too?
>
> **Kiara:** I was wondering the same thing! Who just leaves and doesn't warn other people? Something isn't right there, and the article already says they were basically pretty stingy.
>
> **Me:** Kiara, can you share that part? What makes you infer that they were "stingy"?
>
> **Kiara:** (*Reads aloud*) ". . . the Triangle bosses organized other owners and refused to surrender, paying prostitutes and police to beat the strikers." Kiara continues, "Triangle owners finally agreed to higher wages and shorter hours. But they drew the line at a union."
>
> **Me:** Thanks for sharing that evidence. It helps us see your claim of them being "stingy" better.
>
> **Kiara:** I literally wrote "STINGY" in all caps right next to it!

Standards Skills:
- Determine what the text says explicitly and make logical inferences from it.
- Determine central ideas or themes of a text.
- Draw evidence from literary or informational texts to support analysis, reflection, and research.
- Analyze how two or more texts address similar themes or topics in order to build knowledge.

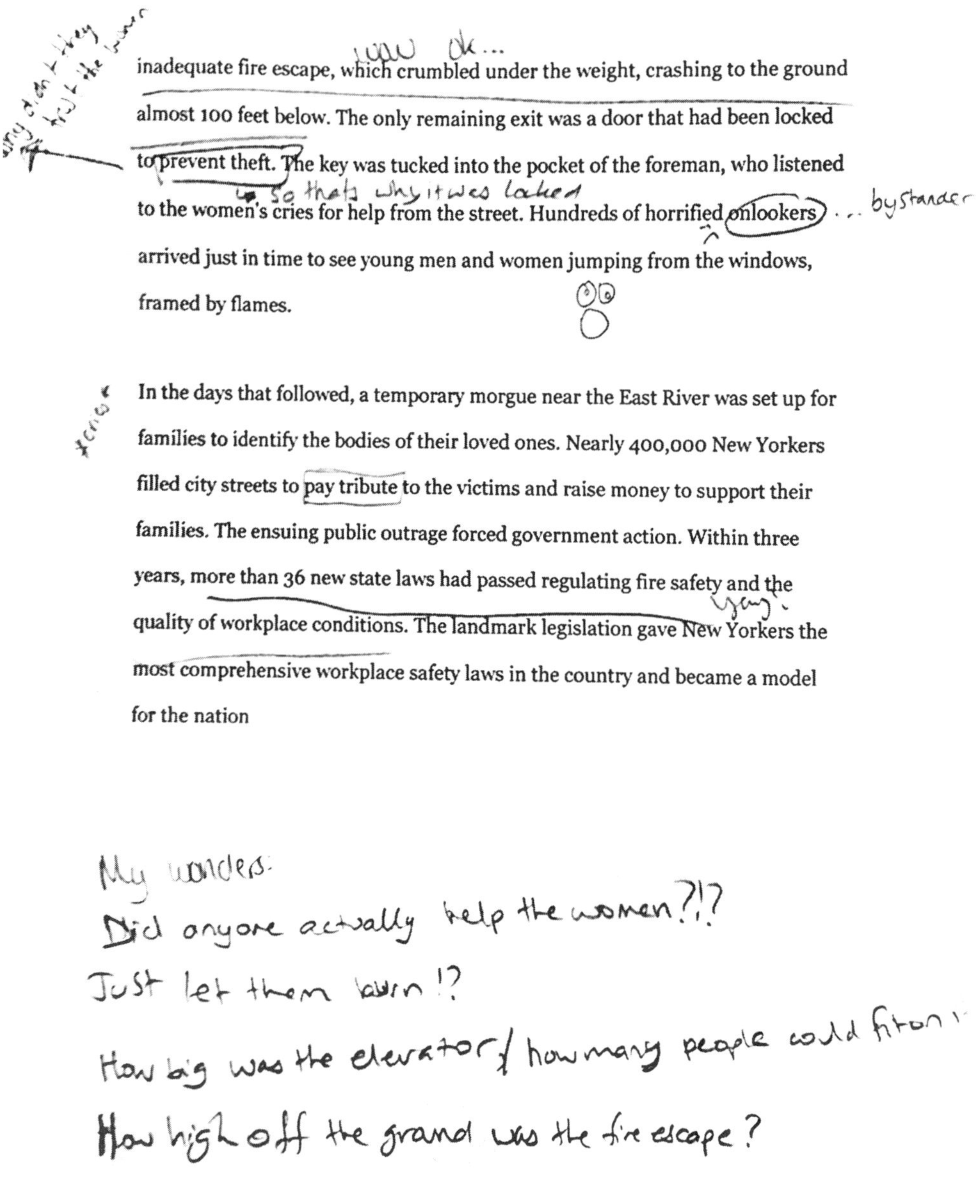

inadequate fire escape, which crumbled under the weight, crashing to the ground *wow ok...*

almost 100 feet below. The only remaining exit was a door that had been locked

to prevent theft. The key was tucked into the pocket of the foreman, who listened

so that's why it was locked

to the women's cries for help from the street. Hundreds of horrified onlookers ... *bystander*

arrived just in time to see young men and women jumping from the windows,

framed by flames.

In the days that followed, a temporary morgue near the East River was set up for

families to identify the bodies of their loved ones. Nearly 400,000 New Yorkers

filled city streets to pay tribute to the victims and raise money to support their

families. The ensuing public outrage forced government action. Within three

years, more than 36 new state laws had passed regulating fire safety and the

yay?

quality of workplace conditions. The landmark legislation gave New Yorkers the

most comprehensive workplace safety laws in the country and became a model

for the nation

My wonders:
Did anyone actually help the women?!?
Just let them burn!?
How big was the elevator / how many people could fit on:
How high off the ground was the fire escape?

Figure 8.6 One student's annotations and question building from the second section of the article.

Harry: I have heard the word *union* before, but what is it again? Also, what is a shirtwaist? I remember when you told us about the teachers' union at your old school being on strike.

Me: Great questions, Harry, and good memory! Let's talk that one out together. Think of just the word *union*; what does it mean? Maybe the article can help us. Turn and talk with someone.

Jina: It means you are like, together.

Iberia: (*Showing with her hands clasped*) Like together, like a marriage is a union. So when they use it in the article, it must mean that they needed to come together to get these rights.

Tana: If you read right before it, it talks about wages, time, and being fair so it must mean they are coming together as workers to make things better for them.

Me: Thanks for going back to the article, Tana.

Ellie: I want to piggyback off Tana and just add that when Ibi and I were talking, we said that marriage is like a union and you are together and have the same interests and stuff, and you are better as a pair than just one person. Stronger. My grandpa used to be part of a union for his electrical business and he organized the meetings for all the workers. It definitely is a group that works together.

Me: Awesome, guys. Thinking together like this helps us dig deeper into all this new information. It must mean that the workers have some power too, because Harris and Blanck "drew the line at a union," didn't they? Like they didn't want the employees to organize around their common interests.

In Chicago, my friends in the teachers' union went on strike last year because there were some things in their working conditions at school, both for the kids and themselves, that they didn't agree with. As a collective group, they stood up and said that they were not happy and there needed to be a change. Unions also make sure that one person, like a factory owner, doesn't have too much power over a group.

I am seeing some natural groupings forming for a deeper inquiry into this event. Some of you want to know about Harris and Blanck, some of you want to know more about Anne Morgan. We all want to know more about this fire, and it seems like we can get the answers from the key actors of this

Standards Skills:

- Determine what the text says explicitly and make logical inferences from it.
- Determine central ideas or themes of a text.
- Draw evidence from literary or informational texts to support analysis, reflection, and research.
- Analyze how two or more texts address similar themes or topics in order to build knowledge.
- Listen attentively to others in formal and informal settings.
- Participate effectively in a range of conversations and collaborations, building on others' ideas and expressing their own clearly and persuasively.

story. Let's look at the board together and see where people are matching up about their wonders.

Annie: Who is T.A.?

Tana: That's me!

Annie: OK, sorry. Layne, Tana, and I all want to know more about Anne Morgan.

Sahil: If we are choosing, then I want to know more about Harris and Blanck, if anyone is interested in that.

Me: It looks like Scotty, Harry, and Kiara all want to know more about those "stingy" guys, as Kiara put it. Does that sound good to you?

They all nod, but Kiara grimaces a bit at the thought of working with all the boys.

Me: Is that too much, Kiara?

Kiara: No, I can handle it.

Me: Thanks. Keep them in line.

Kiara: I will! I got this, Ms. Ahmed.

SMOKEY: *Using humor and banter with kids can work well—but only when you get the tone just right. You have to know them really well. Here, Sara is "kidding on the straight" about some difficulties these kids might have being grouped together. She cajoles Kiara into partnering with some boys who can be challenging. Sara draws on her own playfulness as she jokingly cautions Kiara to keep the boys in line. The boys enjoy being labeled as mini-troublemakers. This allows all the kids to accept the challenge, and go into the work with awareness of the possible pitfalls.*

Choice Articles (45 minutes)

As our conversation continues, Loren says, "I noticed there were some other women mentioned in the articles someone posted to Edmodo. It's not on the list, though." I'm glad she has noticed. I tell her, "That's OK. I have four biographical articles for you on Anne Morgan, Harris and Blanck, Clara Lemich, and Pauline Neuman. Those last two, we haven't learned as much about them yet. Let me give you some background.

> Clara Lemlich was a fighter. She wrote opinion articles in the paper, organized picket lines and protests, and motivated women all over the city. She was like total Girl Power! She said: "I am one of those who are on strike against intolerable conditions. I am tired of listening to speakers who talk in general terms. What we are here for is to decide whether we shall strike or shall not strike. I offer a resolution that a general strike be declared now."

Pauline Newman started working in the factory when she was eight years old, working seventy to eighty hours a week for $1.50 in wages. Meanwhile, she secretly taught herself to read and write in English [she grew up in Lithuania]. Pauline eventually became an important member of the union movement and went on to work with First Lady Eleanor Roosevelt. "All we knew," Newman wrote in a letter, "was the bitter fact that after working 70 or 80 hours in a seven-day week, we did not earn enough to keep body and soul together." (PBS 2013)

I also do a quick talk to highlight the other articles on Anne Morgan and Harris and Blanck.

"OK, we have some good background knowledge on the strike and the fire. We have already examined and posted tons of resources, but now we are going to go even deeper in our groups to see who the real perpetrators, victims, bystanders, and upstanders are in this story. The articles may lead us to the answers we are looking for: how this all came about, and who was responsible for the poor working conditions and the fire itself."

I copy each article in a different color for easy management. I give kids a minute to think about their choices. The historical figures' names are on the board so kids have a visual reminder of their options. Now it's time for some **guided practice**.

 ❯ 61

"These are your goals for the rest of the class period and for homework:

1. Group yourself with three other buddies who chose different people (a different color article).
2. Each person in the group reads and annotates their own article. How is this individual introduced to you? What type of person do they seem to be? What was their specific role in Triangle? Be sure to mark specific passages that give you key information about your chosen character.
3. Everyone in your group needs information on all four key players.

Key Actor and Characteristics	Connection to Fire/Factory	Questions I Would Ask

Figure 8.7 Chart for deeper reading of biography articles.

4. I have provided a chart (Figure 8.7) for you to get this information in one place. This is posted for you on Edmodo if you want to type your answers. I also have the paper version here, or you can just draw it in your journals. Whatever suits the way you want to read and take notes.

Standards Skills:

- Determine what the text says explicitly and make logical inferences from it.
- Determine central ideas or themes of a text.
- Draw evidence from literary or informational texts to support analysis, reflection, and research.
- Analyze how two or more texts address similar themes or topics in order to build knowledge.
- Listen attentively to others in formal and informal settings.
- Prepare for and participate effectively in a range of conversations and collaborations, building on others' ideas and expressing their own clearly and persuasively.
- Clarify research questions and evaluate and synthesize collected information.
- Narrow or broaden the major research question, if necessary, based on further research and investigation.

"You can choose how to do this. You can read and annotate your own article, then pass articles around like a carousel, and discuss them at the end; or read and mark your individual article, then discuss each one as a whole group. You will be responsible for negotiating your process; be sure to discuss the pros and cons of each approach before you decide. All articles are posted on Edmodo in case you don't finish them in class."

SMOKEY: *Here is another example of Sara giving kids choices and responsibilities. It would be so much easier for her to simply dictate the one, correct way of doing this jigsaw. But instead, she gives kids a chance to consider valid alternatives—and the necessity to negotiate work processes with other team members. Talk about college and career readiness!*

This is a variation of a jigsaw, where the color-coded articles are used to form expert groups (same color) and the base groups (all different colors). I dismiss them from the rug by group, and they come over to grab articles from me. Back at their seats, I hear them negotiating in groups.

"I think we should just read the articles we each got, fill out our charts, and then pass them."

"Well, what if someone finishes faster or slower?"

I walk over to this group and offer a solution—if anyone finishes a little early, I remind them to reread the text to see how much more they can add to their chart. I always grab new info when I reread.

"Let's all share our charts at the end, too."

Some kids decide that if anyone finishes early, they can go online to find even more information about their person. Others assign that as homework. I like this idea so much that I stop the class to have the groups tell the rest of the class their idea to dig into even more research about their key actors.

Day 3: Synthesizing Learning Online (40 minutes)

When the students arrive, the directions on the board say "Log in to **Edmodo**." I have a prompt posted there for them to answer: "What exactly caused the Triangle fire? Use text evidence from your wide reading to answer this question." For the rest of the lesson, I keep the live Edmodo feed projected so kids can watch as the whole class' thinking emerges. I also know that I can save and print out this whole conversation later, as evidence of everyone's learning and thinking.

 〉69

Of course, we are mainly doing this writing to synthesize all the learning from the last few days' inquiry. But it also serves as a formative assessment that tells me:

- If kids have been doing their reading
- If they are using our nonfiction texts to infer meaning and draw defensible conclusions
- If they can locate evidence from a text to support a claim
- If they can think quickly and incorporate all their discussion skills in an online conversation
- If my shy kids can use this "protected" time and space to share their thoughts.

> ### Standards Skills:
> - Prepare for and participate effectively in a range of conversations and collaborations with diverse partners, building on others' ideas and expressing their own clearly and persuasively.
> - Use technology to produce writing and to interact and collaborate with others.

I can also jump in and be part of the discussion, but always give kids the lead. I am mostly there to coach and redirect if needed.

〉70

The online **written conversation** goes on for fifteen to twenty minutes. I can easily monitor the dialogue since I am projecting it on the big screen. Periodically, I stop the discussion (no one is allowed to post) and have them go back, slow down, and carefully read the responses. I prompt them to be thoughtful: Are there are any gaps in the conversation? Is the conversation staying on track? Are kids pushing each other and asking for evidence from others? If they are seeing a place where they want to jump back in, I tell them to jot it down on paper so they don't forget. In the past, we have done this same type of discussion on paper or talked out loud on the rug. But today, I wanted kids to really see and learn from all their peers, and a running feed from Edmodo is a good way to do this.

The kids are so engaged with the discussion that I need to slow them down. They react the same way they do when I ask a question in a group discussion. The same kids shoot their hands up without thinking really deeply about what is about to come out of their mouths. Now, I hear quick fingers jamming at the keys right away because they all have their opinions about how this fire started. I am thrilled they are so engaged, but to give all learners a chance at voicing their opinions, I tell them to stop typing and put their screens at forty-five degrees so they cannot type for a while. This management move forces them to shift their focus from their computer screens to me.

Their reaction to this is really entertaining. They are frustrated with me for stopping them. "WAIT! I am almost done!!!" "I want to finish my thought or I'll forget it!" Then they get really mad at any classmate who tries to sneak in and finish the thought they were in the middle of before we stopped. They turn into the Posting Police. I tell them to all take a deep breath, read their notes and the articles for two minutes, and really dig deep into the text to find solid evidence to back up their thinking. I am still seeing too many superficial comments at this stage. Once they read and collect their thoughts, I allow them to go back on Edmodo.

"Go on to the conversation and do not type! Just read your friends' posts and 'listen' to what others are saying. Take a minute to see who you can connect with or disagree with. Consider how you can push each other's thinking with a question. I don't want to see or hear any fingers moving. Just read."

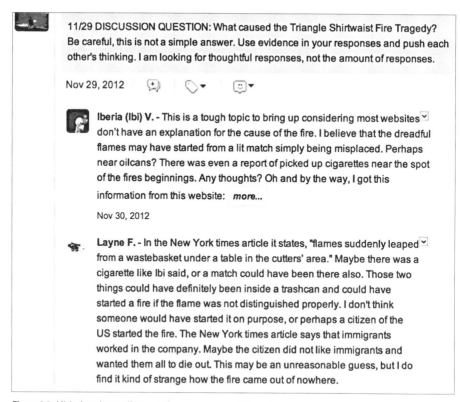

11/29 DISCUSSION QUESTION: What caused the Triangle Shirtwaist Fire Tragedy? Be careful, this is not a simple answer. Use evidence in your responses and push each other's thinking. I am looking for thoughtful responses, not the amount of responses.

Nov 29, 2012

Iberia (Ibi) V. - This is a tough topic to bring up considering most websites don't have an explanation for the cause of the fire. I believe that the dreadful flames may have started from a lit match simply being misplaced. Perhaps near oilcans? There was even a report of picked up cigarettes near the spot of the fires beginnings. Any thoughts? Oh and by the way, I got this information from this website: *more...*

Nov 30, 2012

Layne F. - In the New York times article it states, "flames suddenly leaped from a wastebasket under a table in the cutters' area." Maybe there was a cigarette like Ibi said, or a match could have been there also. Those two things could have definitely been inside a trashcan and could have started a fire if the flame was not distinguished properly. I don't think someone would have started it on purpose, or perhaps a citizen of the US started the fire. The New York times article says that immigrants worked in the company. Maybe the citizen did not like immigrants and wanted them all to die out. This may be an unreasonable guess, but I do find it kind of strange how the fire came out of nowhere.

Figure 8.8 Kids begin to discuss the prompt on Edmodo.

After three more minutes, I let them begin again. The discussion seems to be more thoughtful and interactive.

After about fifteen minutes, I stop them and let them finish their closing thoughts.

 Kiara J. - Also, the most of the people who died in the fire were under aged girls. #ChildLabor

Dec 3, 2012

 Evan B. - #Klara Where is your evidence?

Dec 3, 2012

 Tana A. - This is hard to explain what happened because the articles that I read don't really go into detail how the fire started. In the ILR School website that you had posted, I read that the owners said that the building was fireproof. But after the fire investigators checked and found out that "without fire excapes, and without adequate exits ...". There was no excapes and no adequate exits, they also had locked the doors during work hours. Alsi it said that in the factory there were barrels of oil that could catch on fire and there was barrels blocking the exits. There were many problems that had maybe caused the people to die, a couple of examples are like the door was locked to the stair well, the fire excape collapsed, short ladders only reached to the 6th floor, long wooden tables became obstacles, oily floors spread the fire quickly, fire nets failed to catch the jumpers who didn't want to burn, no sprinkler system, only pails of water, and flammable barrel of oil. The fire was a tragedy becuse many people had died and most of them were very young working for money.

Dec 3, 2012

Figure 8.9 Tana slowly begins to zero in on the bigger problem than just the match or start of the fire itself.

 Ellie L. • Dec 3, 2012
Any small thing could have caused the fire; a cigar, anyting dangerous around paper. But it was't just the little things that caused this fire, it was the big problem. The Triangle Shirtwaist Company was going broke, and left its factory in a horrible working condition. If the company had just given ito their workers and let them have suitable working spaces and at least a decent payment; maybe they could have avoided the fire.

Figure 8.10 Ellie was able to really synthesize what the bigger conflict was.

Day 4: History in the Hot Seat (25 minutes)

"Yesterday, you read about four key players in the Triangle fire. Having all the information we do now, especially after our writing together on Edmodo, I want to think about some questions you may have for these figures. Form into your same groups from yesterday. Ready? If you were able to ask one of these persons anything, what would you ask? Write that question next to their name on the chart of Key Actors you already have filled out."

I give them about five minutes to do this. "Today we are going to get an opportunity to pose questions to a historic figure, using one of our favorite dramatic activities, **Hot Seat.**" As soon as I tell the class that we are going to do Hot Seat, they know what to do—we've used this strategy before. Since kids are already in their groups from the previous day, one person is chosen to represent the Key Actor for which that group was formed. The rest of the members prep their representative with any background information, attitude, or possible questioning that may come their way. Anyone from the audience can ask a question to any Key Actor on the panel. My job is to make sure that kids address one another in the appropriate role and that they are using evidence from the articles, discussions, and extensive conversations they have had all week with one another.

Val: This question is for Ms. Morgan. What made you stand up for the women of the Triangle Factory?

Athee (as Anne Morgan): Well, women deserve rights and good working conditions no matter who they are or where they came from. I felt like I wanted to help girls who don't have what I do.

Loren: Mr. Harris, why would you intentionally lock the doors to the fire escapes in the factory?

Scotty (as Mr. Harris): Ummm, I am not sure what you are talking about? I don't think I locked the doors intentionally.

Loren: Well, it says here [points to article] that the fire inspection showed the doors were locked. I think it was after you escaped and left everyone else to die.

Scotty (as Mr. Harris): Is there a way to object, Ms. Ahmed?!

Me: I am only an audience member today; sorry, Scotty.

63 ‹ 🧰

Standards Skills:
- Use comprehension skills to listen attentively to others in formal and informal settings.
- Listen to and interpret a speaker's purpose by explaining the content, evaluating the delivery of the presentation, and asking questions or making comments about the evidence that supports a speaker's claims.
- Evaluate a speaker's point of view, reasoning, and use of evidence and rhetoric.
- Participate productively in discussions.

This can go on as long as the questions are on topic and the dialogue is engaging everyone on the panel. Kids can "tag out" and invite someone else who is also an expert on this person come and be on the hot seat. (This structure also works for book clubs, current events, and any whole-class text.) Kids should be constantly taking notes on what they hear, and writing to remember what they want to say. I give them Post-its for this. They can write notes to themselves, to someone on their "team," or just to celebrate someone for taking the hot seat!

Now it's time to wrap up.

"You guys, thanks so much for being brave and stepping into the shoes of these key players. You are all so great at interrogation. I would love to hear about how you felt during this. What did you notice? Anything we can celebrate or try for next time?"

In the end, the kids were able to use the lens of our social roles to identify the perpetrators, victims, bystanders, and upstanders of the Triangle Shirtwaist Factory fire and all that led up to that fatal day. Through the personal human stories, they learned about New York City in this time period, the connection of immigration and industrialization over time and across the world, and the struggle for workers' and women's rights in America.

In this particular curricular inquiry (and any of our inquiries), kids were free to express their own curiosity, to explore and learn about topics using texts, images, the Internet, primary resources, and more. They built upon their modest initial background knowledge with tons of new information. They read, listened, responded, reacted, and questioned moral and societal choices. They wrote, with evidence to defend their claims. They went public with their knowledge, articulating how they felt and demonstrating their understanding of the human story behind both immigration and industrialization—and the roots of modern-day globalization.

Literature Circle Inquiries

Lifelong readers, engaged citizens, and emerging upstanders have one thing in common: they all devour text. And our middle level kids are ready to encounter the world of ideas at full strength. The time for abridged "kid versions" is coming to an end, and cursory textbook overviews will no longer suffice. Our students can now tackle whole, challenging books—both fiction and nonfiction. They can build the kind of deep knowledge that comes only from sustained engagement with big ideas, developed at length. Indeed, we believe that young adolescents should be reading and discussing many of the same materials as the thoughtful, curious members of the adult community around them.

Of course, we do use our textbooks sometimes, but they are designed to be bland and homogenized, to appeal to the widest possible market. They speak in a neutral, authoritative voice that lacks any human emotion, or particularity, or location. So we enrich kids' reading diets with current and classic nonfiction books, historical novels, and biographies. And we don't always read these as a whole class with the teacher running everything and telling kids what the books are about. Instead, much of the time, we help kids organize themselves into three- to five-member literature circles or book clubs, much like those voluntary reading groups adults join. In this way, kids can choose different books that really interest them and fit their reading levels, the teacher can differentiate instruction, and we can all jigsaw together our different information as a unit of study unfolds.

But for kids to work this way, to be effective book club members, they have to learn a set of social and management skills that makes this kind of autonomy possible. In this chapter, we will share some of those baseline lessons, and then tell you about a powerful novel study Sara has done with several classes of students.

🔼 Book Club Basics

Thirty years ago, nobody had heard of literature circles or book clubs in American schools. Starting in the early 1980s, Smokey, along with pioneers like Becky Abraham Searle, Karen Smith, Jerome Harste, Carolyn Burke, Ralph Peterson, Mary Ann Eeds, Bonnie Campbell Hill, Nancy Johnson, and Katherine Schlick-Noe, led a movement to bring book discussion groups from adult living rooms into school classrooms. The idea drew upon the two most powerful trends of the era: an awakening to the power of independent reading (Fader 1981) and a commitment to sociable, collaborative learning (Johnson and Johnson 1980). A natural combination of these two ideas—as perfect as peanut butter and chocolate—was literature circles. Today, almost every student who enters the American school system will be offered many chances to join in small, peer-led discussions of an interesting book, meeting over a few weeks to share responses, predictions, reactions, questions, and connections, as the author's work unfolds.

Book clubs are one way to meet the varied reading interests and needs of all the kids in your room. Today's young readers have distinct palates for topics, genres, and styles—and also have reading levels all across the spectrum. In English language arts classes, teachers often use lit circles as a kind of small-group independent reading, a collaborative variant of the individual reading workshop. In this version, small groups of kids choose from among a wide variety of novels (at least the ones for which we have assembled multicopy sets) and launch their own differentiated experiences, with each group reading a different book. Some groups may be reading "harder" books, and some "easier" ones, but every group is reading and thinking about a whole book.

Trying out book clubs with your kiddos for the first time can feel like jumping off a cliff. You may feel you can't have a handle on three to six different titles being read at once, not to mention all those groups meeting simultaneously, when you can really only supervise one at a time. It is hard to let go of the control we are accustomed to, and hand it over to the students. But this is one of those great structures that allows kids to surprise us with their responsibility and focus—as long as we give them the careful training outlined in this chapter. So, wherever you may be on the barometer of book club anxiety, trust us, you can still give book clubs a go!

Training Students for Literature Circles

No matter how good a curricular fit any given book might be, this doesn't mean that book clubs are some kind of "natural" structure for eleven- or fourteen-year-olds. Kids are not born knowing how to operate in an ongoing lit circle (or any other kind of extended inquiry structure, for that matter). We have to *teach* them the reading strategies, the social skills, and the conversational "moves" they need to join effectively in deep reading and thoughtful discussion. But, since we are teachers, that presents no problem.

The three upcoming minilessons from Sara's classroom are key in the development of kids' book discussion skills. These are done not with a whole novel, but with very short pieces of text, so kids can read, think, and discuss inside of a few minutes. The minilessons to build kids' discussion skills in general are:

Minilesson 1: Co-Creating Discussion Norms (30 minutes)
Minilesson 2: Making Group Ground Rules (30 minutes)
Minilesson 3: Silent Dialogues (45–60 minutes)

After these initial lessons, we'll take you into a longer literature circle unit, and show some more complex and challenging lessons that deepen and sustain kids' engagement in a whole book. These lessons (and a Behind-the-Scenes peek at planning) will help you to structure an entire book-based unit with literature circles.

Lesson 1: Building Students' Background Knowledge Before Reading (45 minutes)
Behind the Scenes: Making a Reading and Meeting Calendar
Lesson 2: Warming Up for Discussions with a Membership Grid (30 minutes)
Lesson 3: Going Deeper Using Visual Images (90 minutes)

 # Minilesson 1: Co-Creating Discussion Norms (30 minutes)

I often begin literature circles training by talking about my own past book clubs, reading groups that I have joined with friends or colleagues, just to give kids a real-life picture of how this structure works. Often I'll tell a little cautionary story (no names) about how even adult book club meetings can go astray.

Next, I introduce a short piece of text to help create some discussion and help us co-create a list that can capture our thinking (and serve as a rubric for assessment later). I label the two-column T-chart like this:

A Great Discussion	
Sounds Like	**Looks Like**

Now I get ready to read aloud an engaging story. A great collection I draw from is the When I Was Your Age series, filled with adolescent memoirs from some of our favorite YA authors—James Howe, Walter Dean Meyers, Karen Hesse, and the list goes on. Because our upcoming book *Warriors Don't Cry* is also a memoir, we can lift the features of a great memoir—told from one person's point of view, based on a true story, revealing the feelings of the writer, focused on one key event, and so on. I often use *Everything Will Be Okay*, by James Howe, from this anthology. It begins with a vivid description of a sick kitten; it draws the reader in quickly because we have all tried (often unsuccessfully) to save a defenseless animal at least once in our lives.

"OK guys, today we are going to read a short memoir from an author I loved when I was your age, James Howe. It is kind of a sad story he tells about a time he tried to rescue and save a sickly animal."

🧰 › 70

Before I can begin my **read-aloud**, I notice little connection lightbulbs going off in everyone's mind about a time when they had a run-in with a needy animal. A few hands even shoot up to the sky. I tell them, "I know that most of you have some personal story that connects with this, so why don't you turn and talk with a buddy for one minute, greet them, and share your story."

As kids are talking, I write on the chart the first behavior we are practicing under "Sounds Like": *greeting one another and having a minute of fun checking-in talk.* I point this out to them when I bring them back.

"While you guys were talking, I wrote down some things that you did as I watched you. Our chart today focuses on what good small-group conversations look and sound like. Here is what I noticed you doing: you were connecting, greeting each other, smiling. I also saw some people looking grossed out by what they were hearing, which showed me you were listening to each other. Today we are going to focus on what our minds and bodies do when we are really working to listen to people around us. I am going to start us off by reading the text aloud and then I will give you time to finish this in small groups."

Now I read the text aloud to the students, and stop to share my thinking right away. The first lines of the story describe a very sick kitten and the way James Howe handled the situation. The girls are already cooing and sending out sounds of compassion.

Standards Skills:

- Participate in a range of conversations and collaborations with diverse partners, building on others' ideas.
- Work productively with others in teams.
- Listen attentively to others in informal settings.

Me: Hey, earlier I said this was a memoir; what does that mean we are definitely going to see here?

Gabe: It happened to the author.

Ray: Ya, it's the author's thoughts and feelings.

Alyciah: It's a true story.

Me: Yep, you got it, guys. Great recall on the qualities of a memoir.

I continue reading the text and model the language and movements of what we see and hear in good book club discussions, charting along the way.

About halfway through the text, I put kids into small groups (preselected by their table assignments), and send them off to finish the story and practice using the verbal and nonverbal discussion skills we have already noticed on our chart, but also to add other helpful discussion behaviors as they discover and can name them.

"When we meet back as a group, I will want to hear from you about how your small-group discussions went and the great things you heard and did. We will debrief the conversations and finish the chart together."

A Great Discussion

Sounds Like	Looks Like
Greeting one another and having a minute of fun checking-in talk	Eye contact with the speaker
Make connections to our own lives	Turn to a page if someone asks
Use our schema or background knowledge to push our thinking	Positive body language toward the group or speaker
Make connections to other texts	Wait until a speaker finishes before responding
Discuss the author's language	Invite others in
React to a character and their actions	Give everyone a chance to talk
Notice and interpret illustrations or visualizations while reading	Smile and laugh (maybe even cry)
Make inferences	Enjoy the discussion!
Create new understandings together	
Ask questions for clarification	
Agree or disagree, respectfully, and find evidence	

56

Figure 9.1 We typically come up with an anchor chart that looks like this one, and it stays up all year for reference.

We save this list and post it on the wall. With this anchor chart always visible, kids can glance up for a reminder when they are meeting in groups, they can add to it when they discover another attribute, or we can convene as a whole and go back to the chart when we need a refresher or are having discussion problems. The anchor chart also serves as an assessment tool for me to use along the way.

Minilesson 2: Making Group Ground Rules (30 minutes)

The previous lesson helps kids develop general ideas about what makes a good discussion. But every time a new lit circle group is formed, it will have distinctive strengths, challenges, and off-task triggers. And we are working our way toward bigger groups, longer texts, greater time commitments, and more autonomy. So the next step in becoming a highly effective book club is knowing how to set up specific, agreed-upon ground rules for a group meeting before it even begins.

Step 1. I gather the kids on the rug for this minilesson, with the "Great Discussion" anchor chart from the last lesson beside me.

"We have already been having some good conversations about short articles and stories. And we are developing some excellent collaboration skills. But now our groups are going to get larger and our texts longer. Using these charts that we have developed, we are going to set up some ground rules for our groups so we can be successful together."

Step 2. I ask students working together in their groups to come up with three to five common expectations or norms that everyone agrees to and are attainable. These will be their ground rules. I give groups five to eight minutes to create this list while I circulate around the room and push their thinking. In the back of my mind is my own "master list" of nonnegotiables.

Step 3. Next we come back together as a group, and I ask a spokesperson from each team to share their ground rules. These can also be posted on the wall or laid down in the middle of a big circle, so students can do a **gallery walk** around them. I ask students what they notice about each group's ground rules.

 71

Step 4. Now it's time for groups to finalize their norms. Before they commit, I hand out reflection slips with these questions:

- Which rule will be easiest for you to follow?
- Which rule may give you the most difficulty?
- What plans can you make now so that you can avoid letting the group down later?

I give groups another three minutes to confer, review, and revise after completing the reflection slips individually.

Here's a list that a group of Smokey's New Mexico sixth graders came up with. You'll notice they went way beyond the three to five items suggested.

- Bring all your stuff every day.
- Try really hard to concentrate.
- Don't bring anything to the meeting that can distract you.
- Keep your hands to yourself.
- Realize when you're off topic so you can stop.
- Don't look for weird things on the Internet.
- Make someone leave if they are distracting you.
- No going to other groups.
- Use the group seating chart we made to separate Brandy and Charlie.

Standards Skills:

- Participate in a range of conversations and collaborations with diverse partners, building on others' ideas.
- Work productively with others in teams.
- Listen attentively to others in informal settings.

Step 5. Now I ask the kids to talk honestly about their individual reflection slips in comparison with the group norms list. What might be difficult for them to do as a group member? This holds them accountable to one another; they must own their personal challenges in regard to contributing to group work and begin to think about how they can be successful. I really want them to know they can share that something will be a challenge for them, but they are going to do their best to rise up for the group.

Step 6. The next step is to give groups a small piece of text (a short story, poem, cartoon, or excerpt from a nonfiction article) and have them practice the new group norms they have set up. Then they debrief, revise norms as needed, and carry on.

Minilesson 3: Silent Dialogues (45–60 minutes)

This lesson, a variant of **written conversation**, provides a great lead-in for the unit that follows in this chapter if you choose to use it there.

To prepare, make copies of Jesus Colon's memoir piece "Little Things Are Big" for the class (found on the Facing History website, or simply Google it). Copy only as far as the line, "I hesitated. And then . . . " Print the other half of the story separately for timely handing out, or have it ready to project later.

Prepare this list of questions on chart paper but do not show the students yet. They will serve as a guide later in the lesson:

> Will Jesus Colon choose to help the woman, and be an upstander? What makes you say that?
>
> Or, will he decide not to help and thus choose to be a bystander? What makes you say that?
>
> Using evidence from the story, describe your thinking.
>
> What dilemmas did he face?
>
> What risk is he taking if he tries to help?

Step 1. With the whole class gathered, introduce the story and the author. Jesus Colon was a black Puerto Rican newspaperman who wrote a memoir about being faced with a choice to be a *bystander* or an *upstander*. If you haven't already done something like my lesson on pages 86–93, define these words together, write them into the inquiry journals, and chart them to make them visible throughout the lesson.

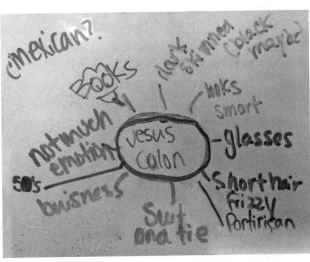

Figure 9.2 One student's identity web for Jesus Colon.

Sometimes I project a picture of Jesus Colon on the board and have students build an **identity web** around him, highlighting what students "see" when they view the photo. A **See, Think, Wonder** chart or a **Mind Map** can also be created from the picture and the memoir.

> ⟩ 70

> ⟩ 64

> ⟩ 67

> ⟩ 65

Game-Time Decision

SMOKEY: *When I teach with this story, I don't like to use the picture; I feel it influences the kids' responses too much. The only pictures we have were taken when he was much older than he was during the subway incident.*

SARA: *I've done it both ways too. I do like the picture because the image draws kids into the story right away. In this case, they have a name and a face. On a metacognitive level, we want them thinking about how they are creating a stereotype, a "single story" for this man, just by looking at him. It is a practice in assumptions, the same assumptions that could potentially affect the characters in the story and how choices in real life are informed.*

Step 2. Preview the silent lit circle activity for the students, and chart the following directions if needed. Working in pairs, they will be writing simultaneous letters to each other in response to a story. Everyone will write for two to three minutes in their own notebooks, until you say "Switch." Then the students will switch letters with their preselected partner. They'll read what their buddy wrote and silently write a response. They can comment, connect, elaborate, ask questions, debate—their job is to keep the conversation going, as if they were talking out loud.

Step 3. Begin reading the story aloud, stopping to answer any questions the kids have. Finally, stop at the designated stopping point: "I hesitated. And then . . . "

Standards Skills:
- Integrate content/ information presented in diverse media and formats, including visually.

Before you invite students to write to their partners, pull out and review the questions you charted in advance, which are different ways of predicting Jesus Colon's decision.

Remind them that this is a letter, so it should start with "Dear _____," and have a closing as well. Now it is writing time. Let kids write, track the time, and call out the letter exchanges every couple of minutes. Give them warnings such as, "You have about fifteen seconds left to wrap up this note." But if they are really into it, allow for more time for each letter. Remind kids to go back to the text for evidence that backs up their claims.

After three switches, give the partnerships two or three minutes to finally chat out loud, sharing their thoughts, clearing up any misconceptions, and debriefing the process in pairs. Then bring the whole class back together and share out how the letters went. If you jot down a list of what went well and what didn't, you can convert your notes later into an anchor chart to help students the next time.

Step 4. If this lesson were only about how to introduce silent lit circles, you could just let the kids continue their work with the story and conclude the lesson when they complete their reading. However, if you're using this specific lesson as a lead-in to a larger discussion about upstanders, fasten your seat belt!

It won't be hard to elicit major anticipation for how the story ends. Did Jesus Colon choose to help and be an upstander? For a kinesthetic response, have the class create a **standing discussion**, reflecting what they think he did. Tell 71 them, "We are going to make a human continuum to show our thinking. Line up at this end if you are sure Jesus helped the woman, and over on the other end if you are sure he didn't. If you are unsure, place yourself where you belong along the continuum. Everyone should be ready to explain where they are standing and why." Once kids are lined up, have them turn and talk to one or two kids standing near them, sharing the specific text evidence they've drawn upon. Then ask for volunteers from different parts of the line to share their predictions, encouraging them to cite evidence from the text that supports their choice.

Now, fold the line so that kids from the ends of the line come together; this means everyone will now be facing someone they disagreed with about the story's ending. Once again, have them talk with adjacent kids about what evidence guided their predictions and have a few volunteers share out. The instruction to "fold the line" sometimes generates puzzlement. In that event, manually walk one end of the line to meet the other end so no one gets lost and everyone gets a new partner.

Because I hold kids accountable for their great thinking and evidence, I ask if there is anyone who wants to move to a new position on the line after having talked to a buddy with a different perspective. If anyone does,

Standards Skills:
- Determine what the text says explicitly and make logical inferences from it; cite specific textual evidence to support conclusions.
- Provide evidence to support understanding.
- Explain how the values and beliefs of particular characters are affected by the historical and cultural setting.
- Write arguments to support claims using valid reasoning and relevant and sufficient evidence.
- Draw evidence from texts to support analysis.
- Write persuasive texts to influence the attitudes of a specific audience.

I ask them to share why they changed positions, giving a nod to the persuasive person with the compelling argument and evidence, and celebrating the other's brave move.

By now, the eagerness to hear the end of the story will be almost unbearable. Hand out, read aloud, or project the last paragraphs of the story. Be prepared for some gasps when kids learn that Colon just "pushed by her like I saw nothing" and bounded up the subway steps two at a time. And make sure to point out that, in a sense, *everyone* made a good prediction; Colon didn't help then, but vowed to always stand up in the future.

Step 5. There are many choices for culminating activities for this silent lit circle lesson.

- Ask kids to write one final letter to their partner reflecting on their prediction about Jesus Colon's decision, now that they know what he did. Some prompts: What evidence in the text led you to the prediction you made? Did you miss or misinterpret anything? Do you think the clues in the story were "fair" to the reader?

- Bring the group back together and have a whole-class discussion. How has the world changed since 1955? Could this sort of situation—and hard decision—arise today? Where, with whom, and under what circumstances?

- Ask kids to rewrite the ending with their position as the perspective. Those who got it right can try the other perspective or write why they made the decision they did.

- Have students write a personal memoir about a moment when they made a choice that they later regretted or still think about today.

- If you have previously been talking about the four social roles—upstander, bystander, victim, and perpetrator—you can use this language as a template for understanding the story. Invite kids to have a one-word go-around; each person chooses the one role that they think Jesus Colon played in this story. As my class shows in Figure 9.3, not everyone thought Jesus was a bystander—several kids thought he was also a victim, dehumanized by the societal norms of his times.

Standards Skills:

- Present supporting evidence such that listeners can follow the line of reasoning and the style [is] appropriate to task, purpose, and audience.
- Prepare for and participate effectively in a range of conversations, building on others' ideas and expressing their own clearly and persuasively.
- Listen attentively to others in informal settings.
- Participate productively in discussions.

Figure 9.3 Seventh graders give their one-word response to Colon's role in this story.

A Whole-Class Literature Circle Unit: Civil Rights

Once kids have gotten comfortable with small-group reading discussions around short texts, we can move them up to whole books that are powerfully linked to the curriculum, and have them engage with a title deeply over a period of weeks.

When we are harnessing lit circles to a curricular unit of study, we have a couple of choices. We can collect sets of four to six copies of several *different* books keyed to the curricular topic—say, six novels set in the colonial period, or six biographies of great scientists, or six nonfiction books about Native Americans. As we collect these book choices, we make sure to include some easier and some harder books, so that every student can find a book that they *can read* and *want to read*. When we use lit circles in this way, we plan ways for kids to jigsaw together the different information, points of view, and interpretations they are getting from all these different books so we all learn about our common subject.

Another choice—the one we will explain in depth here—is to select a *single* whole-class book, fiction or nonfiction, and have all the kids read it in lit circle style, meeting in small, peer-led groups. In choosing a common text, we want to be sure that it has reliable information about the topic—and that, with appropriate supports, it is accessible to all the kids in the class. In conjunction with her oft-taught unit on civil rights, Sara has found a perfect whole-class lit circle book: *Warriors Don't Cry* by Melba Pattillo Beals, one of the teenagers who famously integrated Little Rock Central High school in 1957. Of course, Beals' memoir isn't the only source material for the unit. Sara has already collected a ton of articles, primary source documents, photos, websites, picture books, and more from the civil rights movement. But adding this single special historical book adds unbeatable depth—and raises the issues of integration on a level the kids can connect to: school and friendships.

To support the kids as they dig into *Warriors* over three weeks, Sara provides various comprehension and collaboration lessons along the way. As we have already noted, you could use minilesson 3 from this chapter (pages 161–164) to introduce the whole unit. Here are a few lessons Sara uses:

Lesson 1—Building Students' Background Knowledge Before Reading
Lesson 2—Warming Up for Discussions with a Membership Grid
Lesson 3—Going Deeper Using Visual Images

All of these lessons are listed on the calendar on pages 169–170. For this chapter, we'll zoom in on three more key lit circle lessons, in the order that you might use them with a book of your own choosing. While the details here are about *Warriors* and civil rights, these lessons are generic in their DNA; they can be adapted to any book that fits your curriculum.

Lesson 1: Building Students' Background Knowledge Before Reading (45 minutes)

With some books, especially those set in far-off times and places, we need to provide kids with enough background to enter and understand the text. Sometimes, we can do this by presenting some historical, geographical, or biographical information. This might involve using maps, period artifacts, or historical pictures. But more often, we are not really bringing kids stone-cold, never-heard-it-before information, but rather activating some background knowledge—possibly fragmentary and littered with misconceptions—that kids already have in their memory banks. For this civil rights unit, to provide background for *Warriors*, you might begin by finding articles or first-person accounts.

To build background knowledge, I selected a short piece from the *New York Times Upfront* magazine called "1957, the Integration of Central High."

Here's how I use the text in the lesson:

Step 1. I give students a copy of the text (which is also projected on the screen), two different colored highlighters, and a pencil. I ask them to make a color code key on their handout as I do with mine on the screen.

⟩ 72

"Choose one color that will be your 'schema color,' meaning it's for parts of the text you already know about or have some background knowledge on. The other marker will be your 'wonder color,' meaning when you see something that you don't know, are curious about, or that is a new word for you, you can highlight it. For both kinds of highlighting, I want you to take your pencil and quickly jot down in the margins what familiar or unknown information you found."

SMOKEY: *I'm just wondering why you use a technical cognitive psychology term like* schema *with your students.*

SARA: *We talk about our thinking a lot in my class. In a certain way, I feel like this is my main job: helping kids to become more self-aware, more metacognitive, more active and intentional in their own thinking. So I like for us to know and use the same language that people who study thinking do. This goes in the same category as terms like* inferring, hypothesizing, *and* synthesizing, *which we use all the time.*

Step 2. Now I begin with just the title of the text and perhaps the first paragraph, and I model my thinking here. I let myself **think aloud** in front of the students: "What does the title mean? What connections can I make between the title and my own schema?" I make notes with a pencil and use my highlighters to mark what I'm wondering about and what I can connect to my own background knowledge.

⟩ 60

Step 3. Students work through the text on their own now, as I continue to model silently on the projector.

⟩ 61

"Can you continue on your own through the text? I am going to keep working up here while you do. I will stop you every so often to turn and talk with a partner and share your schema and wonders."

Step 4. As students wrap up their reading and their partner discussions, I hold a quick debriefing to get a feel for what the students have learned from the article. My questions vary depending on the text, but they might include the following:

> Whose stories are in this text?
> What do we know about time and place?
> Can we connect or share any schema about this specifically?

Step 5. Next, I ask students to share what they are wondering about after reading the text. We use our **journals** to write down these questions and wonders. I smile, knowing that we are going to be creating quite a list as we learn more and more.

> What questions do you have for the writer?
> About the time period that the article describes?
> For the people mentioned in the article?
> What does the writer leave us still wanting to know?

As the kids share their questions, there are always some student experts who have lots of schema to offer us. If their information is accurate, I happily let them present. If they enunciate big misconceptions, I'll gently interject with my own background knowledge, but making sure not to squash the intellectual curiosity they are building.

These wonder lists, which begin with the text, serve us all through the civil rights unit. Each day that we have a minilesson or that they meet in their groups, I encourage kids to list new wonders that develop about the era or the book.

Step 6. For homework, I give them another article that will help answer some of the questions that I have anticipated they will have about this time period and these events. It is a well-summarized background piece on the integration of Central High School from the perspective of one of the Little Rock Nine, Elizabeth Eckford (Facing History and Ourselves, *Choices in Little Rock*).

"For homework tonight, set a goal to read this article, annotate the way we did here together, and see if you can find out any answers to the questions we had today. You are also probably going to have more questions, because we know the best readers ask more and more questions as they learn new information, right? Keep working on the list that we started in class and add to it tonight if there is anything that comes up in your reading that you would like to investigate further or that you don't understand."

Standards Skills:

- Read closely to determine what the text says explicitly and to make logical inferences from it.
- Analyze, make inferences, and draw conclusions and provide evidence from the text to support their understanding.

64

Behind the Scenes: Making a Reading and Meeting Calendar

Now we are getting ready to dive into *Warriors*. But first, we need to create a calendar for our reading, literature circle meetings, whole-class minilessons, and, a couple weeks down the road, a culminating experience for our civil rights studies.

To prepare for this lesson, first create your own teaching schedule for the unit. Mark a calendar with predetermined school events, holidays, sports games, or other occasions that may affect reading goals. Identify lessons and minilessons that you already know you will need to teach (the lessons in this chapter are some good candidates for these), and block that time on the calendar. Then, determine consistent days (e.g., Mondays and Thursdays) when you would like to schedule kids' book club meetings, usually one or two a week. Also, choose the date when you would like all books finished. You can use the remaining days or portions of days to apply some of the lessons in Chapter 5 ("The Toolbox"). You may also decide to leave that time uncharted for now: leaving room for minilessons that become necessary as you move through the unit gives you flexibility to adapt the instruction to students' needs.

Figure 9.4 is an example of my own plan from the last time I taught the *Warriors* unit. If this looks complicated, don't panic! It includes some lessons and activities that aren't in this book; it just serves as an example how you balance time between the kid-led lit circle meetings and the teacher-led lessons, and gives some flavor for the additional minilessons you might teach.

Next, on a fresh blank calendar, mark the dates for the book group meetings and make copies for the kids.

Step 1. Distribute the kids' version of the book group calendars to students before they move into groups. Kids should label the top of the calendar with their names and book title, and their period if you meet with multiple classes. Explain that they will meet in their book club groups shortly and negotiate pages to be read before each meeting. Be clear that groups need to finish the book by the given date, and that they must write out the actual page numbers (not just the chapters) they are reading for each meeting.

Step 2. Have students meet in groups and begin the negotiations. As you walk around and listen in, add reality checks, if needed, to accommodate different readers' reading speed. Make sure everyone has a voice. Ask for the logic behind their goal setting in particular areas. As groups finish, hand them another blank

Book Club Calendar

Week 1	Day 1	Day 2	Day 3	Day 4	Day 5
	Introduce book clubs with shared reading ML: See, Think, Wonder Journals: Begin list of wonders	ML: Book Pass Ballot (if multiple titles used)	ML: Intro Membership Grid Read-aloud: Poetry Pass out books and form book club groups	Membership Grid Read Ch. 1	ML: Ground Rules
Week 2	**Day 6** ML: Dealing with the first chapter	**Day 7** Membership Grid Book Club meeting #1 Debrief Post-discussion journaling	**Day 8** ML: What do you do when you disagree? Read-aloud: Article on LR9/ school integration	**Day 9** ML: Going deeper with visual images View images with social role lens	**Day 10** Membership Grid Book Club meeting #2 Journal collection
Week 3	**Day 11** ML: Dealing with unprepared members Share out	**Day 12** Membership Grid Book Club meeting #3 Check-in: Questions for inquiry on civil rights era Debrief and journal	**Day 13** Read-aloud: Article on LR9/school integration Share out	**Day 14** Read-aloud with draw-aloud: *When Mariam Sang, Jackie Robinson*, or equivalent picture book	**Day 15** Membership Grid Book Club meeting #4
Week 4	**Day 16** ML: Noticing our lingering questions Teams shape their beyond-the-book questions	**Day 17** Membership Grid Book Club final meeting Debrief and journal Final journal collection	**Day 18** Work time for civil rights inquiries	**Day 19** Work time for civil rights inquiries	**Day 20** ML: Being an attentive audience Going public

Figure 9.4 A general lesson schedule for our civil rights lit circle unit.

calendar and ask them to fill one out for you to keep. You should have a copy of each group's final calendar. Remind them to check with you if they make any revisions down the road.

Lesson 2: Warming Up for Discussions with a Membership Grid (30 minutes)

In lit circle meetings, we expect small groups of kids to sustain lengthy (twenty minutes or more) and thoughtful conversations without direct teacher guidance. This works better if kids have a brief warm-up activity where every group member speaks. Spending five minutes on this prompts kids to share the air and include everyone, and it reminds shy or reticent members that their voice matters, too. When they begin their book club meeting, kids will feel safer to share their responses to the book. To create this quick warm-up, I use an activity called Membership Grid (Figure 9.5) that I first learned from Nancy Steineke (2002).

Step 1. Have the students brainstorm a list of interesting subjects that everyone can discuss. Kids will come up with topics like places you have traveled, favorite hobbies, the perfect pizza, best (or worst) TV show or movie, coolest band or genre of music, favorite all-time book. Scribe all these suggestions where kids can see them. Explain that book club group members will be conducting informal one-minute interviews to get to know one another better and to get ready for their lit circle meeting.

Step 2. Have students sit with their book club groups and give each student a blank membership grid. The version on page 172 is good for five days of meetings.

Show kids how to record each member's name in a Group Members box and decide which of the brainstormed topics they would like to discuss. They then record the date and topic in the first box under Topics. (You can model this on the document camera.)

When groups gather, each member takes turns being interviewed by the other three members for one minute. The interviewers have to ask good questions, listen carefully, dig deeper with follow-up questions, and jot down key words their classmate said. Then the next kid gets interviewed by the other three, and so on around the group. One minute each, one minute for logistics, that's it. While

Standards Skills:
- Participate in a range of conversations and collaborations with diverse partners, building on others' ideas.
- Work productively with others in teams.
- Listen attentively to others in informal settings.

Membership Grid

Name _____

Book Title _____

Topics	Group Member Names			

Figure 9.5 Membership grid for kids to interview one another.

this is happening, you circulate around the room, encouraging good questioning skills and monitoring the time.

Step 3. The first couple of times you do this, invite students to take a look at their notes and reflect on the process. As a whole group, debrief what went well and what goals could be set for next time. Students may find that better follow-up questions (open-ended, thoughtful) lead to better conversations, and that more detailed notes will help them remember something personal about one of their group members. The same way they do in reading! Celebrate their conversations and explain that they will be opening each of the upcoming book club meetings with Membership Grid.

Lesson 3: Going Deeper Using Visual Images (90 minutes)

It seems quite recent that most of us teachers have finally gotten the technology to project images on a big screen for kids. And now, we can project anything! It's hard to think of a single school subject that doesn't offer an amazing abundance of powerful images, photographs, artworks, maps, or diagrams, just a click away, thanks to Google Images. And when we are teaching historical events or novels, images can enhance kids' understanding, while including everyone. "Reading" an image doesn't depend on your reading level; everyone, definitely including language learners and kids with IEPs, can view and talk about pictures.

We like to do this lesson in one long session, but if that won't work with your schedule, it can easily be divided into two shorter chunks.

Step 1. I begin with a simple invitation to the kids to help them dive into a powerful visual. First-period PE is over and my eighth graders come sifting through the door with a bit more energy (and body heat) than when I greeted them earlier this morning. I welcome them back to class with this note on the projection screen:

> *Good morning! Grab a clipboard, a pencil, Post-its, your* Warriors
> Don't Cry *book, your reading brains, a buddy, and meet me on the rug!*

This kind of invitation gets them thinking right away. Instead of shouting across-the-room questions ("What are we doing now?" "What do we need again?" "What did she say?"), they buzz: "I wonder what we are going to do? Do you think this has to do with those pictures hanging in the hallway?" See Figure 9.6.

Actually, that last question was one I expected to hear. Before school that day, I had hung a gallery of photographs outside our classroom. Each one contained an image related to our current focus on the civil rights movement and our reading of *Warriors Don't Cry*. Some of the photos were images of the very events being portrayed in Beals' book—the nine African American students entering the school, soldiers guarding them, crowds of angry white people screaming and waving signs at the children. Other pictures were from the same era, but depicted different images of school integration, including black and white children happily studying together, saluting the American flag, and even holding hands. I purposely set up these photos in the hallway before kids arrived to pique a little interest and curiosity. It's tough to wake a teenager in the morning, but this one is in my bag of tricks.

Now, I give a ready helper a stack of blank paper and ask her to give one sheet to each student. I shift kids' attention to an image on our big classroom

Figure 9.6 Sara projects images for kids to view and study.

screen (shown in Figure 9.7) with a simple instruction: "Look at this image and talk about it."

Kids view and chat for a minute while I take attendance. This is another version of my consistent "soft starts," replacing individual independent reading for today. By the time the last few stragglers join us, most of my students realize that the people in the image are the main characters of our book. Some are digging into their copies of *Warriors* to connect to a related photo or find a clue that confirms their prediction.

> **Dylan:** That's Melba!
>
> **Ivelis:** Terrence Roberts is the tall one, right?
>
> **Vanessa:** OMG, Elizabeth Eckford isn't in this because she didn't make it that first day, remember?

Step 2. Now that the kids are fully engaged, my next step is to help them dive deeper and analyze the picture more carefully. Before their burst of curiosity fades, I darken the screen and tell them we will get back to that image in just a minute.

"So here we are, about a third of the way through the book. We've met the characters and identified with some, placed ourselves in the setting, grasped some introductory themes, and noticed some early upstanders and bystanders.

©Bettman/CORBIS

Figure 9.7 The image of the Little Rock Nine being escorted away from school.

"Now it's time to really start asking how and why these individuals and historical events interact as we read our way through this text. All year, we have been talking about how effective readers make visual images as they read, right? I know that when you guys read, you always have that movie of mental images running in your mind. I've showed you many times how I stop and carefully think about my own mental images when I read, and how sometimes I even sketch them in my journal or margin?"

There's some good-natured eye-rolling, as it if to say, "Yeah, only three million times."

"Today, I'm going to flip-flop things and give you the image before the text. In fact, it is going to be like one of those wordless picture books you read when you were in first grade, where you had to infer what was happening just from the pictures."

Isaias pipes up. "Oh, I loved those. Those were awesome."

"Good, I have Isaias' approval! So, in just a sec, you are going to be 'reading' some images and hopefully gaining a better understanding of what was really going on when the Little Rock Nine integrated Central High. Now I am going to put that same image up again, but this time we're going to slow down and see it, analyze it, in sections. Take that blank paper that Ana gave you and fold it into three equal sections like this. Follow my lead on the projector or have a buddy help you. Label each part just as I do up here." See Figure 9.8.

When I am doing this viewing exercise with other images, I'll use quadrants, circles, or whatever subdivisions encourage thoughtful attention to all the details in a picture.

Standards Skills:
- Integrate and evaluate content presented in diverse media and formats, including visually, as well as in words.
- Analyze how words [and] images work together to impact meaning.
- Participate in a range of conversations and collaborations with diverse partners, building on others' ideas.
- Work productively with others in teams.
- Listen attentively to others in informal settings.

Left	Middle	Right

Figure 9.8 Three-column chart to record observations.

By now, everyone has their sections labeled as I give the next set of directions. "Each section on your paper goes with the section of the image you are going to see. In that box, I want you to write down what you see. To start with, you can just be literal. The idea is to look slowly and patiently into the image and notice all the details that are there, in the foreground and the background. What does the image make you see, hear, feel, and wonder? And if you are not sure what something is, pose it as a question. So listen to me 'read' a little of the first section. You guys can steal from me if you are seeing the same things."

As I project only the left third of the image, I vocalize my thinking and jot down key words to label my noticings.

Me: I see a tire. I see men with soldier hats.

Forrest: You mean helmets, Ms. Ahmed.

Me: Right, helmets! Thanks, Forrest! I wonder, is that a weapon that soldier is carrying? The picture is old, black and white.

Now I turn it over to the kids, letting them quietly view and write about the first section of the image for another minute.

Me: It looks like you all have some observations down and I know you're eager to talk, so turn to your buddy and share. Feel free to borrow their ideas; it shows you are really listening to them.

I listen in on several conversations as I roam the room, starting with Denzel and Gabe.

Denzel: I noticed all the soldiers are white.

Gabe: Yeah, me too, and there are a lot of them. I also noticed that it is sunny outside, so it is morning or afternoon.

Denzel: They must be the soldiers that turned them away, or maybe they were protecting them?

Gabe: It's hard to tell who would be upstander soldiers or bystander ones.

After a few minutes of talk time, I invite pairs to report out their thinking to the whole class. "I have been hearing some great observations. Anybody want to share?"

While a few kids offer their thoughts to the group, I scribe them on my projected notes, so everyone's thoughts are recorded. Then, over the next four or five minutes, we go through the same process for the middle and right sections of the image (shown in Figure 9.9).

Step 3. Finally, I turn the students loose to write directly about their own reactions. I show the full image once more. This time, I have kids flip their sheet over and write

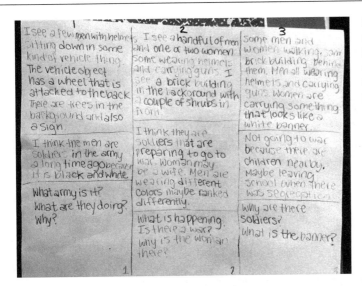

Figure 9.9 One student's response to three sections of the Little Rock school integration photograph.

down their final thoughts. I give them a few prompts: "What are your reactions to the image? What questions would you ask the people in this photo? How do you connect this image back to the *Warriors* book?" Finally, I ask them to give this photo a title or caption.

They set to writing pretty eagerly because they are so consumed with this image and have lots of thoughts and opinions. I let them write for about three minutes before switching to discussion. This time, to add some fresh interaction, I have buddies join with a nearby pair to discuss in a group of four.

I roam the room again, listening and taking notes about what I hear (I will use my observations in my assessment of kids later on, as well as to plan for tomorrow's lesson). I hear a lot of talk about that overarching theme in our class—upstanders and bystanders. There is quite a lot of conversation about whether you can tell what kind of "stander" someone is, just by their body language in a picture.

"I know you were all eager to share with each other. I would love to hear all the titles you guys gave this image, but first let me tell you a few I heard while visiting around the room." I do this to honor the students with great thoughts who aren't always comfortable sharing in the whole group. "Someone titled the picture 'the price of education.' Anyone want to claim that title?" Brenda raises her hand. "Can you say a word or two about what you were thinking?"

Brenda says quietly, "I just thought, this integration is costing everyone so much to go through it, the kids, their families . . . "

"That's very thoughtful, really true," I say. "Thanks for that."

If you need to divide this lesson to fit it into two shorter sessions, you can end the day's work here.

Step 4. Now it's time for an added challenge: taking on another's perspective.

> **Me:** Most of you have noticed there are a lot more photos hanging outside in the hallway today, and some of you have asked about them. All of us are going to go out and "read" those images. Except I am going to challenge you to something, if you are ready. You are going to have to read with a different type of hat on. This side of the room—everyone from Celeste over—is going to view these images with the attitude of an integrationist. Meaning?
>
> **Evan:** We want the schools to mix black and white students.
>
> **Me:** Did you all hear Evan? (*Nods and yeses. Now I point to the opposite side of the room with my arms.*)
>
> **Alexis:** Oh no!

Sympathetically smiling at Alexis' reaction, I nod.

> **Me:** You are going to take on the perspective of a segregationist. Meaning?
>
> **Juan:** We are the most terrible people in the room?

Everyone lets out a tiny, awkward laugh.

> **Me:** Not you personally! But everyone, what does Juan mean by that?
>
> **Sieanna:** That we are supposed to try to see things from the perspective of the segregationists, who are racist and don't want the black students in the white schools.
>
> **Me:** Sadly, yes. Just like some of the characters you are meeting in *Warriors*, right? Thanks, Sieanna and Juan.

I stop a few kids who are trying to inch their way over to the integrationist side.

"With the Post-its on your clipboards, you are going to do just what we did together with the first picture. You are going to walk through the gallery out in the hall and study several of those pictures. You will look deeply into the details, analyze, connect, draw inferences, visualize further, and think about the photographer's motives for taking this photo. You're using your same repertoire of comprehension strategies, except the text is a picture, not a page of print. Does that make sense?" I get a few nods, and I can see that the kids are champing at the bit to get into the hall.

"When you feel you fully understand an image, I want you to give it a title. But you are going to do it with either your integrationist or your segregationist hat on, so you are really going to take on the attitudes, beliefs, and feelings of these

71

Standards Skills:
• Integrate and evaluate content presented in diverse media and formats, including visually.

Figure 9.10 Alexis, a Burley eighth grader, titles a photograph.

people, got it? Your job is to write down the title you would give the specific image you are looking at, put your initials on it, and stick it on the chart paper behind the picture. Try and get to at least four or five."

After reminding the kids about hallway norms and expectations, I set them loose. They pour out into the hall, clipboards in hand. I watch them as they rove around from poster to poster, quietly studying and gradually posting titles as shown in Figure 9.10. After I see that everyone is working autonomously, I go from chart to chart, grabbing compelling Post-its from each one, from both integrationist and segregationist viewpoints.

Once the activity starts winding down, I usher the kids back to our meeting area on the rug. On my document projector, I now put up one of the images with two of the kids' suggested titles, one integrationist and one segregationist. There is a murmur of wonder and looks are shot across the room. The first image shows six students of mixed races, pledging their allegiance to the flag.

> **Dylan:** That's mine.
>
> **Me:** Thanks, Dylan. Read us your caption.
>
> **Dylan:** "One Nation Under God."
>
> **Me:** Explain your thinking on that?
>
> **Dylan:** Well, I was an integrationist and it sounds like a positive message because they are all together doing the pledge like we do.
>
> **Me:** Thanks. What about the other side?
>
> **Jeremy:** I had that same one, but I was writing as if I were a segregationist and I put, "Never the United States," because no segregationist thinks or wants blacks and whites to be united.

Me: Thanks, Jeremy and Dylan. Everyone, I know you all want to share yours, and that's important because I saw some great thinking out there. So I will post them all for a few days so you can look them over and make some notes in your journal about ones that stand out or connect to your own reading. But now, let's dig back into our discussion of the book. Why do you think this was important to do today as we try to get a better idea of what really happened down in Little Rock in 1957? The book already gives us eyewitness testimony from our author, who was one of the Nine and lived through it, right?

Chloe: Well, we are all reading about it and trying to visualize it, but we will never really know what it felt like. Looking at real pictures gives us a better idea because it's not like fiction.

Vanessa: Yeah, back then they didn't have Photoshop, so they like couldn't make it up.

Me: Ha! Good point. Anybody else?

Mikayla: Well, for me personally, I had a hard time in some parts trying to really visualize what it was like in that mob scene or what being escorted by troops really looked like. Then I saw that picture of Elizabeth Eckford and how that girl was screaming at her in that mob and I realized that they really did hate them. It's kinda scary.

Me: Thanks for being honest, Mikayla. I can get stuck like that too, so I'll sketch it out or try and find an image if I don't get it. Thumbs up if you were in the same boat as Mikayla at some point as a reader. *(Lots of thumbs go up.)* So how did reading all of these images help? How will it change the way we go back into *Warriors Don't Cry* and really make sense of what's going on?

Evan: I think it makes us go a little deeper. Like, you will never know how they really felt because it didn't happen to us, but seeing the actual pictures and reading about it at the same time is pretty cool. Well, not cool that it happened, but you know, like cool that it helps us get it.

Me: I'm with ya, Evan. He is right on! Think of all the things you guys did in just that one image. You connected, you questioned, you inferred, you made judgments about what was important, you analyzed, you thought about point of view, and you immediately recalled and retold parts of our novel. Those are all the things that great readers do all the time! You're geniuses. So let's get back into the book with these new understandings and see how this shapes our reading. Let's keep using the author's words, your own mental images, and any historical evidence or artifacts to help us understand this difficult journey of school integration.

A Final Note: Going Public

"Going public," or giving kids opportunities to share what they've learned, is essential in making inquiry meaningful and important. In Chapter 10, we show how you can go through many "going public" options with kids at the end of any inquiry unit.

Throughout our *Warriors* literature circle inquiry, the kids were fascinated with particular historical figures in Beals' book. Students kept a running list of fascinating characters in their journals and I kept one on chart paper as well. Then, as we came to the end of the book, I asked kids to list their lingering questions about these personages.

> How could Governor Faubus do that?
> Did Melba really like, like Link?
> Was Elizabeth Eckford scared when the mob approached her?
> Were there nice white kids in the school too?
> Did Minnijean really throw her chili on those boys on purpose?
> What did the Nine go on to do after Central High? Did they all graduate?

The lingering questions were developed in group discussions, where kids had great conversations about different people's roles in Little Rock. Each lit circle group chose one historical figure as the subject of a further inquiry, and they went off to work.

Right about this time, we got some amazing news. Dr. Terrence Roberts, one of the Little Rock Nine himself, was coming to visit Burley! Through a generous grant from Facing History, we were selected as one of the two schools he would visit on his next trip to Chicago, to share his "Lessons from Little Rock." The kids and I were totally psyched!

Building on our character research, we decided to create a mural scene for Dr. Roberts upon his arrival. Each lit circle inquiry group would create one life-size person on butcher paper, decorating it with texts summarizing their newfound research. The kids went wild with this. They measured as closely as they could get to life size, designed outfits accurate to the time and person, and used their research and writing skills to create informative nonfiction features (captions, titles, labels) for their audience to read and learn from. One group that finished early asked if they could create a mural of the façade of Central High. I couldn't turn them down.

The result was Dr. Terrence Roberts walking into a hallway of familiar faces from his teen years at Little Rock Central High. As he sat on the rug with my class, small groups of students got up and performed a series of tableaux scenes, their own lessons from Little Rock.

This past year, when I taught the *Warriors* lit circle unit at The Bishop's School, I was again fortunate enough to have Terrence Roberts visit. To say that his presence and wisdom had a huge impact on my kids would be an understatement.

I'll admit, I also have a teacher's sense of pride *for* my students—for their hard work, their passion, their curiosity, and their empathy. The email exchange in Figures 9.11 and 9.12 between Simran, one of my students, and Dr. Roberts shows that these upstanders are already making positive change in the world.

Hello Dr. Roberts,
I wanted to thank you so much for coming to Bishops! It was a great honor being able to introduce you and I will never forget being part of the Roberts Team! After listening to you speak, I have noticed a lot about my self that I hadn't noticed before, such as how much I don't bother to find out, and how only my reactions to other people can affect me.

My mom came and listened to both of your talks, one to the student body and your talk in the evening, and she still won't stop talking about how impressed she is and how my sister and I must soak in everything you said! She continues to stress the fact that everyone has an "A brain". Your humbleness both shocked my mom and increased her respect for you by a two-fold and it was my mom who convinced me to type up a list called "My Personal Lessons From Little Rock", so that I never forget what I learnt from you. I have attached the list to this email. Every time I read the list I feel re-inspired in every way!

Thank you for making a positive impact on my personality!

Respectfully,
Simiran Deokule

Figure 9.11 Simran's thank-you email to Dr. Roberts.

Simran,

Thank you for sharing your "Personal Lessons!!" I just returned from a three-day visit to schools in Clark County Nevada and it would have been great to pass out your list to all the students I saw there. Hopefully they too were able to glean as much as you did.

During the Q and A session, one student asked me, "Why do you do this?" Meaning, (I think) why did I bother to come and talk to them. I responded by saying that some of his fellow students were interested in learning as much as possible about everything. It was, in a way, a bit sarcastic and I felt badly afterward but now I have a different answer. Now I will respond: "Because of Simran!!"

Keep learning all the lessons of life!

Ciao,

T. Roberts

Figure 9.12 Dr. Roberts' email response to Simran that absolutely made her year.

PERSONAL LESSONS FROM DR. TERRENCE ROBERTS
Simran Deokule

- *No "likes" or "ums"!!!*
    - If English is going to be the main language of the country you live in, then why not be proficient in the language?
    - We have to invest ourselves in things that will help in the long run, instead of being ignorant out of fear of work.

- *The Insult Grading Scale*
    - What others think about you does not define who you are

- *See the dragon yourself and then figure out how to deal with it*
  - Don't make someone else's fear your own. Face the fear, and then carry out actions according to how YOU feel/react.

- *Fear is portable, but should not interfere*

- *Everyone has an "A brain!"*
  - Everyone has the full capacity/ability to learn and get good grades. Use that ability to its fullest.
  - As a kid, our only responsibility is to learn, so learn!!!!!
    - Be your own executive of learning. Knowledge is the only true power!!
  - Make the reduction of your infinite ignorance your life goal.
    - Be aware and knowledgeable of things around you and how they affect you.

- *I'm just throwing this out there, this is my point of view*
  - Don't be afraid to say your truth or what you believe in. Speak your mind. (ie. Dr. Roberts told everyone that he disapproved of smoking, even if they smoked)
  - COURAGE!!!!
  - Don't EVER compromise your truth because of what others think

- *"There is opportunity in every difficulty"*
  - Experiences that seem negative are actually positive because of what you learn from each experience. Appreciate all experiences and look back on them being grateful of what you learned. (ie. Dr. Roberts has had many "bad" experiences, yet he looks back on them with a smile because these are the experiences that have built his character.)
  - Dr. Roberts knows that so many people look up to him and consider him a hero, yet in none of his speeches did he talk about his personal difficulties or ever seem sad/depressed, even after going through everything he did.
  - Humble

- *My favorite quote*
  - "Since we humans have developed enough fire-power to blow up the entire universe, why don't we stop now and consider how we might use the same brainpower we have employed to take us to the very edge of existence to figure out how to live in peace?"

- *Read one book every week!!!*

Standards Skills:
- Produce clear and coherent writing in which the organization and style are appropriate to purpose and audience.
- Write a letter that reflects an opinion.

Open Inquiries

Open inquiries happen when we say to kids: "I've been choosing the topics and teaching you the school curriculum for a while. So now, what do *you* want to learn? Do you have some curiosities, some hot topics or burning questions you'd like to explore?" The first time we do this, kids will stare back at us blankly as if asking, "What did you just say?"

In the family of inquiry circles, open inquiries are often the last-introduced model of small-group investigation. Sometimes, teachers don't trust kids to stay focused and productive early in the year. Others worry about covering important content before they make room for kids' topics. And in many school districts, teachers don't dare let kids pick their own research topics until the high-stakes testing season ends in the spring. Only then, as teachers so often tell us, does the coast look clear for students "to actually learn something" or (heaven forbid) "just have some fun."

But, we think, why wait? We did the following open inquiry with all five of Sara's classes in October. The idea was to help hook kids on investigating their own topics at the *start* of the year, so they could then apply their budding inquiry skills to curricular topics for all the months to come. Smokey flew in to coteach the first couple of days and then stayed engaged with the classes through Edmodo, Skype, texts, and emails. We begin Day 1 as Smokey invites the first group of sixth graders to the rug, and then introduces open inquiries.

184

Open Inquiry: What Do You Wonder?

Day 1 (60 minutes)

Step 1. Modeling Your Own Curiosity

"When you come to school every day, most of the time the teacher decides what you will be studying, right? She introduces a topic, and that's what you read about, write about, or do research on. Maybe it is the Constitution or photosynthesis or some other topic, and Ms. Ahmed always makes it interesting. Those topics are what teachers call the *curriculum*. This is a body of knowledge that the school or the state has decided is really important for kids to learn.

"But your topics, your questions, your curiosity are really important, too. As you have been learning all these awesome research skills, it's important for you to put them to work on topics you've chosen for yourself. So for the next three weeks, we are turning the tables and asking you: What would *you* like to learn? What are some hot topics or burning questions for you these days? What have you been wondering about or curious about? And, who are some friends who'd like to join your quest?"

Many of the kids look a little lost here.

"It's kind of hard to just suddenly envision this, right? So let me give you a little help to start.

"I have a teacher friend in Wisconsin named James Beane who says that we all walk around with two kinds of questions in the back of our minds. Jim calls one type 'self questions,' meaning curiosities about ourselves and our everyday lives, little things that puzzle or annoy us, or personal problems we are trying to solve. And then we also have bigger 'world questions' about things that affect people around us, across the country, and even around the world. Right now, I am going to share a few of my current self and world questions, to show you how you can notice and list the things that you wonder about, that are maybe percolating in your head. OK?"

Over about ten minutes I gradually share three self and three world topics I am interested in. As I jot down each entry on chart paper, I tell a little story about how I got curious about the topic and answer a few of the kids' questions. Here's how the first one went . . .

"Yesterday, before I got on the plane to come here, I took a hike in the big nature preserve behind my house, and I was stalked by an animal. Yes, really.

"You guys know that I live in the high desert outside Santa Fe, which is very beautiful with mountains all around and lots of wild animals. So I was walking along this trail and suddenly I noticed this large creature who was walking parallel to me, but

Figure 10.1 Smokey modeling observations of a pronghorn in his neighborhood.

about three hundred yards away. I walked ahead and it walked ahead, and every couple hundred feet it would stop and look at me, and I looked back at him. And then we'd walk ahead some more, and every time he was edging a little closer to me. We'd stop and look at each other and then walk on. I finally figured out that he was pacing me, like he was trying to figure out how fast this human could go. There was a fence blocking him right up ahead, and he was going to either run ahead of me or go back behind me. But the second I figured this out, he takes off and just rockets ahead of me and across the trail so fast I couldn't believe it. Want to see a picture of this animal?"

I project a photo here (see Figure 10.1). There are some oohs and aahs from the kids, and in every class someone blurts out, "It's so cute!"

"It was a pronghorn, which is a kind of antelope that lives in small herds around my neighborhood. They are pretty shy and I'd seen them only a few times before. But now after seeing that blazing speed, I was much more curious about these critters. I looked them up on my phone and immediately saw that pronghorns are the fastest land animal in North America. What!? I was amazed, and now I want to learn more about this curious creature.

"So that's one way you might find a 'self question' for an inquiry topic; you have an experience with something that makes you curious or interested."

I offer a couple more of my own self questions, and then switch to the other side of the chart and share some world questions.

SMOKEY'S SELF AND WORLD QUESTIONS

Self	World
Pronghorn antelopes	Asteroid impacts
Choosing a coyote-proof dog	Pueblo/Navajo history
Salmonella poisoning	Child labor rates decreasing

Step 2. Kids Develop Self/World Question Lists
In their **inquiry journals**, I invite kids to draw a similar two-column chart (or fold a page in half vertically) and begin jotting down some of their own self and world questions. Sara and I reassure them that we are just getting started with topics. We'll spend plenty of time to make sure everyone has a really energizing topic, something they really care about and can stick with for weeks of research.

64

We tell kids to think first, then jot entries as they occur to them. Even so, this step is a speed bump in every class. Many kids struggle at this point, and more than a few have completely blank pages in front of them.

Game-Time Decision

We chat about this seeming helplessness between periods. We realize that good students like these, who are so accustomed to cheerfully taking instructional orders, may seem a little floored when someone asks them out of the blue, "What do you want to learn?" So, to provide more support in the next four classes, we encourage the kids to find a partner and talk it over before they write. Gradually, between the thinking, listing, and talking, pages begin to fill with self and world questions.

 73

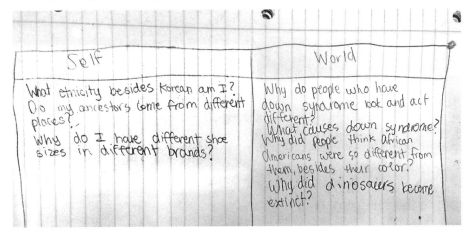

Figure 10.2 Elaine's self and world questions list.

Next, we ask the kids to share out some of their questions. With some classes, we scribe for them on chart paper; with others, we let kids bring a question on a Post-it note and put it up. This results in a brief logjam, but it lets the kids stretch and wiggle—and they do love coming up to the board. Students have developed a wide array of queries as shown in Figure 10.3, from the most idiosyncratic "self" topics to the most momentous "world" concerns.

After the kids have gone home, Sara and I look at the lists from all five classes and smile. What a perfect embodiment of the range of developmental issues among these adorable middle schoolers. We are definitely off and running!

Self Questions

*Could you surf a tsunami?

*What are the best kind of cleats for soccer shoes?

What's the history of the TV show *Psych*?

How come I can't have a cell phone?

Why do we have Daylight Savings Time?

Why do dogs calm people down?

How exactly do you set a spike in volleyball?

*Can I learn to do telekinesis?

Cheese—how did it start?

Why are Apple's products so successful?

How can you be twins, but don't even look alike?

On the first Thanksgiving why did people eat turkey? Why didn't they eat chicken?

Is there a hypoallergenic cat my family could get?

How does 3-D printing work?

*How can I learn more about bonds and how to sell and buy them?

*How long could the average American survive in the wilderness?

Are Native American sports team mascots offensive to the tribes?

Why was Team Oracle penalized in the America's Cup races?

Why did I sleepwalk and reorganize the bookshelf at my house?

Could Scotland become its own country?

World Questions

*What happens when you die?

*What makes people happy?

How was the universe created?

Why does war exist even though there are so many other more peaceful ways to solve conflicts and disagreements?

In the future will animals be able to talk?

Does God even exist?

*Is time travel possible?

What causes déjà vu?

Why do people waste so much food?

Can we stop the melting of the polar ice caps?

*What are the different forms of martial arts?

Why is the U.S. government acting so wacky?

Should we keep orca whales in captivity?

Is global warming really real?

What happens when we run out of oil?

Are there aliens living on other planets?

What was the first animal that appeared in the seas of the world?

Does living today require less intelligence because of modern technology?

How instrumental is philosophy in science and math?

*What do dreams mean?

Figure 10.3 The list of open-inquiry questions from Sara's sixth graders. Items marked with an asterisk developed into group projects later, often with many revisions.

Day 2: Jumping into Research with a Reading Frenzy (60 minutes)

Now we want the kids to do some quick initial research to see which of these varied topics have "legs"—which ones will sustain a substantial small-group inquiry lasting perhaps ten class periods. In *Comprehension and Collaboration*, Smokey and Steph Harvey recommend an initial, deliciously indiscriminate research phase they call a "reading frenzy." The idea is: kids usually cannot pose a very good inquiry question unless they have *some* information about the topic. The Hubble telescope may sound cool, but what is it? Where is it? What does it do? In a reading frenzy, kids get a quick and fun infusion of background knowledge and further research leads. Here's how Sara set them up.

"OK, you guys, here are your awesome question lists from yesterday. Will you please choose from our big list the one topic that has the greatest appeal for you right now. Don't worry, you can change later. This is just for now. Got one? Great. Now jump on your laptops and do some quick searching. Try to figure out if your topic is:

1. Fun and interesting.
2. Researchable—there is plenty of material available about it.
3. Important—complex and significant enough to be worth your time.

"OK? Off you go!"

Kids scatter to the computers and tablets, and begin quick searches into their topics. Most immediately find oodles and googles of research material, images, videos, charts, graphs, you name it. If these hits lead to highly technical information, I remind them to add "for kids" to their searches to locate content at a more sixth-grade-friendly reading level.

Meanwhile, some kids who picked from the smaller "self" topics are getting their questions completely and immediately answered. Johann, who was wondering about the penalty in the America's Cup races, quickly finds that the offending crew had placed five-pound weights in a couple of prohibited locations. When they were caught, race officials dealt a draconian-by-any-measure penalty of three races in a nine-race series. Johann was happy to get this information, but he also said out loud: "Well, that question's done," recognizing that he needed

Standards Skills:

- Ask open-ended research questions and develop a plan for answering them.
- Conduct short research projects based on focused questions, demonstrating understanding of the subject under investigation.
- Gather information from a range of relevant print and electronic sources.
- Gather relevant information from multiple print and digital sources.
- Read closely to determine what the text says explicitly and to make logical inferences from it; cite specific textual evidence when writing or speaking to support conclusions drawn from the text.

to move to something bigger. He turned his attention to the best places in the world to surf and teamed up with some buddies who were focused on all things aqua sports.

Now Smokey and I call the kids back to the rug for one last minute.

"For homework tonight, please chat with each other on **Edmodo**, expanding and connecting your inquiry questions, and being on the lookout for some possible partners with similar interests. Feel free to do some more reading and investigating on possible questions."

SMOKEY: *Of course you can have kids do this homework on paper and bring it in for sharing the next day. But this is an example of when technology inarguably provides a better way for kids to work, doing the research and the conversation simultaneously, on their own time. This is not about any brand or device, but about having this kind of sociable space to work in.*

Looking in on kids' posts that evening, we see some promising connections being made. Melanie, Michael, and Alexander came up with a whole series of subtopics—something every good inquiry team needs.

> **Melanie:** Michael, I care about global warming. I also want to look at energy usage and how we can prevent global warming.
> **Michael:** Really? Yay.
> **Alexander:** I also really want to study global warming, Melanie. I want to learn about the gas shortage and I am interested in seeing renewable energy resources.
> **Michael:** I want to know what happens when global warming takes extreme effect.
> **Alexander:** I am also curious to see what happens when we run out of oil.

Sammie, Morgan, and Bobby quickly decide that they are a team, eager to tackle the exotic/romantic/cinematic topic—time travel:

> **Morgan:** Sammie and I are going to find out if time travel is possible or not. We have already found lot of answers and thoughts from scientists and other people about time travel so I definitely think it is researchable. This is something I would really like to know because it would be very cool to know if it was possible.
> **Sammie:** I am going to research time travel with Morgan. I was wondering how this could even be remotely possible, but it looks like quite a few scientists have theories. This is a topic many people ponder over and I

think scientists are trying to figure it out, so we will have a lot to work with. I think it is researchable even if we don't find the answer to "is time travel possible."

Bobby: I really want to know about time traveling too. Is it really possible (in the future)? Imagine going back in time and watching great historical events—you could even take a trip for a school project back in time. But for this not to be dangerous you would have to be unnoticed when in a future or previous time period.

Day 3: More Research and Group Formation (60 minutes)

When kids come back in the next day, we want to help them continue probing their alternative topics for fun factor, researchability, and significance—and to continue forming groups around similar interests. The just-right tool for this job is a **standing discussion** we call a mingle—a researchers' speed-dating event. As kids finish their soft-start reading, we call them to the rug with journals and pencils.

 ❯ 71

"When we were reading your awesome Edmodo posts from last night, we saw that some new topics have come up, some seem to have been dropped, and a few of you have already started to form groups. We copied down every research topic you mentioned on Edmodo onto this chart paper. Does it look right? Are these all the topics that are still in the running for your groups? Did we miss anything? OK!"

This is a shorter, single-column list now, combining the mostly world questions kids began focusing on yesterday and a couple of new ones from the Edmodo chat, along with the few self questions still under consideration.

"Now we want to take the next step toward choosing topics and forming inquiry groups. Through your conversations last night, you have already winnowed the list down to topics that are capturing the most people's attention. Now, take a good look at what's left on the possible topic list. When you are ready, grab a notecard and write down your own first and second choices. That means pick the two topics you are most excited to spend time investigating with some friends over the next couple of weeks. Take your time."

Casey wonders, "What if I am already sure what I want to do? Can I have just one?" We tell him fine, go ahead.

"OK, everyone ready?

"Today we are going to have a standing discussion, something like our old favorites the 'human continuum' or 'where do you stand?' This one's called a 'mingle.' Have any of you mingled before? Do you know what that word means?"

We define the term as having a short conversation with many people in a row, as you might briefly chat with other guests when arriving at a big family gathering, a party, or a wedding.

Standards Skills:

- Prepare for and participate effectively in a range of conversations and collaborations with diverse partners, building on others' ideas and expressing their own clearly and persuasively.
- Work productively with others in teams and participate productively in discussions.
- Consult with others; decide upon a topic.

"Today we are going to get up and mingle for one minute each with ten other people, sharing your top two research choices. Ten people in ten minutes! That's quick. You're going to have manage the time carefully, make sure that both partners get to share, and then quickly find another partner when the minute is up. Your job is to share your enthusiasm about your topic with others—to 'sell' your idea as a great topic to investigate."

"Before you sit back down you should have figured out who your 'research tribe' is going to be. You'll come back to the rug and sit with them, ready to tell us what your topic is. OK? A tribe needs at least three people. Bring your card along, find your first partner, and mingle!"

We keep time for the kids, stirring them to move to a new partner every minute or so. When time is winding down, we instruct: "Gather your new tribe and sit down with them." When the kids gradually come back to the rug and sit in their newfound tribes, we ask them to share their topics.

During third period, Theo, Dash, and Bobby are wildly waving their hands in the air.

"OK," says Sara, "what are you guys going to investigate?"

"Death!" they holler in unison, giving each other a big high-five.

Smokey asks them to clarify, and they explain that their plan is to research how death is understood in different world religions. When Sara matter-of-factly approves of their topic, they turn to each other and exult out loud, "We made it!"

Game-Time Decision

During the first class of the day, we had kids mingle first and then come back to the rug to try and form groups after even further whole-group discussion. This longer exploration not only slowed things down, but also triggered a few kids to resist being in a research group at all. Of course, there are always these solitary-learning kids in our classes, and sometimes it is wise to let them work alone. And yet, long term, it is not a gift to these kids if we always exempt them from the cooperative work that is so much a part of life in the nonschool world. So, at about 9:15 that morning, we made a game-time decision. We told the next four classes not to come back to the rug without forming a tribe, and this harnessed positive peer pressure to get the teams figured out. There were no more wannabe Lone Rangers the rest of the day.

Not every group is quite as over the moon with their topics as the Death Boys, but solid curiosity and good energy do abound. As the day rolls on, groups are formed on topics like these:

happiness
color spectrum and symbols
cosmic universe
economics
evolution of life
life and death
space and time travel
sports and sporting equipment
telekinesis
domestic animals
war and peace
America's trade partners
surfing spots of the world

As you can see, topics have shifted, been combined, and been renamed to include related subjects and get everyone under an umbrella. You'll notice that many kids have discarded the smaller "self" questions and have gravitated toward broader, more significant questions. Smokey has seen this pattern while doing open inquiries in schools all around the country. Given a patient and thoughtful selection process, most kids are attracted to topics that matter, issues that make a difference.

Day 4: Further Investigation (90 minutes)

Kids have formed their tribes and now it is time for groups to develop some sub-questions within their larger topics. This is an opportunity for individuals to specialize, to choose a narrower part of the topic that's aligned with their interests—or at least to divide up the work into manageable chunks. Now that Smokey has flown home to New Mexico, Sara takes over again.

Step 1. Narrowing a Topic

Before kids dig deeper into their topics, I want to model how to hone and refine a research question, to make sure they don't waste their time with information that's too general or off the mark. So I do a little **think-aloud.**

 60

"So you guys know that my own inquiry question is: What is the best running shoe for me? Well, I think I really need to ask a few things about all the shoes out there and even about myself. When I went to buy a new shoe, the salesperson asked me what kind of runner I am. This led to so many more questions. All I wanted was the pink, glow-in-the-dark shoes! To find out what the best running shoe is for me, I have to trim down my big question to some smaller questions, I think. So here is what I really am wondering":

Standards Skills:

- Ask open-ended research questions.
- Brainstorm, consult with others, and formulate a major research question to address the research topic.
- Work productively with others in teams and participate productively in discussions.

What kind of runner am I?

What shoes best support short-distance running, but can be used for longer distances as well?

What brands are the most trusted?

What is that barefoot running idea all about?

Is my running shoe size really bigger than my regular shoe size?

I ask this one because the last pair I bought are a whole size and a half bigger than my regular shoes. "Can you guys see how I am narrowing down what I really want to know about running shoes? I need to become a mini-expert on some very important details so I can really get to what I am wondering.

 64

"I want you guys to try the same thing right now. In your **inquiry journal**, try and come up with two or three questions that you, personally, are really wondering about your tribe's inquiry topic. What do you think gets to the heart of the subject? I will give you a couple minutes to think on your own before you meet with your group; that way you can have some quiet thinking space. Who knows—there may be someone in your group who is wondering the exact same thing as you. Or something totally different, which would also be awesome."

Kids write in their notebooks and as I move around and visit, I notice that many entries are very broad at first.

What is the history of soccer? (Lila)

What happens when you die? (Matthew)

Is time travel possible? (Morgan)

I kneel down next to a couple kids and talk them through their thinking. Many times, just talking out loud helps them chip away at the topic and find what they are really looking for. I ask questions like:

- What is it about the whole history of soccer that you want to know? The players? The equipment? Where it started? The World Cup?
- Do you want to know about death in actual medical terms? Like your heart stops? Or science? Or religion, as you guys discussed earlier?
- Time travel is such a far-out topic. Do you want to know the science behind it? Wormholes? If anyone has ever done it? What movies have featured it?

These quick conversations help kids to zoom in. I see some erasing, crossing out, and lightbulbs going on. It takes persistence to hand over this responsibility to kids; they are so accustomed to absorbing someone else's information. We haven't taught them to pose their own questions, only to answer ours. So, it requires lots of talking, conferencing, negotiating, and monitoring. This is the essence of the facilitator role we have to add to our repertoires as inquiry teachers.

I give the kids the go-ahead to get into their tribes and share what each of them is hoping to become an expert on. I walk around, listen, and do some more negotiating when needed.

Step 2. Making a Work Plan and Calendar

When I visit with each group, I also pass out a Tribe Work Plan (shown in Figure 10.4).

I explain that this is both a planning tool and a contract. "Once you negotiate and decide what each of you would like to become an expert on, you should write down your sub-questions and then list who will be responsible for each one, so everyone has a clear direction."

The kids talk through some more ideas and questions. Some groups have one person who grabs the sheet and declares that he will do the writing. In others, someone suggests something like: "Guys, everyone write down their own questions, and then write your name next to it. Then pass it on."

I invite everyone back to the rug after about fifteen minutes of hashing it out. "So, let's hear from the groups. What are you going to be experts on?" Kids come up to the doc camera if they want to share the work plan or they can talk to the class from where they are sitting. Their choice. The catch is that they have to share someone else's expert question before they share their own. This helps them (and shows me) that they are becoming great active listeners. A key to being a leader, I tell them: *Listen before you lead.*

TRIBE WORK PLAN

Open Inquiry Topic:_____

Member Names:

1.

2.

3.

4.

What are some specific questions you each plan to pursue? Usually it helps for groups to divide the main topic into several questions or subtopics for different members to specialize in.

Questions we want to explore!	Name: Who will be the experts?

Figure 10.4 Work plan handout.

Louise comes right up to the doc camera. "Well, we are all interested in sports, so we are going to look at different equipment we need for sports we like. So like, soccer, Gavin is going to do snowboarding, things like that."

"Louise, can you tell us in the form of a research question?" I prod.

"Oh ya, so like Arman wonders what soccer cleat is best for strikers to score goals and run fast. Gavin wants to know what snowboard he should get." See Figure 10.5.

When we are making our work plan, it is a logical moment to create another organizational tool—a project

Standards Skills:

- Listen attentively to others in formal and informal settings.
- Create a written plan after preliminary research.

Tribe Work Plan

Topic Sports

Names

1. Jack Scoma
2. Ki Greene
3. Matthew Cohen
4. Craig Devoe
5.

What are some specific questions you plan to pursue? Sometimes it works for groups to divide the main topic into several questions or sub-topics for different members to specialize in.

Questions we want to explore!	Name: Who is responsible?
Scuba diving gear and how it originated.	Craig
NFL and the history and some great players and equipment	Ki and (matthew)
Water polo origins why we play it and facts	Matthew and (Jack)
Lacrosses history and equipment.	Jack

What research resources do you expect you use? (Internet, library, interviews, etc)

Internet - ScoreCenter, Youtube, answers
Books - Sports illustrated

Figure 10.5 Filled-out Tribe Work Plan.

Figure 10.6 Sophie's calendar with target dates.

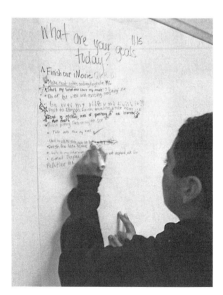

Figure 10.7 Adam during a midcourse correction day: Tasks were getting too big, so we set goals for just that day.

calendar as shown in Figure 10.6. Creating this can be a minilesson of its own, done on the same day or the day after the work plan. The process looks much like the one we use with literature circle inquiries (see pages 169–171). We usually start with a partially filled-out calendar showing the beginning and ending dates of our inquiry project, plug in school holidays and events, and then turn it over to the kids to schedule in the specific steps they need to take. As the project unfolds, we will have frequent "midcourse corrections," during which kids take out their work plans, calendars, and research notebooks to monitor their own goals and adjust schedules as needed.

Step 3. Debriefing the Group Formation Process (20 minutes)

Once groups are formed and work plans and calendars roughed in, I ask kids to debrief how this intensive collaborative process went. I begin by asking how they divided up their possible subtopics. Some teams report that they went around the group and each person took a turn. Others say that some members just blurted out what "I get." In some groups, a couple of people had pretty similar questions and so they decided to both become experts on it. My favorite comment: "We saw how cool everyone's questions are!" There is a lot of momentum building.

Then I point out some things that I noticed as I walked around as well.

"I noticed a lot of what you did and I also noticed something interesting when I passed out the tribe work plans. Some of you want to naturally grab them and do the writing, others don't want to go anywhere near the paper, and some of you suggested that everyone get a chance to write down their own questions.

"Why do you think all these different reactions happened? Can you guys be honest and upfront about how you acted at your tables?"

SMOKEY: *Once again, we see Sara directly asking her kids to be honest and brave.*

> **Maddie:** Well, we all have different personalities, like, I like to write so I wanted to do that.
>
> **Morgan:** Ya, I can't read the paper when other people write (*she shoots a look at some of the boys*), some of us like to write more than others.
>
> **Miles:** Ya, well, the girls just want to do everything and get their ideas down first so no one will take it!

Before we have a gender brawl, I meet them halfway.

"I think it could be all of these things. When we work in groups we have to deal with our friends who are bossy, friends who are quiet, friends who just like to work alone, and friends who always help others. There are so many different types of people we can work with. So we have to be extremely thoughtful about how we talk to others and respond to others, because it is not just you working alone anymore, you're a tribe. So if you are bossy or if you want to do everything yourself, or just by yourself, try and think of the most positive ways you can help the whole group be successful, because you are all going to take good care of each other and help out. Cool? Give me a thumbs up if you are with me . . . "

Thumbs ups. Nods. And "cools."

"Awesome."

SMOKEY: *There's another form of teacher honesty here. When the context and community are just right, Sara can give challenging feedback and directly ask for kids' cooperation.*

Day 5. Extending the Research: Scanning and Assessing Website Information (20 minutes)

Now we are shifting gears into the sustained research work that will occupy the next few days. Kids will be doing much of this investigating outside of class, searching on the web, and I want them to be efficient with this. They need to be able to quickly and accurately scan web content for value, usefulness, and trustworthiness. So I **think aloud** a web search.

I project a Google home page and type in "running shoes." A huge list—millions of pages—comes up and I read the titles of just the first few. These look like stores I can buy from, but I don't want that yet. I find one that looks to be an article from a running magazine and click on it. I model how to scan the page.

As I work, I tell the kids what I'm doing:

"First I check out the title. Then I read the first few lines. Hmmm, this seems relevant.

"Let me scroll down the page to see if there are any other text features like subtitles, charts, photos, et cetera that might help me. These charts might be interesting.

"I read this magazine a lot and I assume it is a reliable source, but you never know. I'm going to get over to the home page and see who publishes this . . . Oh, I see they also publish *Men's Health* and *Women's Health*; those are really solid mags. Yep, this could be a good one for my research from what I can see."

I copy the link and send it to myself on Edmodo with a small note reminding me what it is: "Running magazine article on shoes."

"You can do it just like that. Try and find a few good resources tonight and remember to help others as well."

Now I review the homework for them.

"1. Go back to **Edmodo** and post your chosen expert questions to the group. This way, if anyone happens to come across research that may help you, they know who to post it to. Think of one another as you search.

"2. Continue your research! Using the school's web search tools or your friend Google, begin to create a running list of resources that may help you along the way. You don't need to start reading everything, but scan for what you are looking for. Happy searching!"

Day 6: Refocusing Topics and Supporting Each Other as Researchers (30 minutes)

When kids come back the next day, they have dug into their topics, but their initial findings are all over the map. Two kids walk straight up to me that morning with no intention of a soft start.

> **Lila:** Ms. Ahmed, there are no good websites out there about the World Cup winners, except a stupid chart!
>
> **Louise:** Ya, and I am having a really hard time finding out what goalie gloves are best for keepers except for some random people going on some rant!

Looks like it's time for some reflection on the quality and searchability of topics. And about supporting each other as researchers. I have them sit in their tribes at the rug so we can easily switch between whole-group and tribe talk.

Knowing that there will be some venting, I begin: "I saw your posts and resources you shared last night. How did the research go?"

Matthew triumphantly exclaims to the group: "I found a lot of websites about my topic!"

Annie looks exasperated. "How? I couldn't do my homework because I didn't find any websites really. Can I change my topic?"

"There wasn't much about my question. Some stuff looked good at first but when I looked back it was really dumb."

Ki wonders, "Did anyone else have a hard time finding answers or research to their question?" and quite a few hands go up.

"Let's think about this a little. Why are some questions highly researchable and some not? Why were some of you immediately successful and others had more trouble?"

Andrew offers a solution: "Maybe it is a yes or no question and that's it. So you guys can't find much."

Rocco offers: "Like my question about survival in sailing is one that will have specific answers, but some are just people's opinions too."

Quinn also connects to our research talks on mini-inquiries: "Some questions are just maybe too narrow when you type them in or too big to find the answer you're looking for. Like Annie, you want to know about the whole history of cycling; that is a huge topic! Maybe you could zoom in on like the bikes or the people or something."

Standards Skills:

- Determine, locate, and explore relevant sources addressing a research question.
- Gather relevant information from multiple sources; assess the credibility and accuracy of each source.
- Clarify research questions and evaluate and synthesize collected information.
- Narrow or broaden the major research question, if necessary, based on further research and investigation.

Ryan describes what he did: "I tried to type in the exact question we were looking for and that doesn't always work. I got a bunch of weird people on Yahoo answers just talking."

"Why don't you guys turn and talk with your other tribe members and check in. Who needs support?"

Now I want groups to support their members who haven't had a lot of luck with their questions. I already know from last night's Edmodo posts who might be struggling. I suggest that they try searching as a group and see what they come up with. I send them off to talk it out.

While the groups work, I target a few necessary conferences with kids I know need attention. I start with Lila, who walked in frustrated about her measly one-chart resource about World Cup winners. We talk about what she really wants to know and look over the chart together. We both notice that Brazil has won so many tournaments and I ask her why she thinks that is. What is their secret? She is able to form a more developed question: What makes certain teams so successful at the World Cup?

Day 7: Interviewing an Expert (30 minutes)

Books, magazines and websites aren't kids' only sources of information. About halfway through the inquiry process, I suggest that kids interview experts in the field to gain more information about their topics. A good place to start is by sharing an exemplar interview, either on video or in text.

"Guys, so far you have been reading books, magazines, and the Internet for research. All of these resources have experts behind them sharing their knowledge with us. We want to take this even further and try and get hold of a live expert we can talk to face to face, or at least over the phone, to really dig in and get the best stories, information, or thoughts that we can. What better than someone who has actually studied one of the religions you are investigating or experienced one of the greatest surf spots in the world?

"To be really prepared for this, though, we need to be thoughtful about who we choose, what questions we will ask, and how we will follow up with them to say thank you.

"We are going to watch an interview today and I also have a transcript of it if you want to follow along. While we are watching the interview, we are going to notice things that the interviewer and the interviewee are doing.

"Let's make a T-chart. On the left side put 'interviewer' and on the right side put 'interviewee.' Let's watch them for the way they act, how they speak, what they say to one another. You guys are kind of going to act like an interviewer by writing down what you hear and see while you are listening. You'll see that it happens really fast, so try and keep up!"

I choose a video interview with a sports hero or a YA author that they are all more or less familiar with. *Sports Illustrated for Kids* has great video interviews online, and celebrity interviews are everywhere, including *Nickelodeon Kids*. As kids watch, I pause a few times so they can catch up with their observations and turn and talk with a buddy.

When the interview is over, we discuss what they noticed as a whole group. I have an anchor chart ready: "What Makes a Good Interview?"

"This was a great interview! What did you guys notice that we can maybe take away and use in our own interviews?"

Here's what we came up with:

> Listen carefully.
> Nod your head to show you are listening.
> Make eye contact.
> Ask questions that get you longer answers—not just yes or no.
> Ask open-ended questions.
> Let the interviewee do the talking.
> Try and write it down or record it another way.
> Ask follow-up questions.
> Smile.
> Thank your interviewee.

I type this up so kids can glue it in their journals the next day and use it as a reference. It will also serve as part of our co-created rubric at the end.

"How do you guys think the interviewer came up with questions?" Kids say, "They did their research before the interview and really knew what they were going to say" and "They wanted answers about certain things, so asked those questions."

"Right, so we want to start thinking about our own questions and what we want to know more about. And then, we have to be thoughtful about who to approach for an interview.

"For example: if I want to interview someone about my running shoes, I am going to go to Road Runner Sports and talk to a sales associate. They know so much there!

"Then we need to think about what we will ask them. I will probably ask them things like:

> What is the best shoe in your opinion for people who have higher arches?
> What shoes are great for shorter distances? Longer distances?
> Does a lighter shoe mean it is better for my feet?

Standards Skills:
- Create a written research plan.
- Determine, locate, and explore the full range of relevant sources addressing a research question.

"These are all things that I have found in my research, but I want to dig deeper.

"Finally, I will make sure I get my expert's name and contact information so I can send a thank-you note (even after I thank them in person).

"I am going to give you guys a chance to try and think of some experts you can contact. Start with parents, friends' parents, teachers, and adults you are familiar with. If we can get hold of some of these experts we are reading from, that would be awesome too! OK, off you go to try and find your expert and think of some questions you will ask them."

SMOKEY: *We always try to include live expert interviews with these open inquiries. It is a wonderful way to bring the research process, which kids sometimes find cold and abstract, very much to life. Where we might have trouble motivating students to make notes on their library research, they can easily see how important it is to prepare a list of interview questions—a protocol—before they sit down with a real adult who is granting them some time. Of course, all these benefits only accrue if we are ready to help kids to find their expert. We rely on our own contacts list pretty often, and we learn to make cold calls to strangers who are almost always delighted to help out a curious student. Best of all, kids often end up truly inspired by the people they've interviewed, their knowledge, their profession, their enthusiasm.*

Day 8: Co-Creating Our Inquiry Project Rubric (25 minutes)

Now that kids are well into the research, it's time to think about their final goals and what they value most about the work they have been doing. We gather on the rug, where else?

"So here we are, eight days into this, and you have all these materials, notes, articles, videos. Some of you guys are drowning in information! We are moving toward our Celebration Day, and we have all these moving parts. We need to develop a checklist to help us get ready to share our learning—and we can also develop that checklist into a rubric we can use to assess ourselves at the very end.

"So let's have a conversation about what elements of the inquiry process we want to monitor as we go—and formally assess at the end."

I will do this with all five classes and chart their suggestions. Here are some of the things kids from the first period wanted to address in our rubric:

- *Sources.* Kids wanted to set a standard of using at least four sources to inform their research, including one book and an interview. I welcomed this, since I don't want kids to be solely Internet dependent.
- *Notetaking.* Kids have been working hard taking research notes, both in alphaboxes and in their notebooks.
- *Calendars.* The kids felt they have been doing a great job keeping track of things on their calendars, so we added that as something we value highly.
- *Home court.* The kids felt they'd really exercised their collaboration and kindness skills while working in their groups.

As the day goes by, I leave up the charts from the previous periods, and we use those as starting point. Naturally, the later classes need shorter discussions to affirm or add to these criteria. At the end of the day, I photograph all five charts and draw on all of them to create an official rubric. The next day, I ask kids to review it and affirm a final version. Once we agree on this, we don't put the rubric aside until the end. Kids start using it right now as a checklist to help them prepare for their Celebration Day presentations. After our celebration, I confer with individual students to discuss and assess the inquiry project using the rubric we created together. See Figures 10.8 and 10.9.

Day 9: Deciding How to Go Public (30 minutes)

As we *X* off the days of our calendars, Celebration Day (aka going public, aka due date) is coming up soon. Kids have been eagerly reading, writing, scouring books and websites, and interviewing experts to find reliable information. To keep their enthusiasm going, I am still trying to find more articles and resources on their topics and pass them along, check in with the tribes on Edmodo, and confer with individuals and tribes about all their new learning.

But at this stage, especially since we have created our rubric, kids are getting antsy about how they will present their findings. I try to stall them a bit longer. I know what will happen once we decide on the sharing format: they will immediately shift to planning their presentations, and pull the plug on finding the answers to their wonderings. Their fruitful discussions in class and on Edmodo will cease. They will focus only on the product.

SMOKEY: *Why are you so sure they'll respond this way? I know you are doing this open inquiry early in the year, before you've had a chance to completely Ahmed-ize these kids. But still, you sound a little fatalistic.*

INQUIRY RUBRIC

Tribe_____ Name_____ Period____

Resources (*required)	4	3	2	1	N/A	Comments
*Book: 　• Title: 　• Author:						
Website(s): 　• Title: 　• URL:						
*Interview: 　• Interviewee: 　• Evidence/notes:						
Film/Show/Media: 　• Title: 　• Location/format:						
Notetaking						
Alphaboxes: 　• Resources listed 　• Thorough						
Journal: 　• Resources listed 　• In own words						
Calendar and Edmodo: 　• Daily use 　• Goals set 　• Organized						
Group Work						
Final Project (one score)						
How did you go public? 　• Was it my best work? 　• Interactive 　• Teachable 　• Entertaining 　• Research displayed						

Figure 10.8 Inquiry rubric.

STUDENT REFLECTION

How did it go for you as a tribe? (Pros, Cons, Wishes, Celebrations)

How did it go for you as an individual? (Pros, Cons, Wishes, Celebrations)

What would you give yourself as a final grade? _____/_____
(How many 4's, 3's, 2's, 1's do you have?)

What would you give your group? _____/_____

Final grade (conference with teacher) _____/_____

Figure 10.9 Student reflection.

SARA: *Maybe just realistic? By the time many kids these days get to middle school, they have been acculturated that it's the product, not the process, that counts. They are goal and grade oriented. So I think prematurely focusing on culminating performances can undermine the enjoyment—and the extended practice—of wide-ranging inquiry. You saw, firsthand, the enthusiasm in the room when they didn't have to talk about the product or grades for a few days. If my focus is on the wonders, reading, collaboration, researching, and collecting evidence, theirs will be, too.*

SMOKEY: *You're a true contrarian. In the standard dogma of grading and scoring, all the requirements of any final performance are supposed to be laid out for kids way earlier, like at the very beginning of the whole inquiry project.*

SARA: *I think that timing prematurely focuses kids on performing, not on finding out. To create such a rubric at the outset of a long unit, the teacher inevitably constrains what the kids might imagine doing. I use a final rubric all right, but we don't create it until toward the end, when kids have thoroughly marinated in information. They are perfectly capable of co-creating and managing an assessment later in the process. As we go through the process, we identify what we value enough to assess. They should be deciding what outcomes matter, with me, so they can be successful in manifesting them in their sharing, with no ambiguous expectations and no surprises.*

When we are ready to talk about going public, I refer back to my own inquiry about running shoes and do a little more modeling. All signs point to going public when kids have collected, winnowed, and weighed abundant information and they start asking, "What are we doing with all of this information? I have pages of notes! Do we have to make a PowerPoint or something about this?"

OK, so now we are on final approach to our "go live" sharing time. Time for another **research-aloud** from me.

 60

"I have been collecting so much information about my feet and shoes, it is ridiculous! And now, I am wondering how I can show all that I have learned to my audience. My research has included lots of diagrams and visual images of feet and shoes, and I think I will need a really visual presentation, so people can understand my new learning.

"There are things I really need to think more about, though. My initial question was all about stuff I was personally motivated by, but now I need to think about making the information interesting and useful to my audience—and how best to do that. I am thinking about my favorite museums where I go to learn, like the Abraham Lincoln museum in Springfield, Illinois, or the Newseum in Washington, D.C. What makes me such an attentive audience there? How are they teaching me? If I want to teach someone about running shoes, how do I best communicate as a brand-new expert?

"Here are some things we all need to consider as we go public." I write them on the board as the kids write in their notebooks:

> Is it engaging? (Can all learners learn from it?)
> Is it teachable? (Does it show, not just tell, all that I have learned?)
> Is it interactive? (Can I help people experience it directly?)
> Is it interesting? (Does it keep the audience's attention?)

I continue with my own plan-aloud.

🧰 〉60

"I think I am going to do a diagram with labels and captions that show both my foot (to indicate what kind of runner I am) and a shoe that will suit my needs. Then I'll need to find a way to explain the reasons and use my evidence."

Now I tell the kids, "Why don't you guys turn and talk for a few minutes about the different ways you have shared your learning with others in the past?" I roam the rug and monitor the conversations.

"Let's come back and talk some more about the ways we can go public with our learning. What are some ways you have showed your learning in school before?"

The kids immediately suggest the usual—a poster or trifold board, an essay, a speech, a PowerPoint. Then I ask them to look around the room and notice the objects we learn from, and we grow our list to include magazines, books, a globe or map, poetry, art, and models.

Standards Skills:
- Produce clear and coherent writing in which the development, organization, and style are appropriate to task, purpose, and audience.
- Organize and present ideas and information according to the purpose of the research and their audience.

"OK, those are all great. Let's continue to think of ways to share. Maybe between us we can grow the list." We brainstorm for a while, and I add any ideas the kids don't think of, until we come up with a list.

"Now, I want you to get in your tribes and discuss the best ways you can go public, as individual members and as a group. Should you all be responsible for a part of a bigger presentation? Should you make individual artifacts or performances that work together? Come up with a few ideas and give yourselves some time to continue researching today."

Students break up into tribes and start making some decisions. They are excited and have gained some new momentum; a few kids immediately start scouting the room for any art supplies, scrap materials, or odd objects they can use. Some sit down and think together, "Why don't we all build a model?" When we come back as a class, we share our possible plans. Kids turn and talk, describing what they are thinking they might create and why. How does their research support this final product?

One tribe wants to build elaborate mazes where the audience has to go on a hunt to find the information. The Life and Death group wants to produce a newspaper on the various religious perspectives on death. The Dreams group has recorded each member's dreams every night in a journal they co-created, so now they will analyze and explain to others what their dreams mean.

I hear a variety of presentation ideas and help navigate kids to good choices. When a few of them start leaning toward PowerPoints, I jump in with some coaching.

"When you use PowerPoints, there are some well-known pitfalls, and I am speaking from the adult world. You often end up with lots of similar slides that each have a title or question followed by some bullet points with the information. This can get tremendously boring to the audience. So the person presenting can't just read the slides, bullet by bullet, word for word. You have to give information beyond what people see or read. PowerPoints can be a really great tool to show your learning, if you go beyond them and bring the audience in."

Standards Skills:
- Marshal evidence to explain the topic and give relevant reasons for conclusions.
- Present findings in a meaningful format.
- Write expository and procedural or work-related texts to communicate ideas and information to specific audiences for specific purposes.

At this point, I have to decide how much more time to allow for performance preparations. There is definitely a slippery slope factor; the kids can get creatively carried away, and the next thing you know they are rehearsing a three-act play with costumes and makeup. Back in Chicago, one of my classes decided to recreate the original Coney Island amusement park to culminate a study on the turn of the twentieth century. It was a huge success with the parents who came to visit, but it took weeks to prepare. For any inquiry project, I carefully keep the prep time proportional to the significance of the subject matter being engaged.

Days 10, 11, 12, and 13: Preparation for Sharing Learning

We take four more days of work time for teams to complete their research, crystallize their findings, and develop powerful ways of sharing knowledge with others.

Day 14: Celebration Day

The kids come in with displays, self-published books, how-to videos, homemade board games, sports-equipment-turned-live-models, props I don't even understand, you name it. I have some tables set up to display projects and ask the kids to meet me on the rug.

"We have worked so hard over the last couple weeks to become experts on our topics and to share our learning with others. Today, you guys will get to see everyone's hard work and teach each other so many new things.

As we discussed earlier, "Rather than having groups perform for the whole class one at a time, we are going to set up in stations by tribe. We will have half the tribes at their station, ready to greet a group of visitors, who will be the other half of the tribes. It will be like a gallery walk, where we can move around the room and stop to look, listen, and react to things we see and hear. Each tribe will visit three other groups. When the first round of visits is over, we'll have a break while the second group of tribes sets up their displays.

"Presenting groups, you will have five minutes to teach each tribe that comes to visit your station. Your job is to show your learning through your demonstration or model, by presenting what you learned, by any posters or handouts you provide, and by answering visitors' questions.

"I have a response form here that we will use when we visit groups. When you are a visitor, you will write the name of the tribe you are visiting and any celebrations you have for them, naming specific things that are really successful or impressive in their work. Then you can add questions for them or ideas you may suggest for next time. Be careful about the 'Goals for next time' section. This is not a time to be hypercritical, but to offer your constructive support to a friend. As audience members, we may notice something the creator of this work never did, because they were so involved. For example, maybe their text size is really hard to read or you are not sure how their model works. In fact, when it is your turn to be an expert, you can take a risk and ask the visitor if they have any suggestions for next time, or how you can improve on your project. Remember that you will be on the giving and the receiving end of this."

I send half the tribes to set up their stations, while the other half stays with me on the rug. We decide what tribe each group will visit so

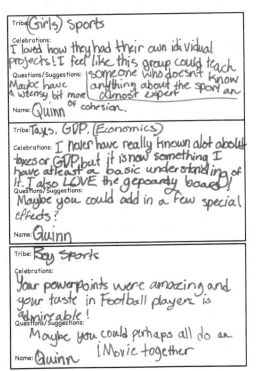

Figure 10.10 Quinn's response form.

there will be no traffic jams and no favorite-friend-only visits. I pass out the response forms and we write down the tribe we will be seeing first and our own name. While we wait another minute, we talk about the things we can notice and comment on as we go around our gallery. I do this by asking this half of the class what they are most proud of on their own projects. Some of them say they worked really hard on technology, some said their creative writing and drawing, others said they built their model and worked on it forever. This is an important conversation; I want kids to recognize the value in the work of others, just as they appreciate their own efforts.

Now, the visitor groups go to the tables of their choice. I walk around with them, clipboard in hand, and fill out the same response form the kids are using. I like this better than taking the rubric around and evaluating them on the spot. This way, I am engaged as a learner alongside everyone else. I can ask questions like: What made you build or create what you did? What surprised you as you researched? What do you know about your topic that you didn't know before? And I can savor how excited they are to share. The forms can serve as notes for my assessment later, in addition to the photos and videos I take all day long. See Figures 10.11–10.18.

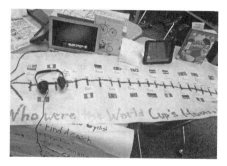

Figure 10.11 For the Sports tribe group, Lila's contribution was a time line of World Cup winners.

Figure 10.12 Poster and artifacts explaining the Tang Soo Do form of martial art.

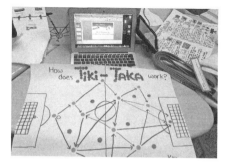

Figure 10.13 The Sports tribe discovered that this soccer strategy had led many teams to World Cup victory.

Figure 10.14 The Telekinesis group trained your mind as they spoke to you, and then gave you a shot at it yourself when they were done!

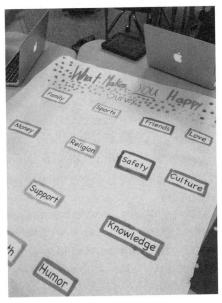

Figure 10.15 The group investigating happiness surveyed visitors about what makes them happy.

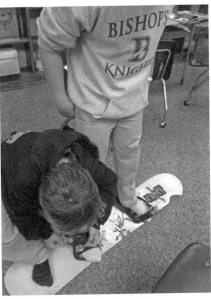

Figure 10.16 Gavin had a trifold board about snowboarding but he also did demos for people so they could experience what he was talking about. Hands-on learning!

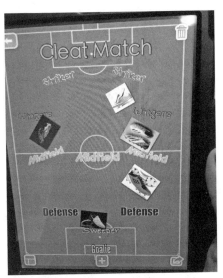

Figure 10.17 Sammy gave visitors a quiz to see if they were listening. Audience members had to move the specific shoe model to the position where it is best utilized.

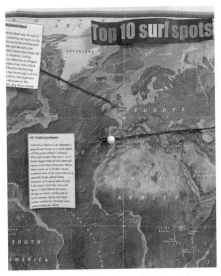

Figure 10.18 After switching topics at the beginning, Johann and his group came up with a map on which they pinned the ten best surf spots in the world, giving their geographic and climate qualities.

Final Assessment

Naturally, we pull out our co-created rubric on Celebration Day. I get kids started with whatever time is left after the presentations and then they complete them for homework.

For the next couple of days, I confer with kids individually, comparing my rubric to theirs and negotiating perceptions. This conferring is very important in the final grade: in any human evaluation process, there should be a dialogue rather than a one-sided review. When we keep this in mind, kids aren't just receiving an arbitrary number or letter grade, but having an honest conversation about what they have been doing well and how to improve.

The final rubric is one key ingredient, but there has also been a tremendous amount of ongoing, formative assessment during the whole inquiry project, all of which now factors into culminating grades. We are constantly listening to the kids, reading their work, conferring with them, observing their habits and behaviors, and recording or charting their work. I use a notebook for this, in addition to my camera for snapshots and videos. I draw upon all these sources when I have grading conferences with kids in the end.

Name Ryan Tribe Sea Life, sports, and survival P 5 Date 12/3		
A new skill I learned or tried?	What did I learn about working in a group?	Next time I will...
• How to setup an interview in a polite way	• To always setup times to meet rather than trying to find them	• Find a better way to express information ✓
• How to edit imovie videos	• Helping group members can improve efficiently	• post more to edmodo
• How to take notes in an organized fashion.	• That disagree-ing is not bad	• finish early rather than late or last minute
• How to find whether a website is credible	• To always check in with your group, so everyone is on the same page	

Figure 10.19 Ryan's reflection.

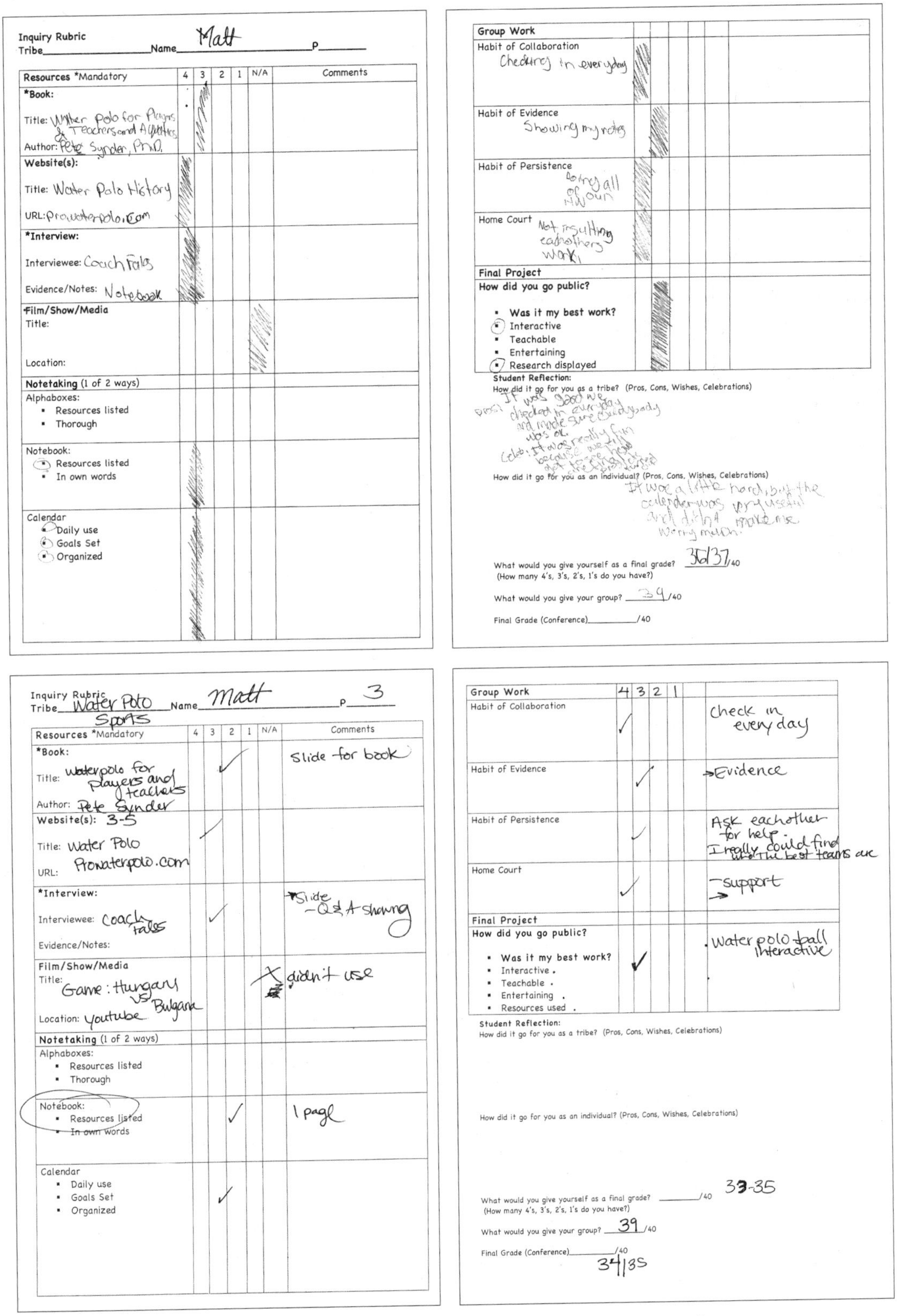

Inquiry Rubric
Tribe______________ Name **Matt** ______________ P______

Resources *Mandatory	4	3	2	1	N/A	Comments
*Book: Title: Water Polo for Players & Teachers and Athletes; Author: Pete Synder, PhD.		✓				
Website(s): Title: Water Polo History; URL: Prowaterpolo.com	✓					
*Interview: Interviewee: Coach Fales; Evidence/Notes: Notebook	✓					
Film/Show/Media: Title: ; Location:					✓	
Notetaking (1 of 2 ways)						
Alphaboxes: ▪ Resources listed ▪ Thorough						
Notebook: ▪ Resources listed ▪ In own words		✓				
Calendar: Daily use; Goals Set; Organized		✓				

Group Work					
Habit of Collaboration: Checking in everyday	✓				
Habit of Evidence: Showing my notes		✓			
Habit of Persistence: Doing all of my own		✓			
Home Court: Not insulting eachothers work		✓			
Final Project					
How did you go public? ▪ Was it my best work? ▪ Interactive ▪ Teachable ▪ Entertaining ▪ Research displayed		✓			

Student Reflection:
How did it go for you as a tribe? (Pros, Cons, Wishes, Celebrations)
Pros: It was good we checked in everyday and made sure everybody was ok. Celeb: It was really fun because we did not force the fighting

How did it go for you as an individual? (Pros, Cons, Wishes, Celebrations)
It was a little hard, but the calendar was very useful and didn't make me worry much.

What would you give yourself as a final grade? 36/37/40
(How many 4's, 3's, 2's, 1's do you have?)
What would you give your group? 39/40
Final Grade (Conference)________/40

Inquiry Rubric
Tribe **Water Polo Sports** Name **Matt** P **3**

Resources *Mandatory	4	3	2	1	N/A	Comments
*Book: Title: waterpolo for players and teachers; Author: Pete Synder			✓			Slide for book
Website(s): 3-5; Title: Water Polo; URL: Prowaterpolo.com	✓					
*Interview: Interviewee: Coach Fales; Evidence/Notes:		✓				*Slide – Q&A showing
Film/Show/Media: Title: Game: Hungary vs Bulgaria; Location: Youtube					X	didn't use
Notetaking (1 of 2 ways)						
Alphaboxes: ▪ Resources listed ▪ Thorough						
Notebook: ▪ Resources listed ▪ ~~In own words~~			✓			1 page
Calendar: ▪ Daily use ▪ Goals Set ▪ Organized			✓			

Group Work	4	3	2	1	
Habit of Collaboration	✓				Check in every day
Habit of Evidence		✓			→Evidence
Habit of Persistence		✓			Ask eachother for help. I really could find the best teams are
Home Court	✓				–support →
Final Project					
How did you go public? ▪ Was it my best work? ▪ Interactive ▪ Teachable ▪ Entertaining ▪ Resources used		✓			Water polo ball Interactive

Student Reflection:
How did it go for you as a tribe? (Pros, Cons, Wishes, Celebrations)

How did it go for you as an individual? (Pros, Cons, Wishes, Celebrations)

What would you give yourself as a final grade? ________/40 33-35
(How many 4's, 3's, 2's, 1's do you have?)
What would you give your group? 39/40
Final Grade (Conference)________/40 34/35

Figure 10.20 Matt's self-assessment (top) and rubric completed with teacher (bottom).

So Worth It

In open inquiries, you get the biggest possible bang for your instructional buck. As teachers, we really step back and let the kids take full responsibility for their own learning. We truly do become facilitators. While this can be a challenge, the payoff is huge. In this open inquiry, the kids did the work. They chose their topics and then scoured books, magazines, and the Internet. They sought out real people to interview and learn from so they could become experts. The kids grappled with the reality of research, learning why and how to validate outside sources for information, and they grew to be critical readers of today's informational universe.

Even with all the structures and supports I built for them, it was sometimes chaotic, messy, unpredictable, and even exhausting. But here's what I saw:

- Kids bringing pieces of their identity into the classroom
- Kids talking to each other, writing with each other, and offering a collaborative hand to others
- Researchers knee deep in books, magazines, models, graphs, and charts, combing for evidence and facts to feed their curiosity
- Curious and critical readers continuing to question the text, the authors, and the experts and asking, "So what?"
- Teams negotiating dates, agendas, and goals, and stopping to make corrections in order to stay on track
- Kids creating and co-creating expectations, goals, and outcomes so they are clear on what they need to do to be successful
- Kids becoming teachers—sharing their knowledge with others, modeling how things work, and clearing up misconceptions
- Kids helping kids, kids teaching kids, kids being kids

We didn't do the thinking or the learning for them; they did it all on their own. It was awesome.

The next few days after the celebrations, we practice "thank-you letter" writing to appreciate everyone who helped us with our research.

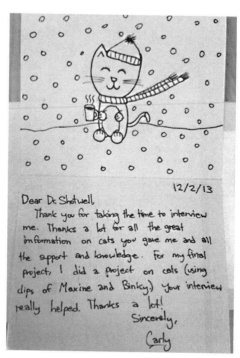

Figure 10.21 Carly thanks her family veterinarian for her interview.

coda

SARA: *About midway through this school year, I had to deal with an emergency and was absent for a few consecutive days. I don't like to be away without warning my kids, but it was unavoidable. Upon my return, I was welcomed with a few great big hugs. "Ms. Ahmed! You're back!" and "Where were you, Ms. Ahmed?"*

But I was not quite prepared for the utter disappointment and scolding I got from Elaine: "Ms. Ahmed, how could you miss my birthday?!"

It made perfect sense. Here was the flawless embodiment of the developmentally self-centered and completely endearing middle schooler. I gave her an extra-big hug and a sincere apology for my negligence. I knew where she was coming from.

Middle school may be the most turbulent years of a kid's social and academic life, and most people shudder to think back on their own experience there. But if we get middle school right, maybe fewer of its graduates will depart with such sad and troubling memories. Those of us who choose to work with young teenagers must bring perspective, wonder, and a broad sense of humor to this gig. Why? Because middle schoolers give us the most authentic version of themselves each day. That may change by the minute, but who can blame them? They bring their best selves to the game if we invite them to do so.

We don't get into power struggles with them, because no one will win. We give them opportunities for shared autonomy and voice. We help them navigate the many choices that will be in front of them soon, and for the rest of their lives. We invite them to wonder about identity and difference, not to practice hold-your-nose tolerance, but to live with genuine compassion. We model for them. We mentor them. We watch them mentor each other. We let them mentor us.

We all have mentors. I was privileged enough to write this book with mine: Smokey Daniels and some of the greatest middle school kids in the world. We have learned so much from kids that we (the kids, me, and Smoke) want to share those gifts with you, the coolest middle school educators in the world.

Laugh with your kids. Tell them how awesome they are, and tell others, too. Seek to know more about them, more than any pieces of "data" can ever give you. Celebrate their curiosity. See the world through their eyes. Listen to them. See the upstander in them. Get to know their hearts. Get to know their minds. Get to know their amygdalas. And please, do not miss their birthdays.

works cited

Allington, Richard, and Rachel Gabriel. 2012. "Every Child, Every Day." *Educational Leadership*. 69 (6): 10–15.

American Psychological Association. 2013. "Teens and Stress." www.apa.org /helpcenter/stress-teens.aspx.

____. 2014. "Teen Suicide Is Preventable." www.apa.org/research/action/suicide.aspx.

Apple, Michael, and James Beane, eds. 2007. *Democratic Schools: Lessons in Powerful Education*, 2d edition. Portsmouth, NH: Heinemann.

Atwell, Nancie. 2007. *The Reading Zone: How to Help Kids Become Skilled, Passionate, Habitual, and Critical Readers*. New York: Scholastic.

Barr, Dennis J., Beth Boulay, Robert L. Selman, Rachel McCormick, Ethan Lowenstein, Beth Gamse, Melinda Fine, and M. Brielle Leonard. 2014. "Randomized Controlled Trial of Professional Development for Interdisciplinary Civic Education: Impacts on Humanities Teachers and Their Students." *Teachers College Record* 117 (4).

Beane, James. 1997. *Curriculum Integration: Designing the Core of Democratic Education*. New York: Teachers College Press.

____. 2005. *A Reason to Teach: Creating Classrooms of Dignity and Hope*. Portsmouth, NH: Heinemann.

Brown, Dave, and Trudy Knowles. 2014. *What Every Middle School Teacher Should Know*, 2nd edition. Portsmouth NH: Heinemann.

Counts, George S. 1932. *Dare the Schools Build a New Social Order?* New York: John Day Company.

Daniels, Harvey, and Elaine Daniels. 2013. *The Best Kept Teaching Secret: How Written Conversations Engage Kids, Activate Learning, and Grow Fluent Writers, K–12*. Thousand Oaks, CA: Corwin.

Eastwood, John D., Alexandra Frischen, Mark J. Fenske, and Daniel Smilek. 2012. "The Unengaged Mind: Defining Boredom in Terms of Attention." *Perspectives on Psychological Science* 7 (September 2012): 482–495.

Fader, Daniel. 1981. *The New Hooked on Books: Program and Proof*. New York: Penguin.

Graves, Donald H. 1983. *Writing: Teachers and Children at Work*. Portsmouth, NH: Heinemann.

Harvey, Stephanie, and Harvey Daniels. 2009. *Comprehension and Collaboration: Inquiry Circles in Action*. Portsmouth, NH: Heinemann.

____. 2010. *Inquiry Circles in Action* (Video). Portsmouth, NH: Heinemann.

Harvey, Stephanie, and Anne Goudvis. 2007. *Strategies That Work. Teaching Reading to Enhance Comprehension,* 2nd edition. Portland, ME: Stenhouse.

Harvey, Stephanie, Anne Goudvis, Kristin Ziemke, and Katie Mutharis. 2013. *Connecting Comprehension and Technology*. Portsmouth, NH: Heinemann.

Hoyt, Linda. 2002. *Make It Real: Strategies for Success with Informational Texts*. Portsmouth, NH: Heinemann.

Hoyt, Linda, and Lynette Brent Sandvold. 2009. *Interactive Read-Alouds, Grades 6 and 7*. Portsmouth, NH: Heinemann.

Johnson, David, and Roger Johnson. 1980. *Learning Together and Alone: Cooperative, Competitive, and Individualistic Learning*. Edina, MN: Interaction Books.

Krashen, Steven. 2011. *Free Voluntary Reading*, 2nd edition. Westport, CT: Libraries Unlimited.

Massalias, B. G., and Jack Zevin. 1967. *Creative Encounters in the Classroom*. New York: Wiley.

Miller, Donalyn. 2008. *The Book Whisperer*. San Francisco: Jossey-Bass.

National Governors Association and the Council of Chief State School Offices. 2010. *The Common Core Standards for English Language Arts*. Washington, DC: National Governors Association.

NGSS Lead States. 2013. *Next Generation Science Standards: For States, By States*. Washington, DC: The National Academics Press.

Pearson, David, and Meg Gallagher. 1983. *The Instruction of Comprehension*. Urbana, IL: Center for the Study of Reading.

Perkins, David. 2010. *Making Learning Whole*. San Francisco: Jossey-Bass.

Postman Neil, and Charles Weingartner. 1969. *Teaching as a Subversive Activity*. New York: Delta.

Public Broadcasting Service. 2013. "The Triangle Shirtwaist Fire Teacher Resources." www.pbs.org/wgbh/americanexperience/features/teachers-resources/triangle-guide/.

Steineke, Nancy. 2002. *Reading and Writing Together: Collaborative Literacy in Action*. Portsmouth, NH: Heinemann.

Trelease, Jim. 2013. *The Read-Aloud Handbook*, 7th edition. New York: Penguin.

Wiggins, Grant, and Jay McTighe. 2005. *Understanding by Design*. Alexandria, VA: Association for Supervision and Curriculum Development.

Wood, Chip. 2007. *Yardsticks. Children in the Classroom Ages 4–14*. Turners Falls, MA: Northeast Foundation for Children.

Zemelman, Steven, and Harvey Daniels. 2012. *Best Practice Video Companion: Watching the Seven Structures That Create Exemplary Classrooms*. Portsmouth, NH: Heinemann.

Zemelman, Steven, Harvey Daniels, and Arthur Hyde. 2012. *Best Practice: Bringing Standards to Life in America's Classrooms*, 4th edition. *Portsmouth*, NH: Heinemann.

index

Reading, *cont.*
    independent, 14–15, 155
    meeting calendar and, 169–171
    modeling, 60–61
    of nonfiction resources, 140–141
    read-aloud, 70, 88–89, 140–141, 157, 164,
        170
    for research, 193–200
    shared, 60–61
    think-aloud, 60–61, 141–143, 167,
        194–195
Reading and Writing Together (Steineke), 95
Reading Zone, The (Atwell), 16
Refocusing topics and supporting each other as
        researchers, 201–202
Relationships, between students and teachers,
        33–34
Research, students conducting, 19, 24, 30, 37,
        39, 67, 71–72, 76–77, 84, 118, 120,
        123, 133, 139, 143, 146, 148, 150, 184,
        186, 193, 201–216
Responsibility: building and protecting your
        brand, 98–101
Risk-taking, 81, 94–95
Roberts, Terrence, Dr., 181–182
Roosevelt, Eleanor (First Lady), 147
Routines in classroom, 14–15
Routman, Regie, 59
Rubrics, 56–57, 156, 204–206, 208

S

Schlick-Noe, Katherine, 155
Screens for worthwhile content, 134
Search-alouds, 60, 200
Searle, Becky Abraham, 155
See, think, wonder, 67–69, 115–117, 161
Self-assessment, 63, 185
Self/world question lists, 65, 186–188
Shared learning, 210–213
Shared practice, 61, 141
Shared reading, 60–61
Shoeless classroom, 14

Silent dialogue, 70–71, 91–93, 104, 136, 149,
    161–164
Silent literature circles, 161–164
Sit-In (Pinkney), 70
Skype, 129–130
Smith, Karen, 155
Smogor, Sharon, 10
Social roles/structure, 86–88, 93, 164
"Soft start" classroom, 13–17
Sports Illustrated (magazine), 33, 203
Standards skills
    analyze texts, 123, 143, 145, 148, 168, 175
    ask open-ended research questions, 189,
        194
    collaboration, 129
    comprehension skills, 116, 129
    conclusion, give reasons for, 210
    conduct research projects, 109–110, 189
    consult with others; decide upon a topic,
        192
    create a written research plan, 197, 204
    determine central ideas, 135, 138, 143,
        145, 148
    draw evidence, 138, 143, 145, 148, 163
    evaluate a speaker's point, 152
    gather relevant sources, 189, 201, 204
    integrate and evaluate contents, 116, 138,
        162, 175, 178
    listen attentively, 145, 148, 152, 158, 160,
        164, 171, 175, 197
    logical inferences, 135, 138, 141, 143,
        145, 148, 163, 168, 189
    narrow or broaden research questions,
        148, 194, 201
    organize and present ideas and
        information, 113, 209
    prepare for and participate in
        conversations, 145, 148, 149, 152, 158,
        160, 164, 171, 175, 191, 192
    presentation, written or oral, 113, 164, 210
    produce clear and coherent writing, 183,
        209